WORTHY DR. FULLER

By the same author

EPPING FOREST
ITS LITERARY AND HISTORICAL ASSOCIATIONS

THE ENGLISH COUNTRY PARSON

ESSEX HEYDAY

DR. FULLER
The Cranford Portrait

WORTHY DR FULLER

by

WILLIAM ADDISON

A merrier man,
Within the limits of becoming mirth,
I never spent an hour's talk withal.
Love's Labour 's Lost.

*Illustrated with
twelve pages of half-tone plates*

LONDON: J. M. DENT AND SONS LTD

Made in Great Britain
by
The Temple Press · Letchworth · Herts
First published 1951

CONTENTS

v

ILLUSTRATIONS

PEPYS ON FULLER

10*th Dec.* 1663.   To St. Paul's Churchyard, to my bookseller's, and having gained this day in the office by my
stationer's bill to the King about 40s. or £3, I did here sit two
or three hours calling for twenty books to lay this money out
upon, and found myself at a great loss where to choose, and
do see how my nature would gladly return to the laying out
money in this trade.   I could not tell whether to lay out my
money for books of pleasure, as plays, which my nature was
most earnest in; but at last after seeing Chaucer, Dugdale's
History of Paul's, Stow's *London,* Gesner, *History of Trent,*
besides Shakespeare, Jonson, and Beaumont's plays, I at
last chose Dr. Fuller's *Worthies, The Cabbala or Collections
of Letters of State,* and a little book *Delices de Hollande,* with
another little book or two, all of good use or serious pleasure;
and *Hudibras,* both parts, the book now in greatest fashion
for drollery, though I cannot, I confess, see enough where the
wit lies.

10*th April* (*Lord's Day*) 1664.   Lay long in bed and then up
and my wife dressed herself, it being Easter Day, but I not
being so well as to go out, she, though much against her will,
stayed at home with me. . . .   We spent the day in pleasant
talk and company one with another, reading in Dr. Fuller's
book what he says of the Cliffords and Kingsmills.

INTRODUCTION

*There never was a merry world since the fairies
left dancing, and the parson left conjuring.*

SELDEN.

THOMAS FULLER was a conjuring parson. He was Southey's
'prime favourite author'; Lamb's 'dear, fine, silly old angel';
and to Coleridge, 'incomparably the most sensible, the least
prejudiced, great man of an age that boasted a galaxy of
great men.' Yet to-day he is little read. Perhaps the
reason for this neglect is that his reputation has not yet recovered from its series of prolonged and acute attacks of
Victorian reverence. Between 1844 and 1884 Fuller under-
went three major biographies. It was too much for any
reputation, for, as E. M. Forster said in introducing the
Reverend George Crabbe's life of his father, the poet,
'Nothing kills like reverence; it is the cruellest tribute one
can pay to the deceased.' Such ruthless tributes were paid
to Fuller by John Eglington Bailey, a painstaking antiquary
who collected everything that could be collected about him,
and by two others whose tributes were pious rather than
painstaking. Between them they all but killed him. Fuller
was a parson, and in Victorian days parsons were valued
chiefly for their sermons, and sermons for their gravity.
Now, Fuller believed—as he confessed while writing of that
estimable man, Jeremy Dyke of Epping—that 'an ounce of
mirth, with the same degree of grace, will serve God farther
than a pound of sadness.' His three biographers, though
acceptable to their own generation, missed the point with
him by taking him too solemnly, while we, if we read him at
all, react from this by going to the other extreme. We take him
too flippantly, as though his works were a mere collection of

> Quips and cranks and wanton wiles,
> Nods and becks and wreathed smiles.

Fuller has all the mirth that any one could ask of him. As
Leslie Stephen, who understood this side of his character

xi

perfectly, said, he would 'extort laughter from a bishop at a funeral.' But he has also the second part of his own mixture, 'the same degree of grace.' To take either without the other is to miss the best in Fuller, which comes from his own blending of the grave with the gay, and his enlivening of both with a quality that was essentially his own. While this 'doctor of famous memory' is a seventeenth-century divine whose works may be found in huge folios on the shelves of old libraries, he is also the best of cronies.

Several of the 'reverend old authors' whose works still live have been given epithets that express in a word their distinctive character—Judicious Hooker, Honest Izaak Walton, Holy Mr. Herbert. And in Elysium, or in whatever place these gentle and learned men now forgather, Fuller must be known as the Worthy Doctor. Such titles imply affection as well as honour, and receive a special character from the name they adorn. Holy, as it rests on Herbert, has a grace it might not have on another. The judicious quality of Hooker is different from the judicious quality of one of His Majesty's judges. To-day, Fuller's reputation rests chiefly on his *Worthies of England*. He is thus Fuller of the *Worthies*. But worthy suits him for his own sake, as also does the doctorate, which—if we think of it as simply the D.D.—was not conferred on him till the end of his life. In anticipating the degree, however, we have sound precedent to support us. Those who are used to glancing through parish registers will know that the parson is often described there as doctor to distinguish him from the assistant curate or lecturer. But apart from this, doctor was in common use in Fuller's day for many who did not hold an appropriate degree. He himself is our best authority here. In the *Appeal of Injured Innocence* (part ii) he says: 'The name of Doctor is threefold: 1. For a teacher at large, extant in Scripture, "Art thou a Doctor in Israel?" 2. As a title of dignity, fixed by a society of learned men on some eminent person amongst them. 3. For one solemnly and ceremoniously graduated by a professor in some particular faculty, and the word in this sense is not of so great seniority.'

On all these counts Fuller was a worthy doctor. But

perhaps the title fits him best for the modern reader because among old authors it is now instinctively associated with one who had much in common with him: Samuel Johnson, who, incidentally, once visited Fuller's native county in the company of Goldsmith and Garrick, and supped with Dr. Percy at Easton Maudit. Both were pre-eminently men of their own times, yet of such rich humanity that they belong to all time. Consequently both were greater as persons than as writers. They were alike in their appeal to common sense and in their dislike of cant, though Fuller, as it were, flourished a cane, while Johnson wielded a club. They were alike in that both were large in physical bulk; different in that one was personable, the other repulsive. One was a careless, the other a greedy feeder. Boswell says that at table Johnson would pay no attention to the company until he had 'satisfied his appetite, which was so fierce, and indulged with such intenseness, that while in the act of eating, the veins of his forehead swelled, and generally a strong perspiration was visible.' Fuller, on the other hand, would eat a penny loaf without knowing. They were equal in learning, in sociability, and in the strength of their affections. Both had extraordinary powers of attraction and natural ascendancy in any company. Both compiled dictionaries: Johnson of England's language, Fuller of England's worthies. Above all, both were stout Church and King men, and of such universal curiosity that each had probably the readiest mind, the readiest ear, and the readiest tongue of his generation. They were not equally fortunate in their biographers. Johnson had Boswell; Fuller had Bailey.

To say that Bailey, who was a fine scholar, did not give us a living likeness of the man is not to disparage what he did, and did well. No man could have been more industrious in collecting data, more conscientious in scrutinizing, or more painstaking in assembling his material. It is true that the first marriage baffled him completely—he never so much as discovered the name of the lady, though once or twice he was near it—and that later research has brought other new material to light; but Bailey's remains the standard biography. His faults are simply the faults that go with his

virtues.   The doctor is burdened with belongings till he can
hardly breathe.   So the present work is an attempt to relieve
him of this redundant luggage.   It is also an attempt to
remove him from the nineteenth century of his biographers,
and restore him to his own seventeenth century.   If any one
is interested in the trappings they can still be found in
Bailey.

Happily, his physical likeness was sketched for us by an
early anonymous biographer whose work, though brief and
not always accurate, is of singular charm.   In it the doctor
is presented to us as 'of stature somewhat tall, exceeding the
mean, with a proportionable bigness to become it, but no way
inclining to corpulency; of an exact straightness of the whole
body, and a perfect symmetry in every part thereof.   He was
of a sanguine constitution, which beautified his face with a
pleasant ruddiness, but of so grave and serious an aspect, that
it awed and discountenanced the smiling attracts of that
complexion.   His head adorned with a comely light-coloured
hair, which was so by nature exactly curled (an ornament
enough of itself in this age to denominate a handsome
person, and wherefore all skill and art is used), but not
suffered to overgrow to any length unseeming his modesty
and profession.

'His gait and walking was very upright and graceful,
becoming his well-shapen bulk: approaching something near
to that we term majestical; but that the doctor was so well
known to be void of any affectation or pride.   Nay, so
regardless was he of himself in his garb and raiment, in which
no doubt his vanity would have appeared, as well as in his
stately pace; that it was with some trouble to himself to be
either neat or decent; it mattered not for the outside, while
he thought himself never too curious and nice in the dresses
of his mind.

'Very careless also he was to seeming inurbanity in the
modes of courtship and demeanour, deporting himself much
according to the English guise, which for its ease and simplicity suited very well with the doctor, whose time was
designed for more elaborate business: and whose motto might
have been "Sincerity."'

For a reflection of his mind we go to his books. In the following pages they have been quoted at large for two reasons. First, because Fuller talked at great length about his friends and his interests, and by careful selection and collation we can learn far more about him from his works than from external and incidental facts, which often hang about him as loosely as did his clothes. Secondly, because no one can put the doctor's case better than he, though it is often implicit rather than explicit in what he writes. For all that, he wrote so much, and on such a variety of topics, that in reading him we need a selective magnet if we are to draw out the metal.

To glance through a list of his works, bearing in mind the range and magnitude of the subjects, is to see that he wrote too much for excellence. He was a popularizer rather than a scholar, and as such has had few equals. It was his boast that no bookseller ever lost by him, and two hundred years after his death his books were still selling. There were twenty-six medleys, anthologies, and selections, either entirely or largely from his works, published during the nineteenth century, and all his books came into print again between 1810 and 1891. Many of them, however, can now be laid aside. *The History of the Worthies of England* will always be a valuable work of reference. *The Church History of Britain* will continue to be consulted by students for eye-witness accounts of events in its author's lifetime, and by a wider public for its delightful digressions. Some of his miscellaneous writings are as fresh as ever, and will be reprinted. But as writer the Fuller of to-day and to-morrow cannot be either the Fuller of the seventeenth century, or the Fuller of the nineteenth. His most popular work, *The Holy State and the Profane State*, fascinating as it is to the student, is a museum piece. It is the man that lives, and those parts of his work that reflect his personality. To be sure, he carries an enormous folio under his arm, as Dr. Johnson might carry his *Dictionary* and Izaak Walton his fishing tackle. What of that? The man is more than the book. Leslie Stephen summed up his worth briefly when he wrote in the *Dictionary of National Biography*, the lineal descendant of the *Worthies*:

'His power of fascinating posthumous as well as contemporary friends is easily explicable. His unfailing playfulness, the exuberant wit, often extravagant, rarely ineffective, and always unforced, is combined with a kindliness and simplicity which never fails to charm. If not profound, he is invariably shrewd, sound-hearted, and sensible.' He is indeed a worthy doctor.

CHRONOLOGICAL TABLES

CHRONOLOGICAL

PUBLIC

1603 Accession of James I.
The Puritans petitioned the king for ecclesiastical reforms.

1611 Authorized Version of the Bible; Speed's *History of Great Britain.*

1616 Death of Shakespeare.

1620 Voyage of the *Mayflower.*

1621 Burton's *Anatomy of Melancholy.*

1623 'First Folio' of Shakespeare.

1624 Donne's *Devotions.*

1625 Death of James; accession and marriage of Charles I; Bacon's *Essays* in final form; Milton entered at Christ's College, Cambridge.

1626 Death of Bacon.

1629 Hobbes's translation of Thucydides.

1631 Birth of Dryden at Aldwincle.

1633 *Declaration of Sports* reissued.

1634 Milton's *Comus* at Ludlow Castle; Laud enforced conformity in the Church of England.

1635 Quarles's *Emblems.*

1637 Chillingworth's *Religion of Protestants.*

1640 'Short Parliament'; Ben Jonson's *Works.*

1641 Laud impeached and sent to the Tower; Strafford executed; Milton's *Of Reformation touching Church Discipline.*

1642 Civil War; Sir Thomas Browne's *Religio Medici.*

1643 Solemn League and Covenant; George Fox set out on his travels.

TABLES

PUBLIC — *continued*

1645   Directory substituted for the Prayer Book; Laud beheaded; poetical works by Milton, Quarles, Waller, and Wither published.

1646   End of first Civil War; poetical works by Quarles, Suckling, Crashaw, Shirley, Vaughan.

1647   King given up to Parliament; Hall expelled from bishopric of Norwich; Herrick left Dean Prior; Andrewes's *Private Devotions*; Taylor's *Liberty of Prophesying*.

1649   King's trial and execution; Commonwealth; *Eikon Basilike*; Milton's *Eikonoklastes*; Lord Herbert's *Henry VIII*.

1651   Charles II crowned at Scone; battle of Worcester; confiscation of royal estates in England and Scotland.

1652   Heylyn's *Cosmography*.

1653   Izaak Walton's *Compleat Angler*.

1655   Cromwell dissolved Parliament, 31st Jan.; Taylor's *Golden Grove*; vol. i Dugdale's *Monasticon Anglicanum*.

1656   Second Protectorate Parliament; Dugdale's *Antiquities of Warwickshire*.

1657   Cromwell inaugurated as Protector.

1658   Death of Cromwell; Sir Thomas Browne's *Hydriotaphia* and *Garden of Cyrus*.

1659   Third Protectorate Parliament; Dryden's *Heroic Stanzas on the Death of Cromwell*; Milton's *Civil Power in Ecclesiastical Causes*; *Way to Remove Hirelings*, etc. Rushworth's *Historical Collections* (1659–1701).

1660   Charles II landed at Dover, 25th May; Royal Society inaugurated; Bunyan imprisoned; Pepys begins *Diary*; Donne's *Sermons*; re-opening of the theatres.

1662   Royal Society incorporated; Act of Uniformity.

PERSONAL — *continued*

1645   *Good Thoughts in Bad Times.*

1646   Bodley Lecturer at St. Mary Arches, Exeter; reached London, June, after the surrender of Exeter, April; *Andronicus, or the Unfortunate Politician.*

1647   *Good Thoughts in Worse Times.*

1649–58   Perpetual Curate of Waltham Abbey, Essex, and chaplain to the Earl of Carlisle.

1650   *A Pisgah Sight of Palestine.*

1652   Married Mary Roper, daughter of Sir Thomas Roper and sister of Thomas, Viscount Baltinglass.

1653   *The Infant's Advocate.*

1654   *A Comment on Ruth.*

1656   *The Church History of Britain*, Jan.–Mar., dated 1655. *The History of the University of Cambridge* and *The History of Waltham Abbey in Essex* as supplements to the *Church History.*

1658–61   Rector of Cranford, Middlesex, and chaplain to George Berkeley, afterwards Earl of Berkeley.

1659   *The Appeal of Injured Innocence.*

1660   *Mixt Contemplations in Better Times*; accompanied Berkeley to The Hague for the meeting with Charles II; Doctor of Divinity, August.

1661   Chaplain in extraordinary to the king; died at Covent Garden of a fever, probably typhus, 16th August; buried in Cranford church.

1662   *The History of the Worthies of England.*

CHAPTER I

ST. PETER'S PARSONAGE

Northamptonshire . . . situate in the very
middle and heart, as it were, of England.
CAMDEN'S *Britannia.*

WE might almost suppose that Aldwincle in Northamptonshire, an unpretentious village near a crook of the river Nene
between Oundle and Thrapston, had obligingly divided itself
into two parishes, Aldwincle All Saints' and Aldwincle St.
Peter's, solely to accommodate two men of genius. John
Dryden was born in 1631 in the pleasant thatched parsonage
opposite All Saints' church; Thomas Fuller in 1608 in a
rectory that no longer stands, close to St. Peter's. It is one
of those straggling stone villages found in this part of England, with low cottages, some thatched, some slated, set at
odd angles behind the grass verge of its one winding street.
The surrounding country gives, perhaps, more to the mind
than to the eye. It has neither the luminous freshness of the
east nor the romantic scenery of the west. Both the elegance of the south and the grandeur of the north are foreign
to it. In tone, colour, and configuration it is landscape in a
minor key, and particularly suited to the reflective genius of
its two poets, Cowper and Clare.

In this subdued, pastoral landscape, predominantly green
and grey, streams and spires are the essential features. The
Welland, the Nene, and the Warwickshire Ouse rise in
Northamptonshire, and drain its meadows. The county,
therefore, appeals most to such contemplative riverside men
as anglers, bargees, and saunterers of various kinds who cultivate the reflective calm

> Which shows with what an easy tide
> The moments of the happy glide.

Fuller was of this company. No matter what his destination
might be, to the joy of the general reader and the dismay of

I

the scholar, he never reached it by toiling along a highway. His was the field path. Indeed, we might almost say it was the primrose path if that did not suggest idleness and indulgence when Fuller was, in fact, extremely industrious all his life.

St. Peter's old rectory stood north-west of the church in the field between the present rectory and the road. Only the well remains. But the small enclosure, surrounded by chestnuts, beeches, and hawthorns, known in the village as Tithe-yard Close, preserves the memory of the rambling, half-timbered house, with high-peaked roof and tower of three diminishing storeys. Before it was pulled down in the seventeen-eighties it had long been something of a curiosity in the neighbourhood. Visitors to the county are said to have come miles to see it. The best rooms, which appear to have been large, faced south and were hung with tapestries. The end of the house was to the road, and originally the rooms seem to have enclosed a courtyard. The kitchens were below ground level, with windows high in the walls. The staircase was broad and substantially built, with stout posts and heavy timbers, similar to many still found in the old halls of the district, formerly renowned for its great oak staircases built from local timber. There is one of them still in that fine old hostelry, the Talbot Inn at Oundle.

The outbuildings as well as the house have now disappeared from St. Peter's glebe; but in the seventeenth century, when the parson farmed his land, a tithe-yard, with cattle-sheds on one side and stables and barn on the other, lay between church and parsonage, and across this the infant would be carried for baptism on the 19th June 1608. His godfathers were his uncles, two learned and sober divines, Drs. Townson and Davenant, afterwards successive bishops of Salisbury, or Sarum; but if the host of heavenly witnesses attended that baptism, they must have returned to their celestial quarters excited and alarmed. The age had been planned as one in which theology would make history and occupy the attention of statesmen and poets as well as divines, yet the infant who was that day baptized Thomas, and who, it had doubtless been rumoured in heaven, was to be both divine and historian, cannot, even at that early age, have looked anything but inconsequently gay, as with due and solemn ceremony he was received into the congregation of Christ's flock.

The father of this alarming infant was also named Thomas. He had been educated at Trinity College, Cambridge, where his tutor had been the great Dr. Whitaker. Of his family we know little. Fuller was a common name, particularly in the south-eastern counties, where the wool trade flourished, and as it is not a patronymic but a trade name, there is no reason to suppose that the many families who held it were related. Nor does the baptismal name help. Many of the Fullers in Suffolk and Essex, and doubtless elsewhere, named their sons Thomas. His father was probably of London, which Fuller knew intimately from childhood, and where his maternal grandfather, John Davenant, citizen and merchant of the parish of St. Mary-le-Bow, evidently flourished. Although this last named gentleman was buried at Croydon, Surrey, he was of Essex stock: the son of William Davenant of Sible Hedingham, great-grandfather of Sir William Davenant, poet laureate, as well as of Fuller. The Davenant family had been settled at Sible Hedingham since the time of Henry III, so on his mother's side, if not on his father's also, Fuller had roots well down in the clay of Essex, the county he was later to serve as curate of Waltham Abbey during the most fruitful ten years of his life.

But while Fuller gave ample proof of his affection for Essex, his heart remained faithful to the county of his birth, Northamptonshire. 'There is a secret loadstone in every man's native soil,' he wrote in *Abel Redevivus*, 'effectually attracting them home again to their country, their centre.' If Northamptonshire thought it no disgrace to have him as a son, he said, he for his part esteemed it an honour to have such a county for his birthplace. He used to tell his friends that his native village lay between Achurch, where Robert Brown, founder of the Independents, was rector for forty years, and Liveden, where Francis Tresham of Gunpowder Plot fame—executed on Tower Hill in 1605—'had a large demesne and ancient habitation.' He would then add quizzically that his nativity was thus emblematic of his own moderation, for his cradle, as he put it, was suspended between two rocks, 'the fanatic Anabaptist on the one side, and the fiery zeal of the Jesuit on the other.'[1]

The region was full of interest for an imaginative child. Fotheringhay Castle was near. It had been the birthplace of Richard Plantaganet, of whom Fuller says: 'He was somewhat rumpled in his mother's womb (which caused his crooked back): otherwise handsome enough for a soldier,' and, only twenty-two years before Fuller's birth, the scene of the trial and execution of Mary Queen of Scots. Sir Robert Cotton, a friend of the family and founder of the famous library, who lived at Conington, west of Aldwincle, is said to have bought the entire furnishings of the room the queen died in, and to have had them installed in his own house. The castle seems to have fallen into decay during Fuller's boyhood. Much of its stone was taken away to repair other buildings, and the breaking up of this historic home could not fail to stir the child's imagination, as also did Sir Robert Cotton himself, later described in *The Appeal of Injured Innocence* as 'one who had as much of the gentleman, antiquary, lawyer, good subject, and good patriot, as any in England.'[2]

> Camden to him, to him doth Selden, owe
> Their glory: what they got from him did grow.

There is an interesting reference to Sir Robert immediately after a note on Harvey's theory of the circulation of the blood. After suggesting that 'gentle blood fetcheth a circuit in the body of the nation,' Fuller says: 'My father hath told me from the mouth of Sir Robert Cotton, that that worthy knight met in a morning a true and undoubted Plantagenet, holding the plough in the country.' Such a story, told at the rectory table, was not likely to be forgotten, and its influence is found again in the passage: 'I have reason to believe that some who justly hold the surnames and blood of the Bohuns, Mortimers, and Plantagenets, though ignorant of their own extractions, are

---

[1] *Mixt Contemplations in Better Times*, part II, xliii
[2] *The Appeal*, part i, p. 427.

hid in the heap of the common people; where they find that under a thatched cottage which some of their ancestors could not enjoy in a leaded castle—contentment, with quiet and security.'[1] At the end of his life he was still ready, whenever occasion offered, to put in a word for the countryman. In the Hertfordshire section of the *Worthies*, under 'Proverbs,' he says: 'But the finest cloth must have a list, and the pure peasants are of as coarse a thread in this county as in any other place. Yet, though some may smile at their clownishness, let none laugh at their industry; the rather because the high-shoon of the tenant pays for the Spanish-leather boots of the landlord.'

Later in life Fuller was to make full use of the Cottonian library, 'our English Vatican for MSS.,' which became the property of the nation in 1702, and fifty-one years later formed part of the nucleus of the British Museum library. 'Give me leave,' he says in the *Worthies*, 'to register myself amongst the meanest of those who, through the favour of Sir Thomas Cotton, inheriting as well the courtesy as estate of his father Sir Robert Cotton, have had admittance into that worthy treasury.'

At Geddington, west of Aldwincle, there was the tradition of an ancient palace; at Grafton-under-Woods, it was claimed, Elizabeth Woodville, queen of Edward IV, was born. 'Beauty,' says Fuller, again in the *Worthies*, 'is a good solicitress of an equal suit, especially where youth is to be the judge thereof. The king fell much enamoured of her feature; whilst the lady put herself into a chaste posture, and kept a discreet distance, neither forward to accept, nor froward to decline, his favour. She confessed herself too worthless to be his wife, yet pleaded too worthy to be his wanton; till at last the king was content to take her upon her own terms, though a widow, and his subject.' Elizabeth Woodville had more than common interest for the Fullers, because she completed Queens' College, Cambridge, for a time under the presidency of Dr. Davenant, afterwards Bishop of Salisbury, and later to be Fuller's first college. The favourite of another Queen Elizabeth—Gloriana herself

[1] *Worthies.*

—Sir Christopher Hatton, was born at Holdenby House. He went to court in a mask, Fuller tells us, and the queen loved him 'for his handsome dancing, better for his proper person, and best of all for his great abilities.'

On such memories as these Fuller's joy in history was fostered. In his father's parsonage he formed the lifelong habit, as pleasant as it was profitable, of associating persons with places, the habit which produced the *Worthies*, for of his chosen study—history—he was to say late in life, 'they must spring early who would sprout high in that knowledge.'

There seems to have been nothing about Northampton-shire that Fuller did not recall with pleasure. The peasant speech fascinated him. He claimed that it was the best in England, and remembered how a labourer had said to him: 'We speak, I believe, as good English as any shire in England, because, though in the singing psalms, some words are used to make the metre unknown to us: yet the last translation of the Bible, which no doubt was done by those learned men in the best English, agreeth perfectly with the common speech of our country.'

Whether this is a reasonable claim or not,[1] there can be no question of the idiomatic quality of Fuller's own diction. He wrote a pure, clear, vigorously figurative English, if somewhat slipshod, as also did Dryden. Both, indeed, illustrate in a notable way the value of provincial gifts to the national culture, and both drew freely on the speech of countrymen.

Robert Brown, who was related to the Cecil family and owed to them his preferments, was probably the most discussed character in Aldwincle while Fuller was a boy there. After starting the movement that took his name, he returned to the Church of England in 1590, and within a year received from his kinsman, the Earl of Exeter, the comfortable Achurch living. But by nature he was a contentious person and always involved in dispute with someone in the neighbourhood. Rumour had it that he got along with his wife no better than with his church. Fuller says that in his time

[1] Dr. W. G. Hoskins, in *Midland England*, Batsford, 1949, says (p. 15): 'And it is here, in this part of England, in the early monasteries of the Nene valley, that the east Midland speech became the standard English tongue.'

Brown had a wife with whom for many years he never lived, and a church in which for many years he never preached, though he enjoyed the revenue; while common report, whether rightly or wrongly we cannot know, said bluntly that 'he was a common beater of his poor old wife' when he did live with her. Of his last days there is an amusing account in the *Church History*: 'Being by the constable of the parish (who chanced also to be his godson), somewhat roughly and rudely required the payment of a rate, he happened in passion to strike him. The constable, not taking it patiently as a castigation from a godfather, but in anger as an affront to his office, complained to Sir Rowland St. John, a neighbouring justice of the peace, and Brown is brought before him. The knight, of himself, was prone rather to pity and pardon than punish his passion; but Brown's behaviour was so stubborn that he appeared obstinately ambitious of a prison, as desirous, after long absence, to renew his familiarity with his ancient acquaintance. His *Mittimus* is made, and a cart with a feather bed provided to carry him, he himself being so infirm (above eighty) to go, too unwieldy to ride, and no friend so favourable as to purchase for him a more comely conveyance. To Northampton gaol he is sent, where, soon after, he sickened, died, and was buried in a neighbouring churchyard; and it is no hurt to wish that his bad opinions had been interred with him.'

To the Fullers, Brown was probably an oddity and a subject of amusement rather than a menace to the Church. They knew him too well to take him seriously. Fortunately his sect, though extremely unpopular with the magistrates for many years, and mocked at by Shakespeare's Sir Andrew Aguecheek, who would 'as lief be a Brownist as a politician,' was taken up by honest and scholarly men who built up the Independent movement, soon to become an important body in English Nonconformity.

Fuller's references to such men as Brown are invariably kindly, and it is evident that he inherited his tolerance from his father—perhaps tolerance, to be free from guile, can only be inherited. At all events, the elder Fuller did his utmost to live at peace with his clerical neighbours, which in

seventeenth-century Northamptonshire was far from easy.
Fuller's account of Nonconformity in his native county,
found in the ninth book of the *Church History*, is remarkably
unbiased. Nothing, surely, could be friendlier than his
portrait of John Dod—silenced for his views and ejected
from his livings—in the Cheshire section of the *Worthies*.
Dod was, we learn, 'by nature a witty, by industry a learned,
by grace a godly divine.' Then, after reflecting in his
whimsical way upon the false conceit of certain Jewish
Rabbins that Methusalem lived in a cabin on Noah's ark,
Fuller adds: 'But most true it is, that good Father Dod,
though he lived to see the flood of our late civil wars, made to
himself a cabin in his own contented conscience; and though
his clothes were wetted with the waves (when plundered)
he was dry in the deluge, such his self-solace in his holy
meditations. He died, being eighty-six years of age, *anno*
1645.'

The unknown anonymous biographer—suspected, though
without much evidence, to be Dr. Fell, Dean of Christ
Church, a graceful biographer of the day—is our authority
for the elder Fuller's good relations with his Puritan neighbours. And as he was thirty years vicar of St. Peter's at a
time when men 'laboured under the fatigues of most importune Puritanism and pleading Popery,' this was much to his
credit. There can be no doubting that the elder Fuller was a
scholarly man, and his influence on the son's mind was permanent. It is easy to see throughout his works that Fuller's
life was all of one piece, and that the pattern was started by
threads of kindly thought and genial wisdom spun in his
parsonage home. No tale that he heard in his father's house
was thought too trivial to adorn a work of learning, until, in
fact, it became a matter of reproach that so many scraps of
knowledge, gossip, superstition, picked up in the most casual
way, should have been used to savour and garnish histories
and biographies.

There was, perhaps, one shadow on his boyhood. He
was put to school early, and his first teacher seems to have
been an ignorant if not a brutal man. From 1612 to 1616 he
was in the charge of a Mr. Smith, a product of Emmanuel

QUEENS' COLLEGE, CAMBRIDGE, AFTER BURFORD

College, Cambridge, in its Puritanical early days, who was afterwards assistant curate to Robert Brown at Achurch. The anonymous biographer says Fuller 'had lost some time under the ill menage of a raw and unskilful schoolmaster.' The victim says nothing of this, but he does say in the Norfolk section of the *Worthies* that he had often been beaten for the sake of William Lily, author of a Latin grammar in universal use at the time.   Smith was, in fact, the only one of Fuller's schoolmasters not mentioned with respect and affection in one or more of his books.   He has one obvious reference and one only.   In the Cheshire section of the *Worthies* we are informed that this pedagogue was related to Captain John Smith, the explorer.   Perhaps our author had the same unhappy man in mind when he wrote of teaching in *The Holy State*: 'There is scarce any profession in the commonwealth more necessary, which is so slightly performed. The reasons whereof I conceive to be these: First, young scholars make this calling their refuge, yea, perchance, before they have taken any degree in the university, commence schoolmasters in the country, as if nothing else were required to set up this profession but only a rod and a ferula. Secondly, others who are able use it only as a passage to better preferment, to patch the rents in their present fortune till they can provide a new one, and betake themselves to some more gainful calling.   Thirdly, they are disheartened from doing their best with the miserable reward which in some places they receive, being masters to the children, and slaves to their parents.   Fourthly, being grown rich, they grow negligent, and scorn to touch the school but by the proxy of an usher.'

But what he missed from his schoolmaster he gained from his father.   The anonymous biographer says that 'In a little while such a proficiency was visibly seen in him, that it was a question whether he owed more to his father for his birth or education.'   He seems to have loved books from infancy, for the same writer says: 'he was admirably learned before it could be supposed he had been taught,' and our friendly old gossip, John Aubrey, who was intimate with members of the family, has this delightful picture: 'He was a boy of pregnant witt, and when the bishop and his father were discoursing, he would be by and hearken, and now and then putt in, and sometimes beyond expectation, or his yeares.' [1]

As Fuller was intended for the Church from boyhood, the society of his many clerical relations must have been a great advantage to him, and we may be sure that they did not think meanly of the clerical profession to which they gave such distinction, though it is to be noted that even in that age it was a common reproach that parents put their dullest child into the Church. In *Abel Redevivus* Fuller says, 'like to many nowadays, who begrutch their pregnant children to God's service, reserving straight timber to be beams in other buildings, and only condemning crooked pieces for the temple; so that what is found unfit for city, camp, or court (not to add ship and shop) is valued of worth enough for the Church.'

A curious example of Fuller's family-mindedness is to be found in an account of Stephen Gardiner, described in another place as 'that cruel bloodhound.' It appears in the *Church History* in a paragraph headed, 'The Author's Gratitude to Stephen Gardiner': 'However (as bloody as he was),' it runs, 'for mine own part, I have particular gratitude to pay to the memory of this Stephen Gardiner, and here I solemnly tender the same. It is on the account of Mrs. Clarke, my great-grandmother by my mother's side, whose husband rented Farnham Castle, a place whither Bishop Gardiner retired, in Surrey, as belonging to his see. This bishop, sensible of the consumptionous state of his body, and finding physic out of the kitchen more beneficial for him than that out of the apothecary's shop, and special comfort from the cordials she provided him, did not only himself connive at her *heresy*, as he termed it, but also protected her during his life from the fury of others. Some will say that his courtesy to her was founded on her kindness to himself. But, however, I am so far from detaining thanks from any, deserved on just cause, that I am ready to pay them where they are but pretended due on any colour.' [2]

He would hear this tale about great-grandmother's bishop

---

[1] *Brief Lives.*   [2] *Church History*, book viii.

from her daughter, old Mrs. Davenant, who has a memorial in the chancel of St. Peter's Church at Aldwincle. The Fuller parsonage must have abounded in good stories. Less than a year after Mr. Fuller had been instituted rector of the parish, the new king, James I, on his journey southward, passed through the district and received the loyal services of his new subjects. If Mr. Fuller did not actually see him at the time —and most probably he did—he would hear about the festivities and pass the stories on to his family. At Boughton, for example, the great house best known to the Fullers, James was entertained both lavishly and expectantly to good purpose by Sir Edward Montagu, whose six sons brought in the first six dishes of the feast, and were later rewarded with three knighthoods and three baronies.[1] There were still more splendid scenes at Hinchingbrooke, Huntingdon, the home of that stalwart Royalist, Oliver Cromwell, the Protector's uncle, who received a knighthood for his loyalty. It was on this occasion—the 28th April 1603—that the heads of the Cambridge colleges, clad in their scarlet gowns and corner caps, attended to offer services to His Majesty in an eloquent Latin oration, and also to entreat him to confirm their charter and privileges, which he graciously did. At the same time, with more loyalty than tact, they 'presented his Majestie with divers bookes published in commendation of our late gracious Queene.'[2]

Fuller knew the story well, and says of the occasion that 'Master Oliver Cromwell . . . made all former entertainments forgotten, and all future to despair to do the like. All the pipes about the house expressed themselves in no other language than the several sorts of the choicest wines.'[3] In the *Worthies* we read of Sir Oliver that he was 'remarkable to posterity on a four-fold account. First, for his hospitality and prodigious entertainment of King James and his court. Secondly, for his upright dealing in bargain and sale with all chapmen; so that no man whosoever purchased land of him was put to charge of threepence to make good his title. Yet

---

[1] Samuel Ward's *Diary*: Sidney-Sussex, Cambridge (see Bibliography).
[2] Nichols's *Progresses*, i. 101.
[3] *History of Cambridge*, viii. 46.

B

he sold excellent pennyworths, insomuch that Sir John Leamon (once Lord Mayor of London), who bought the fair manor of Warboise in this county of him, affirmed, "that it was the cheapest land that ever he bought; and yet the dearest that ever Sir Oliver sold." Thirdly, for his loyalty; always beholding the usurpation and tyranny of his nephew, godson, and namesake, with hatred and contempt. Lastly, for his vivacity, who survived to be the oldest gentleman in England who was a knight; though not the oldest knight who was a gentleman; seeing Sir George Dalston, younger in years (yet still alive), was knighted some days before him.'

Court and university topics would be common fare at the rectory table, or when neighbouring divines stretched their legs before the study fire. Mr. Fuller himself was a fellow of Trinity and a person who moved in distinguished circles both scholastic and social. Drs. Townson and Davenant, the learned uncles, were frequent visitors, and the gossipy references to the bachelor of the pair, Dr. Davenant, show how intimate he was with the Fullers.

Dr. Davenant was always the great man of the family. His influence over Fuller will become increasingly apparent. Here we may notice two trifling references which could only have come from old Mrs. Davenant. 'When an infant,' Fuller relates in the *Worthies*, 'newly able to go, he fell down a high pair of stairs, and rising up at the bottom smiled, without having any harm; God and his good angels keeping him for further service.' In another intimate note he illustrates his uncle's candour. When a child he was in tears about something, and the servants in trying to soothe him, said that they could not believe that it was John who was crying, it must be one of his brothers. Whereupon John piped out 'that it was none of his brothers, but John only cried.' We can imagine Mrs. Davenant telling this story about her forthright son, already Lady Margaret Professor of Divinity at Cambridge and President of Queens', as she sat with her family drinking malmsey wine.

Frankness and courage were two qualities John Davenant never lost. While President of Queens' he voted against the election of a kinsman, John Gore, afterwards knighted, of Gilesden, Hertfordshire, and owned to the disappointed candidate that he had opposed him.

'Cousin,' he said, 'I will satisfy your father that you have worth but not want enough to be one of our society.'

Even the king could not tempt him to wink at his conscience. When summoned to attend His Majesty at Newmarket he refused to travel on Sunday, and when he explained the reason for his belated appearance, it is said, the king not only pardoned but commended him for his principles.

Fuller's enthusiasm for his uncle is evident in everything he writes about him, though he claims to be restraining himself, for, he says, 'let others unrelated unto him write his character, whose pen cannot be suspected of flattery, which he when living did hate, and dead did not need.'

Dr. Townson was the husband of one Mrs. Fuller's sisters, and like his brother-in-law was on excellent terms with the Aldwincle family. He was another Queens' man, elected fellow at the same time as Davenant, and he held Northamptonshire livings within easy reach of the Fullers. When Fuller was nine his uncle Townson was presented at court. Shortly after this he became chaplain to the king and Dean of Westminster. A year later he had the duty of attending Raleigh at the scaffold, and Fuller's great admiration for Raleigh probably—we might almost say certainly— came from his uncle's account of the last hours. Dr. Townson, in fact, left a moving record of the scene in Palace Yard, and of Raleigh's resolute and noble bearing at the end, and it was probably from his uncle's lips that Fuller heard the familiar story related in the *Worthies*, of how Raleigh 'spread his new plush cloak on the ground; whereon the Queen trod gently.'

In 1620 Dr. Townson became Bishop of Salisbury, but held the see for less than a year. His death was a serious matter to the family, for he left a widow and thirteen children. The Fullers could do little to help them because they also had shown annual increment until there were now seven of them. But the king was gracious enough to provide a happy solution to the problem by bestowing the see upon Dr. Davenant, whom he also allowed to retain for two or three years the livings he held already, so that the revenues of the see could be set aside during that time for Mrs. Townson and her family.   It was from these two uncles that Fuller acquired much of his knowledge of the inner workings of the Church, which proved so useful to him in writing the *Church History*.

Thus, the picture we get of Fuller's childhood from references scattered through his many works is unusually pleasant and lively.   He loved his country home:

> A land of waters green and clear,
>   Of willows and of poplars tall,
> And in the spring-time of the year
>   The white may breaking over all— [1]

and at the rectory there appears to have been none of the tension between young and old so often found in families of strong character.   He was obviously entirely happy with his parents, and none the worse for spending so much of his time in their company, though it is doubtful whether child psychologists of to-day would approve of such a boyhood. They would probably say that he spent too much time with his elders.   And most damaging of all—according to theory —he spent hours poring over that museum of horrors, Foxe's *Book of Martyrs*, a book calculated—in theory—to produce a criminal or a fanatic rather than a well-disposed and genial antiquary.   He seems to have been enthralled by the gruesome illustrations, yet to have had no bad dreams in consequence.   In *Good Thoughts in Bad Times* he confides: 'I thought that there the martyrs at the stake seemed like the three children in the fiery furnace,[2] ever since I had known them there, not one hair more of their head was burnt, nor any smell of the fire singeing of their clothes.   This made me think martyrdom was nothing.   But oh, though the lion be painted fiercer than he is, the fire is far fiercer than it is painted.' [3]

Of his early knowledge of the Bible there is abundant evidence in his frequent use of phrases from Bibles earlier

---

[1] Andrew Lang.   [2] Dan. iii. 27.   [3] 'Mixt Contemplations.'

than King James's, while his unquestioning and lifelong adherence to his father's philosophy of life is remarkable when we remember that he lived in a revolutionary age. The truth is that he was never a thinker. Though the world of his parents collapsed in the 1640s he still saw life in the 1650s as his father had seen it. Whether this was wholly to his credit or not, it makes his childhood exceptionally important because it was the lasting foundation of his life. And how much energy this unquestioning faith saved him! Most outstanding men have had to spend a great part of their young manhood mastering their environment and establishing themselves in life. There was none of this for Fuller. He accepted, affectionately and cheerfully, every circumstance of his environment. He had joy from infancy in his county, his village, his home, his family, and that joy never left him, with the result that he could begin where his father and uncles left off. The difficult half of his life had been lived for him. He had been born with a silver spoon in his mouth, and had used it to cut his teeth on.

CHAPTER II

QUEENS' MAN

And kings shall be thy nursing fathers,
and their queens thy nursing mothers.

ISAIAH.

FULLER had been thirteen for ten days only when, on the 29th June 1621, he was entered at Queens', Cambridge, the college of which Dr. Davenant had been president since 1614. He was young for such a move, but after all he was only leaving his father's house to live in his uncle's. Apart from the family link, Queens' was a happy choice for one who, like Wordsworth's skylark, was always 'true to the kindred points of heaven and home,' because architecturally it was, and remains, the most domestic of the Cambridge colleges. Some of the timber of the original fifteenth-century building, carved and set up by Thomas Sturgeon, the village carpenter of Elsenham in Essex, is still to be seen. It came, no doubt, from the stout oaks for which north-west Essex was then famous. And if the warm brick and stout beams of the President's Lodgings made him feel at home, there was no danger of smugness, for there were other associations to give wings to his mind, particularly in the turret at the south-west corner of the principal building. This, it was said, though wrongly, had been occupied by Erasmus from 1511 to 1515, while he taught Greek in the university and lived at Queens' as the guest of its most esteemed president, John Fisher, the saintly bishop of Rochester, who 'sat here governor of the schools not only for his learning's sake, but for his divine life.'

Fuller, in his *History of Cambridge*, refers to Erasmus at Queens', and says that he may have chosen it for 'love of his friend, Bishop Fisher, then Master thereof; or allured with the situation of this College, so near the river (as Rotterdam, his native place, to the sea) with pleasant walks thereabouts.'[1]

[1] *History of Cambridge*, v. 39.

Since then a great deal of romantic nonsense has been written about Erasmus at Queens'. Andrew Pascall, a fellow of the college, in 1680 wrote an account of the visit and placed the honoured guest in the turret where pious memory has seen fit to keep him. He says: 'To that [the turret] belongs the best prospect about the college, viz., upon the river, into the cornfields and country adjoining. So that it might very well consist with the civility of the house to that great man . . . to let him have that study.' With this before them, it was easy for romantic writers to visualize the scholar climbing the turret stairs to his quiet oratory, from which he could look out across the cornfields, and at night bend his head over his book while the moon shone in at the window to light his page. We wonder if Milton had Erasmus in mind when in *Il Penseroso* he wrote:

> Or let my lamp, at midnight hour,
> Be seen in some high lonely tower,
> Where I may oft outwatch the Bear
> With thrice-great Hermes, or unsphere
> The spirit of Plato, to unfold
> What worlds or what vast regions hold
> The immortal mind, that hath forsook
> Her mansion in this fleshly nook.

Thus embowered in romance, it only remained for him to be sanctified with poverty, and this accordingly was done. But the true picture was somewhat different. Erasmus had 'the best and most spacious apartments in the college,' according to J. H. Gray, the historian of Queens', and if the turret was in fact part of his suite, it was probably used only by his servitor. Even that did not satisfy the scholar. He was, as Fuller says, 'a badger in his jeers: when he did bite, he would make his teeth meet.' As for his attributed poverty, he had in actual fact a most comfortable competence, though no amount of money could be adequate reward for the work he did, particularly in preparing his New Testament, published at Basle in 1516, for which he claimed: 'These books present us with a living image of his [our Lord's] most holy mind. If we had seen him with our own eyes, we should not have so intimate a knowledge as they give of Christ, speaking, healing, dying, and rising again, as it were in our actual presence. . . . I long that the husband-man should sing portions of them to himself as he follows the plough, that the weaver should hum them to the tune of his shuttle, that the traveller should beguile with their stories the tedium of his journey.'

Among its own sons, the Elizabethan Sir Thomas Smith was the most revered in Fuller's day, and with good reason. He had done so much for Queens' that his biographer, John Strype of Leyton in Essex, said Queens' got such glory from his renown 'that it had like to have changed her name from Queens' to Smith's College.' To appreciate this we have to remember that in a sense the universities owed their very existence to Sir Thomas Smith, who, incidentally, was a Saffron Walden man. When the dissolution of the monas-teries was completed in 1540 it was thought almost certain that the universities would fall next. Sir Thomas Smith was Clerk to the Queen's Council at the time, and begged Her Majesty—Catherine Parr—to use her influence with the king on behalf of the colleges. In his history of Cambridge, Mullinger relates how successful Sir Thomas was. He con-trived to have the reporting of the college assets done by actual members, men of 'notable virtue, learning, and know-ledge.' These, without straining their virtue we hope, demonstrated that the alleged wealth of the universities was, in fact, most lamentable poverty, and that they were not worth plundering.

But Smith's greatest service was through an Act of 1576, which required that when new leases were made for letting college land and property, it should henceforth be a condition that one-third at least of the old rent should be paid in corn, 'that is to saye in good Wheate after VIs. VIIId. the quarter or under, and good Malte after VIs. the quarter or under . . . . The same Wheate, Malte, or the money cominge of the same to be expended to the use of the Relief of the Com-mons and Diett of the saide Colledges.'

Sir Thomas argued that as land and its produce was limited, while other forms of wealth were practically un-limited, the value of land must rise. He was so right in this forecast that in course of time the third payable in corn rose to be worth six or eight times its nominal value, and thus of greater value to the colleges than the two-thirds payable in money. But for this increasing income it is hardly likely that the colleges would have survived the civil wars.

With these and other illustrious shades at Queens', Fuller must have felt that he was living in a place where

> High potentates, and dames of royal birth,
> And mitred fathers in long order go.[1]

For all that, the mitred father most dear to him, his own uncle, was about to leave. He had already been appointed Bishop of Salisbury when Fuller arrived at Cambridge; in the following November he was consecrated. In the *Worthies* we have the story of Dr. Davenant taking leave of an old college servant, John Rolfe, which besides doing honour to both the bishop and servant shows that Fuller himself was unchanged by the intellectual atmosphere of Cambridge, that he still had the joy in every condition and degree of life which had shown itself in his first years at Aldwincle, an engaging characteristic that was to continue to the end of his life. As the bishop bade John farewell, he asked this faithful man to pray for him. John replied respectfully that he had greater need of his lordship's prayers, whereupon the bishop returned, 'Yea, John, and I need thine, too.'

When the bishop had gone, Fuller still had a kinsman in the college in Edward Davenant, the bishop's nephew and his own cousin, who was described by Aubrey as 'of middling statue, something spare; and weake, feeble leggs; he had sometimes the goute.' This Edward Davenant was the son of another of the same name, who, again according to Aubrey, was 'a better Grecian than the Bishop,' and a rare man in his time,' one who deserved to be remembered. The younger Edward Davenant was one of Fuller's tutors at Queens', and it was from him that Aubrey learned much of what he tells us about Fuller. All who knew this younger Edward Davenant, including Sir Christopher Wren, spoke well of him. He was 'not only a man of vast

---

[1] Thomas Gray.

*B

learning, but of great goodness and charity.' It is evident
that he was a favourite with the bishop, for he received
several preferments from him and figured prominently in his
will. Thus in 1623 he became a prebendary of Salisbury, in
1630 treasurer of the diocese, and, in the same year, Arch-
deacon of Berkshire. Later in life he and Fuller were to
become more intimately linked when both were Dorset
country parsons, Fuller at Broadwindsor and Davenant at
Gillingham. Perhaps the greatest gift they had in common
in their Cambridge days was an exceptional memory. Both
were renowned for it. This may have been a family trait,
but it was obviously cultivated with some care, and the
pupil must have learned much from the tutor. Aubrey, who
calls Davenant 'my singular good friend,' says that 'he
would make one of them read a chapter . . . and then . . .
repeate what they remembered, which did exceedingly profitt'
them; and so for sermons, he did not let them write notes
(which jaded their memorie) but give an account *vivâ voce*.
When his eldest son, John, came to Winton-schoole (where
the boyes were enjoyned to write sermon notes), he had not
wrote; the master askt him for his notes—he had none, but
sayd, "If I do not give you as good an account of it, as they
that doe, I am much mistaken."' [1]

Fuller gives his own views on memory-training in *The Holy
State*, and no reasonable person could question his right to
speak on the subject. Aubrey indeed tells us how 'he would
repeate to you forwards and backwards all the signes from
Ludgate to Charing-crosse,' and Pepys has a tale belonging
to Fuller's last years of how 'he did lately to four eminently
great scholars dictate together in Latin, upon different subjects of their proposing, faster than they were able to write,
till they were tired.' [2] Other references to Fuller's remarkable
memory are to be found in many seventeenth-century works.
In *The New Help to Discourse* (1669), for example, the
question is asked: 'Who is the most renowned for memory
that we have read or heard of?' and the answer given is: 'In
former times *Seneca*, who writes of himself that he was able

---

[1] *Letters*, p. 302.
[2] *Diary*, 22nd January 1660-1.

to recite two thousand words after they were once read unto him; and of late days we find Mr. *Fuller* to be therein most exquisite, who is reported that he would walk any street in *London*, and by the strength of his memory tell how many and what signs they were hanging in that street, from the one end to the other, according as they were in order: As also if five hundred strange names were read unto him, after the second or third hearing of them he would repeat them distinctly, according as they had been read unto him.' His rules and maxims, therefore, should be worth having. Briefly, they are:

'First, soundly infix in thy mind what thou desirest to remember.... It is best knocking in the nail overnight, and clinching it the next morning.

Overburthen not thy memory to make so faithful a servant a slave.... Have as much reason as a camel, to rise when thou hast thy full load.

Spoil not thy memory with thine own jealousy, nor make it bad by suspecting it. How canst thou find that true which thou wilt not trust?

Marshal thy notions into a handsome method. One will carry twice more weight trussed and packed up in bundles than when it lies untowardly flapping and hanging about his shoulders. Things orderly fardled up under heads are most portable.

Adventure not all thy learning in one bottom, but divide it betwixt thy memory and thy note-books.... A common-place book contains many notions in garrison, whence the owner may draw out an army into the field on competent warning.

Moderate diet and good air preserve memory; but what air is best I dare not define when such great ones differ.

Thankfulness to God for it continues the memory.... Abuse not thy memory to be Sin's register, nor make advantage thereof for wickedness.' [1]

The tails of these principles are so characteristic of Fuller that we may accept them as his and his only; but the heads,

---

[1] *Holy State:* 'Of Memory.'

we cannot doubt, came from the excellent Edward Davenant.
Memory had to serve Fuller as maid-of-all-work during the
Civil War, when he was often without books or home, so it is
important that we should recognize how early in life it came
into training, and how sound that training was.   Fuller
always warned his young friends against artificial tricks for
memorizing, which he said served for ostentation rather than
for use.   We may note also that his rules for good memory
were harmonious with his rules for good living.   He merely
advocated method, moderation, trust, thankfulness to God,
and the genial, confident bearing towards life that he cultivated in every field.

The relating of parts to a whole was a common preoccupation of students in Fuller's day, for specialization had not
then disintegrated scholarship.   For a sketch of university
education at the time, when a course in what were called
'the liberal arts' occupied seven years—*Quadriennium* and
Triennium—we cannot do better than glance at the chapter
in *The Holy State* entitled 'The General Artist,' remembering,
however, that it represents a Renaissance ideal by no means
fully achieved.   The first paragraph maintains that 'all
learning, which is but one grand science, hath so homogeneal
a body, that the parts thereof do with a mutual service relate
to, and communicate strength and lustre each to other.'
Eight maxims follow in which the university course is sum-
marized.   Grammar comes first, as the instrument of
learning.   Latin and Greek are the literate student's first
studies: 'On the credit of the former alone, he may trade in
discourse over all Christendom; but the Greek, though not so
generally spoken, is known with no less profit and more
pleasure.'   From these he turns to Hebrew, and next to
Logic and Ethics—'The latter makes a man's soul mannerly
and wise; but as for Logic, that is the armoury of reason,
furnished with all offensive and defensive weapons. . . .
From hence he raiseth his studies to the knowledge of
Physics, the great hall of Nature, and Metaphysics, the closet
thereof. . . .   He is skilful in Rhetoric, which gives a speech
colour, as Logic doth favour, and both together beauty. . . .
Nor is he a stranger to Poetry, which is music in words; nor

to Music, which is poetry in sound: both excellent sauce, but they have lived and died poor that made them their meat.'

Edward Davenant's particular subject comes next: 'Mathematics he moderately studieth to his great contentment, using it as ballast for his soul, yet to fix it not to stall it; nor suffers he it to be so unmannerly as to jostle out other arts. As for judicial Astrology (which hath the least judgement in it) this vagrant hath been whipped out of all learned corporations. If our Artist lodgeth her in the out-rooms of his soul for a night or two, it is rather to hear than believe her relations.' History, his own subject, follows, without which 'a man's soul is purblind. . . . He is also acquainted with Cosmography, treating of the World in whole joints; with Chorography, shredding it into countries; and with Topography, mincing it into particular places.

'Thus taking these Sciences in their general latitude, he hath finished the round circle or golden ring of the arts; only he keeps a place for the diamond to be set in, I mean for that predominant profession of Law, Physic, Divinity, or State-policy, which he intends for his principal Calling hereafter.'

The normal college day started at five with prayers in chapel, followed by a short homily delivered by one of the fellows. Between this and twelve o'clock dinner came studies, which were of two kinds: college studies under the direction of college tutors, and university exercises attended by students of all the colleges—either lectures or disputations. There was a further short session for disputation or lecture in the afternoon, followed by evening service and seven o'clock supper. The large proportion of the day given to disputations had a marked influence on the period. It produced divines and statesmen with a command of language and skill in debate that might well astound us in our more literary but less loquacious age.

If we go to Fuller's works for a general description of university life as he knew it, we find the *Church History* in general a richer source than the *History of Cambridge* itself. His personal notes are not sown for profit in any one field, but blow like East Anglian poppies wherever the wind of his humour carries them. The population of the town in 1621 seems to have been about eight thousand, and the number of students about three thousand.   In the *Worthies* Cambridge is described as 'the chief credit of the county, as the University is of Cambridge.   It is confessed,' the description continues, 'that Oxford far exceeds it for sweetness of situation; and yet it may be maintained, that though there be better air in Oxford, yet there is more in the colleges of Cambridge; for Oxford is an University in a town, Cambridge a town in an University, where the Colleges are not surrounded with the offensive embraces of streets, but generally situated on the outside, affording the better conveniency of private walks and gardens about them.'

One important difference between the Cambridge life of Fuller's day and the Cambridge life of ours is in their respective relations with the court.   James had a lively interest in scholars, and on his frequent visits to Newmarket would turn to the colleges for diversion when tired of the usual country pastimes.   George Herbert, public orator at Cambridge from 1619 to 1627, says that the king's 'entertainment was comedies suited to his pleasant humour'; and our Essex divine, John Gauden, Dean of Bocking, goes so far as to say that the king found his best entertainment in the learned exercises of scholars.   Those scholars, it seems clear, knew how to make their 'learned exercises' tickle the king's ears.   In Bishop Hacket's *Life of Archbishop Williams* we read that George Herbert in 1618, being Reader in Rhetoric that year, 'passed by those fluent orators that domineered in the pulpits of Athens and Rome, and insisted to read upon an oration of King James, which he analysed, showed the concinnity of the parts, the propriety of the phrase, the height and power of it to move affections, the style utterly unknown to the ancients, who could not conceive what kingly eloquence was, in respect of which these noted demagogi were but hirelings and triobolary rhetoricians.'   The intimate connection of court and colleges must be understood if we would know how Fuller came to be so ardent a Royalist as well as so diligent a student.

James I enjoyed nothing better than an intellectual cockfight, or battle of wits between two rival scholars.   When he

visited the university in 1615 the two Divinity professors,
Drs. Richardson and Davenant, were put up to dispute before
him, with Bishop Harsnett as moderator. Davenant had
the easier case. He had to maintain the proposition that
'the pope had no temporal power over kings.' When he
denied that the pope had the right to excommunicate a king,
Dr. Richardson objected and used the excommunication of
Theodosius by St. Ambrose as an example. At this point
the king interrupted angrily and said that in his view St.
Ambrose had acted most arrogantly. Dr. Richardson could
only bow to the king's pleasure and abandon the case.

The best story of the king interrupting a learned disputation in philosophy is told of an occasion when John Preston
of Queens', of whom we shall have more to say presently, and
Matthew Wren of Pembroke, uncle of Sir Christopher and
afterwards Bishop of Ely, made sport with the question:
'Can dogs make syllogisms?' Preston said they could.
'The major proposition in the mind of a harrier,' he maintained, 'is this:

'"The hare is gone either this way or that way," and with
his nose he smells out the minor, namely,

'"She is not gone that way," and follows the conclusion,
"Ergo, this way," with open mouth.'

Wren objected, and tried to draw a distinction between
sagacity and sapience:

'Dogs especially in things of prey and that did concern
their belly might be *nasuti*, but not *logici*.'

The king, as a sporting man and dog-lover, was delighted
with Preston's argument, and when the moderator, Dr. Read,
attempted to interrupt a second doggy syllogism, James
intervened to relate how one of his own dogs, that had been
right when the others had been wrong, marked the point of
division, then ran after the others and 'by such yelling
arguments as they can best understand prevailed upon a
party of them to go along with him.' Could Dr. Read himself have done better? asked the king. And turning to the
unfortunate moderator he bade him 'think better of his dogs,
or not so highly of himself' in future.

Preston, delighted with the king's intervention, asked

leave to pursue His Majesty's game to the kill.   But Wren
was equally adroit.   He protested that 'His Majesty's dogs
were always to be excepted, who hunted not by common law,
but by prerogative.'   James was in high glee at this, and
when Dr. Read also rallied and in conclusion prayed His
Majesty to consider how under his illustrious influence even
dogs, especially His Majesty's, could now make syllogisms,
every one retired in the best of spirits.[1]

It was probably with this discussion in mind that Fuller
wrote of Preston that he was 'a perfect politician, and used
(lapwing-like) to flutter most on that place which was furthest
from his eggs; exact at the concealing of his intentions, with
that stimulation which some make to be in the marches of
things lawful and unlawful. . . .   He never had wife or care
of souls.'

Fuller's first sight of James I at Cambridge would be in
1623.   The royal visit was expected, and two plays had
been prepared for the court's diversion.   One, *Loyala* by
John Hacket, afterwards Bishop of Lichfield, was eminently
suited to the king's views.   But unfortunately both a Roman
Catholic ambassador from Spain and a Protestant ambassador from Brussels were with him, and it could hardly be
adapted to the pleasure of both.   The problem was actually
referred to James himself; but he, bent on mischief, sent word
to the Master of Trinity College, with whom he intended to
stay, that the play was to be performed and that both ambassadors would be present.   The king, however, was himself
subject to a ruler enthroned in his own joints, namely gout,
which intervened on this occasion, causing him to be detained
at Newmarket.   This made it possible for the university to
entertain the ambassadors in a less provocative way than
planned, and they left well pleased with their visit.   In the
absence of the Earl of Suffolk (the chancellor), his son, Lord
Howard de Walden, was in attendance on them, and afterwards they stayed as his guests at Audley End.

As soon as the gout permitted, James fulfilled his promise
to visit the university, arriving on the 12th March between
nine and ten o'clock in the morning.   It was his third visit,

[1] Ball, *Life of Preston*, pp. 80–1.

and as before the colleges vied with each other to do him honour—with the exception, perhaps, of Emmanuel, which had followed its own course on the 1615 visit, as Clement Corbet, Master of Trinity Hall, amusingly recorded:

But the pure House of Emmanuel
Would not be like proud Jezebel,
Nor show herself before the king
An hypocrite or painted thing:
But, that the ways might all prove fair,
Conceived a tedious mile of prayer.

On this 1623 visit, James entered the town from the Newmarket side, and from Jesus gate to Trinity gate the way was lined with students, many of them in brightly coloured gowns with hanging sleeves, stockings of divers colours, and dandified round caps. Before His Majesty's arrival proctors, presidents, and deans of the several colleges had paraded the streets to see that all stood in their proper places, according to their rank and degree. In the court at Trinity College, against the King's Lodgings, the chancellor, the vice-chancellor, the heads of colleges and the doctors stood to receive His Majesty, to whom the Master of Trinity ceremoniously presented a book, richly bound. After dinner in the Great Chamber, the troublesome play was performed, but in shortened form, and Joseph Mede, the fellow of Christ's whose letters are a valuable source of information for this period, wrote that the king sat it out 'with good satisfaction,' but 'expressed no remarkable mirth thereat; he laughed once or twice toward the end.' Then, after further refreshment and a speech from the public orator, George Herbert, His Majesty graciously departed. Afterwards there was an exchange of compliments between the chancellor and the heads of colleges in another ceremony during which the chancellor, his son Lord Howard de Walden, and the bishops of both London and Durham were presented with gloves.

Fuller must have found the royal visit an exciting interlude, and as he watched the course of events he would remember the stories told at Aldwincle about the same king's journey south to his coronation twenty years earlier, and of his uncle's historic disputation of 1615.

Two months later fire broke out among the low thatched houses and untidy barns in Wall's Lane, and this may have been as exciting a spectacle to the students as the royal visit itself. Fire was a constant danger in seventeenth-century Cambridge, with so much inflammable material on the eastern outskirts of the town which a strong wind blowing in from East Anglia could catch and drive inwards towards the colleges. One of the great fire-hooks used for dragging the thatch off a building to prevent the flames spreading is still to be seen in St. Bene't's church, of which Fuller became curate. Many of these barns seem to have belonged to the illustrious Cambridge carrier, Thomas Hobson, who is mentioned by name in an order made by the Privy Council on the 16th May 1623 for the better observance of an order that had been issued in 1619, designed to reduce the risk of such outbreaks. A few years later Hobson was to be Fuller's friend and parishioner.

In the autumn of this same year, on Monday the 6th October 1623, news reached Cambridge that the Prince of Wales was safely home from Spain without the infanta his father wished him to marry. Though he had been more than five months in the country, not once had he seen her alone. The prolonged negotiations had become sadly confused by the subtlety and intrigue of the Spanish court. At home, the match had been dreaded by almost the entire nation, and relief at the escape was proportionately great. The bells of Cambridge were rung for three consecutive days; there were bonfires each night, and on the second day each college was treated to a special speech and, as a more practical demonstration of thankfulness, to an extra dish for supper. The townsmen, not to be outdone, lit their own bonfires in the streets and were as merry without the colleges as the students were within. On the third day, Wednesday, the celebrations were brought to a climax. The entire university assembled in Great St. Mary's for public thanksgiving in the morning, and in the afternoon for one of Mr. George Herbert's orations. That night the fireworks were brighter than ever, and as the court was at Royston, only thirteen miles away, James would have news of the rejoicings and would see the illuminations for himself across the plain that divides the two towns. Such an occasion could not fail to make a lasting impression on the young Tom Fuller of Queens'.

The outstanding event of the following year, the historic contest for the lectureship of Trinity Church, which, like most lectureships, was supported by public subscription of the townspeople, we know impressed him. The townspeople wished to elect the Dr. Preston who had maintained in disputation before the king that dogs could make syllogisms. Preston was a Northamptonshire man, born at Heyford, and by this time he had become the most notable Puritan preacher of the day, and a favourite with the people. He was also a famous crammer. Fuller says of him: 'He was the greatest pupil-monger in England in man's memory, having sixteen fellow-commoners—most heirs to fair estates— admitted in one year in Queens' College, and provided convenient accommodations for them. . . . It was commonly said in the college that every time when Master Preston plucked off his hat to Dr. Davenant the College-Master, he gained a chamber or study for one of his pupils; among whom one Chambers, a Londoner (who died very young), was very eminent for his learning. Being chosen [1622] Master of Emmanuel College, he removed thither with most of his pupils; and I remember when it was much admired where all these should find lodgings in that College, which was so full already. "Oh!" said one, "Master Preston will carry Chambers along with him."'

Preston's nonconformity made him unpopular with his bishop, whom he was sometimes so bold as to defy. On one occasion when a large congregation had assembled to hear him preach, an order came from the Chancellor of Ely requiring service to be read without sermon, and allowing time for the one only, whereupon Preston took upon himself to deliver the sermon and omit the service. As preacher at Lincoln's Inn and chaplain to Prince Charles he had gained much outside influence in high places; but the strangest of his friendships was with the Duke of Buckingham, the king's pet, who, whatever we may think of his mode of life, was no companion for a Puritan. The two meddled together in politics and obviously were useful to each other in that way. Perhaps, like the colonel's lady and Judy O'Grady, they were more closely related under their skins than they appeared to be on the surface. One preached for the people's favour, the other played for the king's.

When Preston was nominated for the Trinity lectureship, the heads of the colleges, jealous of his influence, nominated a candidate of their own; so with the townspeople on one side, and the university ranged behind the Bishop of Ely on the other, the contest seemed likely to imperil the public peace. The king became interested, and, though an admirer of Preston in many ways, he saw the danger of too much Puritan preaching to immature minds, and offered the bishopric of Gloucester as a counter attraction. Preston, however, had set his heart on the lectureship and finally succeeded in gaining it.

In the autumn of this same year the Prince of Wales's marriage again came up for discussion, and it was in Cambridge that on the 12th December James signed the ratification of the treaty with France for the union with Henrietta Maria, an event which Fuller must often have recalled a few years later while he was chaplain to a child of the marriage, the Princess Henrietta. By this time the country had become sufficiently reconciled to the prospect of a Catholic queen for the university to show its loyalty by entertaining the Prince of Wales, the ambassadors, and the noblemen of the court to long disputations in philosophy. The king, however, was relieved of these favours by one of his more convenient attacks of gout.

All these lively events and echoes from the outside world were duly noted by Fuller and took their place in the permanent environment of his mind. At the same time he continued to follow the normal course of studies and at the end of the Lent term, 1625, graduated, receiving his B.A. degree along with fifty-seven others, one of whom was his cousin, Robert Townson, who later that year was elected to a fellowship.

Fuller's dates and statements about his residence at Cambridge are vague and not always accurate, but he had no difficulty with the date of his graduation because it was the

year of the king's death. The year was marked for another
reason. In December the vice-chancellor and eleven heads
of colleges announced that they had been considering the
growing laxity in college discipline—not a new subject,
perhaps, but one that had become more urgent than usual.
Unlettered boys, and even women, they observed, were now
installed in the colleges to do work that had formerly been
done by poor students in order to pay their way. This new
practice was impoverishing the students and causing no little
scandal. So they had resolved, they said, that all men and
boys who were not students, and all women whatsoever,
should be forbidden to enter the colleges unless required to
nurse the sick, in which case the women admitted must be
'of mature age, good fame, and wives, or widows.'

The year 1625 proved to be important in the life of both
Fuller and Cambridge. It was clear from the start of the
new reign that relations between court and university would
not be as friendly as they had been. The first open breach
came in 1626 after the death of the Earl of Suffolk, who had
been chancellor since 1614, and as a near neighbour—he was
the builder of Audley End—had kept in touch with the life
of the colleges. Though his personal character was something short of exemplary, to the students he was simply 'an
hearty old gentleman, who was a good friend to Cambridge,'
and as a favourite of the old king he had been a useful
friend-at-court for the heads. At the earl's death, Charles
demanded the election of Buckingham to succeed him. Most
of the heads were inclined to be loyal. The students, however, were refractory. Queens' in particular was opposed to
the election of Buckingham. Mede tells us that two days
before the votes were taken, 'about dinner time, the Bishop
of London arrived unexpected, yet found his own college
(Queens') most bent and resolved another way to his no small
discontentment. . . . Divers in town got hackneys, and fled
to avoid importunity. Very many, some whole colleges,
were gotten by their fearful masters, the Bishop and others,
to suspend, who otherwise were resolved against the Duke,
and kept away with much indignation.' At the election,
Buckingham won, but by a majority of four only.

While witnessing these public events with the interest to
be expected from a budding historian, Fuller was no less
delighted by the progress of his own family, now under the
benevolent patronage of uncle Davenant, or rather Sarum as
he had become.   Already the elder Fuller had been awarded
the prebendal stall of Highworth, Wiltshire.   Our own 'true
Thomas' was also under the bishop's eye, though being so
well endowed with natural parts his need for help may have
appeared less urgent than that of his father and cousins.   At
all events, Edward Davenant, as senior, naturally came
before him, and it had to be remembered that a further three
years of residence would be required before Fuller could take
his M.A. degree.   All accounts agree that by this time his
peculiar combination of gravity and genial good humour had
made him a general favourite at Cambridge.   In Aubrey's
words, he was 'a pleasant facetious person, and a *bonus
socius.*'

This cheerful progress was suddenly interrupted in the
July of 1626 by the unexpected intervention of the bishop-
uncle, who then, and at intervals during the next two years,
tried to gain a second family fellowship at Queens', by
pressing the claims of Fuller upon the president, Dr. Mansel.
That faithful disciple, the anonymous biographer, says:

'During his residence in this college, a fellowship was
vacant, for which the doctor became a candidate, prompted
thereunto by a double plea of merit and interest, besides the
desire of the whole house; but a statute of the college prevailing against them all, which admitted not two fellows of
the said county of Northampton [and Robert Townson, it
will be remembered, had recently been elected], the doctor
quitted his pretensions and designation to that preferment.
And though he was well assured of a dispensation from the
strict limitation of that statute to be obtained for him, yet he
totally declined it, as not willing to owe his rise and advancement to the courtesy of so ill a precedent.'

This agreeable account of what happened is far from being
a complete one.   Probably the undesirability of appointing
two fellows from one county and one family was the principal
objection, though the president was not so bold as to say so to

the bishop. Fuller himself may have agreed with the president in this and have been equally unwilling to cross his uncle. We cannot know the Cambridge side because every one there was careful not to say much until the election was over. When choice was made in 1628, soon after Fuller received his M.A. degree, and he was not elected, the bishop made no secret of his annoyance. His letters are still extant.[1] To his friend, Dr. Ward, Master of Sidney-Sussex College, he wrote: 'I am informed that they have made a late election at Queens' College and utterly passed by my nephew. I would the Master had but done me that kindness as not to have made me expect some kindness from him.' Dr. Davenant's letters are given at length in Bailey's life of Fuller, so there is no need to reproduce them here. Such matters were decided by influence rather than merit in those days. The upshot of the whole disturbing affair was that Dr. Davenant at once arranged for his nephew to be moved to the apparently friendlier courts of Sidney-Sussex.

[1] The Bodleian, Tanner collection.

CHAPTER III

GENTLE MUSE AND LEARNED WIT

Cambridge, whom as with a crowne
He doth adorne, and is adorn'd of it
With many a gentle Muse and many a learned wit.
SPENSER, *Faerie Queene*, IV. xi. 34.

To the mind, the years of a man's life may vary in length no less than in value. The locusts devour some and spare others, and memory in storing them forgets the calendar. To most men in middle life the years before twenty are the longest, yet in some biographies they count for little. If public achievement is all that matters, childhood and youth may be irrelevant. They can rarely be so with the writer, because with him, as with all whose success depends upon personality, the fruit as well as the flower is usually present in the bud. It was so with Fuller, though we cannot say of him that the child was father of the man, because that would imply that the man succeeded the child, whereas in his case the child was present to the end. Fuller never outlived his youth. As we shall see later, it survived even the sufferings of civil war. And this survival of innocence into experience is what gives his best work its perennial freshness. For all that, there was a date when he might be said to have become a man, and for convenience this may be taken as the time of his admittance to Sidney-Sussex, where his friendships ripened and his talents found their medium. When he entered this new foundation in November 1629 he had been at Cambridge for more than eight years and, according to the anonymous biographer, 'filled the eyes of that university with a just expectation of his future lustre.'

Sidney-Sussex had been built on the site of a Franciscan house founded by Edward I. Its founder was Frances Sidney, an aunt of Sir Philip, who in 1555 became the second wife of Thomas Radcliffe, afterwards Earl of Sussex, a nobleman known to readers of *Kenilworth* as the rival of Leicester.

34

She was learned but temperamental, and had evidently been a ready student of her royal mistress, for Sir James Harrington, her brother-in-law, wrote of her that 'when she smiled it was pure sunshine that every one did choose to bask in; but anon came a storm from a sudden gathering of clouds, and the thunder fell in a wondrous manner on all alike.' Again there were links with home for Fuller, because Lady Montagu of Boughton, the wife of Sir Edward the second and one of the family Fuller was to be intimate with all his life, was Lady Sussex's niece and one of the beneficiaries in her will.

The money set aside by the countess to endow what she described as 'some godly monument for the maintenance of good learning' was a mere £5,000, which she had saved out of the revenues of her estates since the death of her husband five years earlier. This inadequate sum, how-ever, was generously supplemented by her executors, the Earl of Kent and Sir James Harrington (Lady Montagu's father), of whom Fuller writes: 'These two noble executors, in pursuance of the will of this testatrix, according to her desire and direction therein, in her name presented Queen Elizabeth with a jewel, being like a star, of rubies and diamonds, with a ruby in the midst thereof, worth an hundred and forty pounds, having on the back side a hand delivering up a heart unto a crown.[1] At the delivery hereof, they humbly requested of her highness a mortmain to found a college, which she graciously granted unto them. . . . We usually observe infants born in the seventh month, though poor and pitiful creatures, are vital; and, with great care and good attendance, in time prove proper persons. . . . To such a *partus septimestris* may Sidney-Sussex well be resembled, so low, lean, and little at the birth thereof. . . . Yet such was the worthy care of her honourable executors, that this Benjamin College—the least, and last in time, and born *after* (as he *at*) the death of its mother—thrived in a short time to a competent strength and stature.'[2]

The first master of this new foundation was also a member of the foundress's family. He was James Montagu, Dean of

---

[1] Copied from her will.
[2] *History of Cambridge*, viii. 35–6.

the Chapel Royal, the fifth son of the second Sir Edward of Boughton. We have already seen to what good effect his eldest brother, Sir Edward the third, had entertained King James on his journey south. James Montagu on that occasion was one of the Cambridge scholars who waited on the king at Hinchingbrooke, and, perhaps with his entertainment at Boughton in mind, the king had singled him out for special attention: 'Here one might see the king (passing over all other Doctors for his seniors) apply himself much in his discourse to Dr. Montagu, Master of Sidney College. This was much observed by the courtiers (who can see the beams of royal favour shining in at a small cranny), interpreting it a token of his great and speedy preferment, as indeed it came to pass.'[1] Presently Dr. Montagu, while remaining Master of Sidney, was appointed Dean of Lichfield, and in 1604 Dean of Worcester; but he resigned the mastership when he became Bishop of Bath and Wells in 1608. Eight years later he was promoted to Winchester and entrusted with the translation of the king's works into Latin. This version appeared in 1619, and copies bound in velvet and gold were presented to the university by the gratified author. Fuller says James 'did ken a man of merit as well as any prince in Christendom,' but on this occasion merit does not appear to have been the sole consideration.

The family links were agreeably continued for the Fullers, Townsons, and Davenants with Dr. Samuel Ward, the master in Fuller's time, who presided over the college for thirty-four years. Dr. Ward had been Montagu's chaplain and was Dr. Davenant's successor as Lady Margaret Professor of Divinity. Like most of the members of this circle he was inclined towards Calvinism and no friend of Laud's. Sidney-Sussex modelled itself on Emmanuel. Both were Puritan colleges. But Ward and Preston, the respective masters, were entirely different from each other as persons, however similar their tenets may have been. Fuller says of Ward: 'He was counted a Puritan before these times, and Popish in these times; and yet being always the same was a true Protestant at all times.' Fuller loved him. Both had the same kindly,

---

[1] *History of Cambridge*, viii. 47.

moderate, yet grave outlook on life, and many of the intimate details of Cambridge and its personalities that are scattered through the younger man's works must have been passed on by the older in friendly, humorous conversation.

One of the most valued manuscripts in the college library at Sidney-Sussex is Samuel Ward's diary, which besides the usual doubts and despondencies of the Puritan has such ingratiating confessions as that of 'my intemperance in eating plums,' and 'my little pity of the boy which was whipt in the Hall.' Though so enlightened in many ways, Ward, in common with most learned men of that metaphysical rather than scientific age, was prone to superstition. 'How many things served us yesterday as articles of faith, which to-day seem mere fables,' wrote Montaigne. It is important to observe this, because Fuller himself was not free from it, though a careful reading of Bacon had made him at least partially aware of a revolution in reasoning. He understood well enough that the new methods of arguing from earth to heaven instead of the other way round meant the breakdown of medievalism: that many ideas dear to the Fathers of the Church must go. And while his heart was often with the old, his shrewd, inquiring mind was with the new. That such enlightenment was far from common at the time we know from the fuss there was about the celebrated fish-book. If we look at this through Dr. Ward's eyes we shall see how little had yet been done to disperse the mists of superstition from Cambridge. On the 27th June 1626, Dr. Ward wrote to his friend Archbishop Ussher: 'There was last week a Cod-fish brought from Colchester to our market to be sold; in the cutting up which there was found in the maw of the fish a thing which was hard; which proved to be a book of a large 16°, which had been bound in parchment; the leaves were glued together with a jelly. And being taken out, did smell much at the first. . . . The book was entitled *A Preparation to the Cross.* It may be a special admonition to us at Cambridge.'

To this the archbishop replied: 'The accident is not lightly to be passed over, which, I fear me, bringeth with it too true a prophecy of the state to come; and to you of Cambridge, as

you write, it may be a special admonition, which should not
be neglected.'

Such ridiculous alarm at a pious preamble trapped in the
maw of a cod-fish seems centuries behind Fuller's amused
scepticism of a few years later when, in writing of St. Hilde-
gardis in *The Holy State,* he said: 'As for miracles which she
wrought in her lifetime, their number is as admirable as their
nature.   I must confess at my first reading of them, my belief
digested some but surfeited on the rest; for she made no more
to cast out a devil than a barber to draw a tooth, and with
less pain to the patient.'   So ingrained became Fuller's
doubts about anything outside the observable order of nature
that similar confessions of scepticism are to be found in
Book Three of the *Church History* and in several parts of the
Worthies.   We can imagine such doubts first taking form as
he sat listening to the prophets of doom at Cambridge, who,
like their prototypes at all times, had discovered how easily
fear and superstition can be used to bring the ignorant into
submission, and therefore regarded them as useful in dealing
with refractory and mettlesome youth.

Though Sidney-Sussex was a Puritan college, many
families who were not of that persuasion seem to have
patronized it from the beginning, though particularly during
Dr. Ward's long mastership.   Certainly some of its more
distinguished members were not noticeably infected by
Puritanism.   Goring, for example, was a Sidney-Sussex man,
and there was nothing of the Puritan about him, though his
geniality made him the friend of men in both parties.   Fuller's
chamber-fellow at Sidney-Sussex, Rowland Lytton of
Knebworth, Hertfordshire, who was knighted by Charles II
at the Restoration, was as good a Royalist as the doctor.   A
quarter of a century after these relatively carefree college
days, when a Sidney-Sussex man of a different complexion,
Cromwell himself, was in power, Fuller dedicated one of the
books of his *History of Cambridge* to Lytton, and mentioned
there that his friend had studied under Dr. Dugard, who was
a friend of Milton.

It is disappointing not to find more about Milton in Fuller.
It is true that the one went up four years later than the other,

and that they had little in common.   Nevertheless, as the
poet was a Cambridge man it seems odd that he should not be
mentioned by name at least once.   Even if Fuller missed the
poet himself, he must have heard of him later from Christopher Milton, his brother, who was Royal Commissioner of
Sequestrations for three counties during the Civil War, with
his headquarters at Oxford, and was with Fuller at Exeter
for seven months.   Yet the single reference to Milton in
Fuller has no name attached to it and is only of the slightest
value.   In *Of Reformation touching Church Discipline*,
Milton referred disparagingly to the Catholic martyrs.   In
his essay on Ridley in *The Holy State*, Fuller quietly said that
such language as Milton had used was unworthy of him.

In noting this stricture, we have to remember that Fuller
had been brought up on the *Book of Martyrs*, and that in any
case such violence of language as Milton's could never commend its author to so moderate and generous a man as Fuller,
who, where he disapproved, either kept silent or rebuked
humorously.   We must bear in mind also that our worthy
doctor's devotion to his king was second only to his devotion
to God and His Church, and that Milton must have been
regarded as a traitor to all three.   After all, the poet began as
a loyal churchman, and in his second year at Cambridge
wrote Latin elegiacs on the deaths of two bishops, Lancelot
Andrewes of Winchester and Nicholas Felton of Ely.   In
view of their personal divergencies it is pleasant to reflect
that it was Milton's biographer, Masson, who said: 'There
was not a better soul breathing, and certainly not a more
quiet and kindly clergyman than Thomas Fuller.'   But how
we wish the kindly clergyman had left us a picture of the poet
to compare with Wordsworth's imaginary one of him,

in his scholar's dress
Bounding before me, yet a stripling youth—
A boy, no better, with his rosy cheeks
Angelical, keen eye, courageous look,
And conscious step of purity and pride.[1]

It would be amusing to speculate what would have been
the differences in both if Milton and Fuller had shared

[1] *Prelude*, book iii. 288–92.

chambers as Lytton and Fuller did. Perhaps it was better for both that they were kept apart. To be confined with an irascible poet might have tried even the patience of Fuller, whereas he and Lytton looked at life in much the same way. They had the same friends outside their own college, and in later life Lytton also was respected as an antiquary in his own county. Perhaps it was with Lytton in mind that Fuller wrote of Foxe in *Abel Redevivus*,[1] 'he was chamber-fellow with Alexander Nowell, afterwards doctor and Dean of St. Paul's, and friendship betwixt them took so deep an impression in their tender years, advantaged with the sympathy of their natures, that it increased with their age to be indelible. These communicated their studies together, and with harmless emulation, and loving strife, whilst each endeavoured to outstrip others, both surpassed themselves.'

In the twentieth century it may seem strange that we should even look for an association between a poet and a clergyman, however 'quiet and kindly,' but poetry and theology were much nearer to each other in the seventeenth century than they have ever been since. Milton was intended for the Church when he entered Christ's, and Fuller himself, who, incidentally, continued to write verse all his life, made his one ambitious attempt to scale Parnassus at this time in *David's Heinous Sin, Hearty Repentance, Heavy Punishment,* which was published in 1631. The title is not promising; the poem is not rewarding; but it would seem much less absurd to his contemporaries than it does to us. In *They Were Defeated,* Rose Macaulay gives a timely warning against the fickleness of literary fashion in a description of Cambridge life almost at this time. Most of the Cambridge wits of the day were trying their hands at the same kind of thing. The pity of it is that so many of them continued to do so for the rest of their lives.

David's Heinous Sin was reprinted more than once during the nineteenth century; but it is nothing more than a literary curiosity, interesting only for its author's sake. It was dedicated to Edward, William, and Christopher Montagu of Boughton, sons of the third Sir Edward, who had now been

[1] p. 377.

elevated to the peerage as the first baron. These three young gentlemen came to Sidney-Sussex about this time, Edward in 1631, William in 1632, Christopher in 1633, and we may be sure that Fuller would take a friendly interest in them. Later in life, Edward, when he had succeeded his father in the peerage, was to be one of Fuller's most generous patrons.

Perhaps even at this stage our author was not entirely disinterested in drafting his dedication. He was as frank as Bernard Shaw in admitting that he looked for profit from his work, and took note of the wind before setting his sails. This may be a shocking admission to those who have an adolescent's attitude to literature; but as Fuller himself was honest enough to admit it there is no reason why we should be squeamish. He did, in fact, refer later to 'the pleasant, but profitless study of poetry,' and in a sermon written at this time—probably in the year of *David's* publication—he said plainly to his college congregation: 'With our Saviour, let us look to the joys which are set before us, and with Moses, let us have an eye to the recompense of reward, yet so, that though we look at this reward, yet also we must look through it and beyond it.' There was not pietistic humbug about Tom Fuller.

As we should expect from a man with this mundane way of looking at his work, he did not allow the good things he had worked into his poem to be buried with it. It is amusing to find how often he would extract what he considered—often misguidedly—to be gems of felicitous expression from their original setting and use them to adorn essays and brief biographical sketches. He found them particularly useful in writing the fanciful work *A Pisgah Sight of Palestine*, published in 1650. It must be admitted that Fuller was far too fond of his most extravagant phrases. We may smile at them when we read them first. When we find them for the third or fourth time we can only groan. The one thing that redeems this fault in him is his obvious joy in his own verbal dexterity. For once we are not laughing with him but at him, and who could believe that he would begrudge us the pleasure?

But though Fuller cannot be called a poet, he was at times a neat and skilful versifier, and always a clever translator. He had a flair for apt and judicious quotation, sprinkling his chapters liberally with classical verses, which, in the manner of his time, he seldom failed to translate into serviceable English verse, for whatever faults Fuller had as a poet, no one could say of him what Suckling said of Carew:

> His Muse was hide-bound, and the issue of 's brain
> Was seldom brought forth but with trouble and pain.

On the other hand, we cannot say of Fuller what Suckling said of Falkland:

> He was of late so gone with Divinity
> That he had almost forgot his Poetry,
> Though to say the truth (and Apollo did know it)
> He might have been both his Priest and his Poet.

Two of the most popular playwrights of the day in Cambridge, Peter Hausted and Thomas Randolph, were also from Northamptonshire, and must have been friends of his. Hausted was a wit with an itch for reform, whose sharpest arrows were directed against the Church. One of his plays, *The Rival Friends*, was performed along with Randolph's *The Jealous Lovers* before Charles I and his queen when they visited Cambridge in March 1632. According to its author, when first performed *The Rival Friends* was 'cried down by boys, faction, envy, and confident ignorance; approved by the judicious.' His most daring efforts, such as *Senile Odium*, performed in 1633 (MS. in Longleat Library), criticized the abuses of ecclesiastical patronage, which worked so favourably for the Fullers, the Davenants, the Townsons, and their relations while Dr. Davenant was Bishop of Salisbury. Hausted may have had them in mind when writing. He had his own reason for feeling strongly on the subject, because he himself was a clergyman. Later in life he seems to have mellowed somewhat, and who could wonder, for he enjoyed for a time the comfortable living of Much Hadham in Hertfordshire. In 1642 Oxford, not Cambridge, conferred a D.D. on him. Three years later he died at Banbury Castle during the siege.

The other Northamptonshire and Cambridge playwright, flaxen-haired Thomas Randolph, 'contented lived by Cam's fair stream,' and thus placed himself more favourably to receive the plaudits of his audiences, if not the favours of the

THE UNIVERSITY AND TOWN OF CAMBRIDGE

muses.   Unfortunately his talent for placing himself solici-
tously for applause was his undoing.   After a few years of
dissipated life in London he died prematurely in March 1635
in his thirtieth year.   The inscription on the large marble
monument set up in his memory by the friend with whom he
died, William Stafford of Blatherwick, was composed by his
old friend and rival, Peter Hausted, who was evidently less
severe towards moral laxity than towards spiritual pride.
Fuller couples these two poets together in his notice of
Randolph in the *Worthies*, where he says: 'The Muses may
seem not only to have smiled, but to have been tickled at his
nativity, such the festivity of his poems of all sorts.   But my
declining age, being superannuated to meddle with such
ludicrous matters, consigneth the censure and commendation
of his poems (as also of his countryman, Peter Hausted, born
at Oundle, in this country) to younger pens.'

Among the articles issued for regulating the students when
The Rival Friends and *The Jealous Lovers* were performed was
this: 'Item, that no tobacco be taken in the Hall, nor any-
where else publicly, and that neither at their standing in the
streets nor before the Comedy begin, nor all the time there
any rude or immodest exclamations be made; nor any hum-
ming, hawking, whistling, hissing, or laughing be used, or any
stamping or knocking, nor any other such uncivil or un-
scholarlike or boyish demeanour upon any occasion; nor that
any clapping of hands be had until the plaudit at the end of
the comedy, except His Majesty, the queen, and others of the
best quality here do apparently begin the same.'

With a parson as playwright it was necessary to be more
than usually strict.   That was one of the principal social
difficulties of this period in which moralists took to writing
comedies and playwrights took to moralizing.   Peter Hausted
was only one example of the excessive frivolity—intellectually, at all events—of a parson turned poet.   Bishop
Corbet of 'Farewell rewards and fairies' was another, and
better than either, of course, was Robin Herrick; while on
the other side of the dividing stream Milton looked down in
scorn on these poets of Olivet from his superior height on the
slopes of Parnassus.   He wrote of them: 'Many young

C

divines, and those of next aptitude in divinity, have been seen oft in the colleges upon the stage, writhing and unboning their clergy limbs to all the antic and dishonest gestures of Trinculos, buffoons and bawds, prostituting the shame of that ministry, which either they had or were nigh having, to the eyes of courtiers and court ladies, with their grooms and mademoiselles.'

Fuller must have been an amused spectator of this undignified spectacle, in its way as farcical as the traditional comedy of the wrong bedroom. But he had none of Milton's scorn. For himself, he summed it up when he said of Fancy in *The Holy State*: 'To lift too high is no fault in a young horse, because with travelling he will mend it for his own ease. Thus lofty fancies in young men will come down of themselves, and in process of time the overplus will shrink to be but even measure.' Already at Cambridge he realized that he himself was by temperament no less than by talent unsuited for the higher flights of poetry and drama—partly because he was too happy with life as he found it to desire any escape into a dream world, and partly because his innate fair-mindedness made him dislike any kind of exaggeration which, after all, is inevitable in poetry and drama. 'Enough hereof,' he would interject, 'it tends to slanting and suppositive traducing of the records.' The historian had little patience with the poet's slipshod treatment of fact, and an uncharitable estimate of character was always an unpardonable offence to him. That these offences might be committed to improve a play artistically meant nothing. Thus even Shakespeare was criticized for having made too bold with the memory of Sir John Oldcastle in creating Falstaff, so that in writing of this knight in the *Worthies* Fuller said '[I have] worn out the neb of my pen in my *Church History* about clearing the innocency of this worthy knight'; and with that excused himself from saying more. In his use of language, however, Fuller could be charged by the poet with offences quite as unpardonable as any that poets have committed with fact. If, as he said he did, he regarded poetic imagery as sauce for flavouring the meat of life, we can only say that he used far too much of it on his own plate.

The stage, of course, was not esteemed very highly in Fuller's day, though its reputation was reviving in an attempt to reform it.   Fuller had heard from his father that some years earlier there had been an attempt to ban stage plays altogether in the university; but 'some grave governors,' as we read in *Good Thoughts in Worse Times*, 'maintained the good use thereof, because thereby in twelve days they more discover the dispositions of scholars than in twelve months before.'

> There have been more, in some one play,
> Laughed into wit and virtue, than have been
> By twenty tedious lectures drawn from sin
> And foppish humours.

Usually in such matters Fuller took the middle course. He was neither fanatically for nor fanatically against the arts. When, for example, on the king's return from his visit to Scotland with Laud in the summer of 1633, a collection of complimentary verses written by the wits and poets of Cambridge was published under the title *Rex Redux*, etc., Fuller appeared as poet in the company of such scholars as Drs. Ward, Collins, and Love, and of such gifted students as Edward King, Thomas Randolph, Richard Crashaw, Henry More, and Edmund Waller.   Such a medley of authors would make a strange book to-day, but in the seventeenth century it was normal.   Divines hobnobbed with wits, and religious terms were the currency of ribaldry as well as of theology.   Thus when the Mitre Tavern collapsed towards the end of Fuller's period at Cambridge, Tom Randolph sang:

> Lament, lament, ye scholars all,
>   Each wear his blackest gown,
> The Mitre that held up your wits
>   Is now itself fall'n down.
> The dismal fire on London Bridge
>   Can move no heart of mine,
> For that but o'er the water stood
>   But this stood o'er the wine;
> It needs must melt each Christian heart
>   That this sad news but hears,
> To think how the poor hogsheads wept
>   Good sack and claret tears.

> The zealous students of that place
>   Change of religion fear,
> That this mischance may soon bring in
>   A heresy of beer.

Of all the poets at Cambridge in his day, Fuller thought most of Quarles, the fellow Royalist of whom he wrote: 'He was a most excellent poet, and had a mind biased to devotion.' Quarles was an Essex man, which to Fuller was a point in his favour. Another poet from the same county whose friendship he valued, Edward Benlowes of Brent Hall, Finchingfield, is referred to in one of the *Church History* dedications as 'a religious and learned gentleman, no small promoter of my present labours.' Again from the eastern counties Fuller loved so much, this time from Suffolk, there was one whose development was closer to his own in Simonds D'Ewes, the antiquary, who, like Benlowes, was at St. John's. His father, Paul D'Ewes, bought the manor of Lavenham from the spendthrift poet-earl of Oxford in 1611. In later life he became a painstaking student of Tower records and similar sources for a history of England he planned to write. In his antiquarian studies D'Ewes worked with Sir Robert Cotton in what he called his 'sweet and satisfying studies,' which were much more pleasantly pursued in the quiet of Sir Robert's library than at Cambridge, whose courts had no appeal for D'Ewes. In his autobiography he tells us that he left the university with relief at being able to escape from all its swearing, drinking, rioting, and hatred of all piety and virtue. But he was a Puritan, so had a nose for smelling out the less savoury parts of the university, of which Fuller was hardly aware.

Then as now, the wits of Cambridge were sharpened by friction rather than by applause, and there was friction enough in Caroline Cambridge. A dispute that must have excited even the serene Fuller was started in 1627 with the creation of a new chair of history, endowed by Fulke Greville, Lord Brooke, to which a Dr. Isaac Dorislaus, friend of Wotton and Selden, was appointed. This gentleman was of Leyden, where political ideas were then somewhat advanced. He began his first lecture with Cornelius Tacitus and traced the conversion of the state of Rome from government by kings to government by consuls. This might have been completely innocent of offence, but he went on to discourse upon the relative freedom of the people under the various forms of government, and there the trouble started. Dr. Ward of Sidney-Sussex, in a letter to Archbishop Ussher, said he thought the new professor had spoken with great moderation. Others had different views on moderation and complained to the vice-chancellor about the lecture. As soon as he heard of this, Dr. Dorislaus asked to be allowed to meet the heads in order to discuss their complaints with them. This was arranged, and at the interview he gave complete satisfaction. But his patron was nervous about the king's possible reaction. Nothing would satisfy him but that Dr. Dorislaus should resign, which he accordingly did, retiring to Maldon in Essex, his wife's home.[1] The future was to confirm the worst suspicions. It was Isaac Dorislaus who in 1648 prepared the charge of high treason against Charles I. In 1649, while envoy to the States-General, he was assassinated by Royalists at The Hague.

There is no better clue to a man's character than the company he keeps. Fuller was at ease with every one, but he had his more intimate friends, and these were often older than himself. Of all his friends, perhaps Joseph Mede influenced him most during his later years at Cambridge. Mede was a rare soul. He was born at Berden, near Quendon in Essex, and educated at Hoddesdon before going up to Cambridge, where he became one of the three outstanding tutors of the day. The other two were William Chappell, Milton's tutor, and Dr. Power. Power's pupils were called Poweritans; Chappell's, who were more precise and strict, were called Puritans; and Mede's, because midway between the precision of the Puritans and the laxity of the Poweritans, were called Medians. Fuller thought highly of Chappell as a tutor. He went so far as to say that 'No tutor in our memory bred more or better pupils, so exact his care in their education.' He was severe, even harsh with them, and he achieved results. But Mede's influence may have been more

---

[1] *History of Cambridge*, ix. 16–17.

lasting. In himself he was the better scholar and incomparably the nobler character. The Cambridge Platonists regarded him as their spiritual father, and it was from these that the broad and tolerant party in the eighteenth-century Church of England took much of their philosophy. Fuller learned from Mede something of the tolerance that characterized all his work, and that was so lacking in his lifetime. Besides being one of the most learned men in the Cambridge of his day, Mede was a simple, sincere man, loved by all who knew him and the delight of his students, whom he was wont to greet smilingly with '*Quid dubitas?*—What doubts have you met in your studies to-day?' He is said to be the old shepherd Damoetas in Milton's *Lycidas*. His letters, full of notes and sketches on the university life of his time, are now valued more highly than his *magnum opus, Clavis Apocalyptica*, originally published in Latin, which was translated in 1643 and reissued as *The Key of the Revelation*. Biblical criticism was, perhaps, the chief of the half-dozen or so subjects on which he was considered an authority; but we are told that he turned from the 'troublesome labyrinths of metaphysical inquiry to physics as a reassuring study.' Fuller consulted him on the history of the Crusades, citing him in *The History of the Holy War* as 'my oracle in doubts of this nature.' Quoting one of Mede's replies to a question referred to him he says: 'I thought fit to recite, not for his honour, but to honour myself, as conceiving it my credit to be graced with so learned a man's acquaintance.' And again of Mede, that for one 'who constantly kept his cell—so he called his chamber—none travelled oftener and farther all over Christendom.'

Mede was one of many in this age who travelled round the world in imagination without leaving home. Samuel Purchas never went far from his native Essex, yet he knew every ocean. It was a curious difference between the Elizabethans and the Carolines that the former wished to circumnavigate the globe whereas the latter were content to have it served to them between the covers of a stout folio. That way they could outpace the Elizabethans and take in heaven as well as earth. Thus Milton could lose and regain Paradise without setting foot in a stirrup or firing a shot.

CHAPTER IV

ST. BENE'T'S

Mark him the Pastor of a jovial fold,
Whose various texts excite a loud applause.

CRABBE.

THE town and gown of Cambridge meet for worship in several churches; but two, one at the head, the other at the heart of the university's religious life, have neither like nor equal. The church of St. Mary the Great, or Great St. Mary's, is the official church of both the university and the borough. It is the largest church in the town and the most important. St. Benedict's, or St. Bene't's, though small and tucked away, has a tower which is the oldest building in Cambridge, with a fine Saxon arch opening to the nave. What is more important is that St. Bene't's enshrines a tradition that goes back to a date four hundred years before the Norman Conquest. For centuries it was the university church. Before the first college in Cambridge had a building the students would meet in St. Bene't's for lectures, and a bell in the same tower would be rung to convene them. When, therefore, early in 1630—shortly after his admission to Sidney-Sussex— Fuller was presented by the Master and Fellows of Corpus Christi to the perpetual curacy of St. Bene't's, he must have felt sealed to his dual profession of history and divinity. His own account of the appointment is found in the *History of Cambridge*, where he says: 'I most thankfully confess myself once a member at large of this house, when they were pleased, above twenty years since, freely, without my thoughts thereof, to choose me minister of St. Benedict's Church, the parish adjoining, and in their patronage.'

Nothing could be clearer proof of his popularity, for he was only twenty-two, and there is no evidence of any influence being used to gain for him this important pulpit, where, in the anonymous biographer's words, he 'offered the primity of his ministerial fruits, which, like apples of gold in pictures of

silver—sublime divinity in the most ravishing elegancies—
attracted the audience of the university.' Most of his early
sermons are lost, but one series preached at St. Bene't's was
published more than twenty years later with the title, *A
Comment on Ruth*. He may have touched up the manuscript
a little for publication, but it is unlikely that he altered the
text to any considerable extent, for with his usual frankness
he explains that the sermons were preached in his first
ministry, and begs his readers to 'pardon the many faults
that may be found therein.' They have, perhaps, too many
of the 'ravishing elegancies' admired by his first biographer;
but their author's mark is upon them, and they show that in
this early start at twenty-two he was already able to make
his own individual way through a subject, as with all his
peculiar charm he tells the tale of the maiden,

> when, sick for home,
> She stood in tears amid the alien corn.

Published sermons were a fashionable form of literature
in the seventeenth century, and when Fuller's fame was at its
height some of those who had taken notes as they listened to
him at St. Bene't's announced their intention to publish a
report of these sermons on Ruth. It was this announcement
that provoked him to publish the original text and thus avoid
being misinterpreted. To-day, perhaps, we value these sermons chiefly for their Fullerisms; but there is plenty of
evidence that Fuller himself intended them to be plain and
practical. 'Oh that ministers had this faculty of Boaz!' he
said in one of them, 'not to tickle the ears, teach the heads, or
please the brains of the people, but that their sermons might
soak and sink to the roots of their hearts.' He used topical
illustrations freely, and though these would go home at the
time they sometimes puzzle the modern reader. Other
allusions are still relevant. Perhaps the best is one referring
to the emigration of the Pilgrim Fathers. Most of these
pioneers had come from the eastern counties, and many of
Fuller's hearers would have relations among them. By this
time the excitement of adventure had worn off, and sad
stories were filtering into the home country about the hard-
ships the pilgrims had suffered, often through their own

pig-headedness. So, after a quaint dialogue between Elimelech and 'a plain and honest neighbour' who tried to dissuade him from going into Moab, we are given a classification of those for whom foreign travel is legitimate. They are merchants, ambassadors, and 'private persons that travel with an intent to accomplish themselves with a better sufficiency to serve their king and country; but unlawful it is for such to travel which, Dinah-like, go only to see the customs of several countries, and make themselves the lacqueys to their own humorous curiosity. Hence cometh it to pass when they return, it is justly questionable whether their clothes be disguised with more foolish fashions, or bodies disabled with more loathsome diseases, or souls defiled with more notorious vices; having learned jealousy from the Italian, pride from the Spaniard, lasciviousness from the French, drunkenness from the Dutch. And yet what need they go so far to learn so bad a lesson, when (God knows) we have so many schools where it is taught here at home?

'Now if any do demand of me my opinion concerning our brethren which of late left this kingdom to advance a plantation in New England, surely I think, as St. Paul said concerning virgins, he had "received no commandment from the Lord": so I cannot find any just warrant to encourage men to undertake this removal; but think rather the counsel best that King Joash prescribed to Amaziah, "Tarry at home." Yet as for those that are already gone, far be it from us to conceive them to be such, to whom we may not say, "God speed"; but let us pity them and pray for them; for sure they have no need of our mocks, which I am afraid have too much of their own miseries. I conclude therefore of the two Englands what our Saviour saith of the two wines, "No man having tasted of the old, presently desireth the new; for he saith, the old is better."'

In speaking thus of travel Fuller may have been half in earnest, half in jest. He knew that some of his congregation looked forward to touring the countries he named. Such tours were then considered part of a nobleman's education. He seems to have had little desire for travel himself,

* C

and when he came to write an essay on the subject in *The Holy State* he was still inclined to warn rather than to encourage as he recalled how Roger Ascham in the preface to *The Schoolmaster* thanked God that he had spent only nine days in Italy, when in one city, Venice, he had seen more liberty to sin than he had heard of in London in the same number of years.   No doubt Fuller would have agreed with E. V. Lucas, who, in his *Wanderer in Holland*, said that 'many of us are so constituted that we never use our eyes until we are on foreign soil.   It is as though a Cook's ticket performed an operation for cataract.'   And, incidentally, Holland was the European country that received his friendliest comment: 'If thou wilt see,' he said, 'much in a little, travel the Low Countries,' which simply meant that this lover of home, even when abroad, preferred the country most like his own familiar plains and fens.   But perhaps there was another reason for his dislike of travel.   In *Good Thoughts in Bad Times* he confessed: 'When I am to travel, I never use to provide myself till the very time, partly out of laziness, loth to be troubled till needs I must, partly out of pride, as presuming all necessaries for my journey will wait upon me at the instant.'[1]   If the Civil War, then, had not turned him out of his study to wander through the west country with the Cavaliers we might never have had him as a topographer. We cannot, however, say more than 'might' here, because already while at Cambridge he wrote a paper entitled 'Observations of the Shires,' which is to be found in Gutch's extracts from the Tanner manuscripts entitled *Collectanea Curiosa*, and must have been written about 1632.   A hundred years later Fuller's namesake, in *Gnomologia*, had the argument in a nutshell: 'If an ass goes a-travelling he'll not come home a horse.'

Fuller's three years at St. Bene't's were not easy years in Cambridge.   Almost as soon as he received the appointment the life of the university was interrupted by an outbreak of plague, brought into the town—which was none of the healthiest—by one or two soldiers of the King of Sweden's army.   Trinity College closed down completely at the end of

[1] 'Personal Meditations,' xvi.

April. The following month all the students were sent home and sermons were discontinued at Great St. Mary's. Sometimes an outbreak of the dreaded plague scattered parsons as quickly as students. There is a broadside entitled 'A pulpit to be let. Woe to the idle shepherd that leaveth his flock. With a just applause of those worthy Divines that stay with us.' It begins:

> Beloved: and he sweetly thus goes on,
> Now, where 's Beloved? Why, Beloved 's gon;
> No morning Mattens now, nor Evening Song.
> Alas! the Parson cannot stay so long.

Some of the ministers at Cambridge, however, with Fuller apparently among them, along with such loyal heads of colleges as Dr. Ward of Sidney-Sussex and Dr. Butts, vice-chancellor and Master of Corpus Christi, the heads of the two colleges Fuller was associated with, remained to assist the magistrates in caring for the infected and feeding the poor. With the break-up of the colleges most of the townspeople were without work and therefore without means to buy bread. Fuller's register was kept throughout the plague, but he can have had little work at Corpus Christi. At the end of summer, when the plague was most virulent, Dr. Butts wrote to the High Steward of Cambridge, Lord Coventry: 'Myself am alone, a destitute and forsaken man; not a scholar with me in college; not a scholar seen by me without.' In the same letter this generous-hearted man, who, alas, hanged himself two years later, wrote: 'There are five thousand poor and not above one hundred who can assist in relieving them.'

An appeal for outside help stated that there were two thousand eight hundred people in need of public assistance, and not more than a hundred and forty able to contribute to it. This is not quite so despairing a statement as that of Dr. Butts, but it is still tragic, and we can understand how the few responsible people left in the town must have felt. After that, money was no longer a problem. The appeal produced thousands of pounds; the difficulty of inducing the farmers of East Anglia to bring in food remained. On inquiry it was found that there was about seven weeks' supply of grain in the town granaries, and a fairly considerable supply in the hands of the bakers and brewers. But fresh produce was needed at once, and grain would be needed shortly, so an order was made by the king in council obliging the farmers to continue their supplies. Forty booths were set up on commons outside the town, to which the infected were removed. Assemblies were forbidden, and the constables, assisted by gentlemen pleasantly described by Dr. Butts, not as wardens or special constables, but as 'certain ambulatory officers,' walked the streets regularly to keep the people moving and report disorders, while the court sat twice weekly to deal with petty offences and give rulings on questions in doubt.

Among the few university men who remained, several were Fuller's intimate friends. It is possible that he and most of them left for a short time during the summer; but their loyalty to the afflicted town was noble. Besides Ward and Butts, there was the imperturbable Mr. Mede; but perhaps he was too much engrossed in his studies to pay much attention to the plague. At all events he continued in residence most of the year and wrote to Sir Martin Stuteville as usual. In all, three hundred and forty-seven townsfolk died during this particular visitation, and five thousand were eventually reduced to distress. Not until the frosts of winter were believed to have killed infection were the students brought back. The interruption of studies was serious for many, and in his *History of Cambridge* Fuller tells us that many students were given degrees who had done nothing to earn them, so that 'Dr. Collins, being afterwards to admit an able man Doctor, did (according to the pleasantness of his fancy), distinguish *inter cathedram pestilentiae, et cathedram eminentiae*, leaving it to his auditors easily to apprehend his meaning.'[1]

But besides his obligations to Corpus Christi, Fuller had his parish. So humorous and large-hearted a priest could not fail to be popular with the townsfolk, and he on his side was not without his rewards. On the 1st January 1631 he lost his celebrated parishioner, Thomas Hobson the carrier, who must have been the joy of his heart. This astute man was then in his eighty-sixth year and a man of substance in the

[1] *History of Cambridge*, ix. 20.

town. His father, who had been the Cambridge carrier before him, by a will dated the 10th November 1568, had left his copyhold lands at Grantchester to his son Thomas on the condition that he should be ruled and ordered by his mother. This dutiful son was also to have 'the team ware that he now goeth with, that is to say, the cart and eight horses and all the harness and other things thereunto belonging with the nag, to be delivered to him at such time and when as he shall attain and come to the age of twenty-five years, or £30 in money for and in discharge thereof.' From then to the end of his long life Thomas Hobson drove his team backwards and forwards between Cambridge and Bishopsgate Street, carrying letters, parcels, and such human bag and baggage as were entrusted by their guardians or of their own free will to his care.

Hobson's death on the first day of the first month of the new year was singularly appropriate for the man who gave rise to the proverbial 'Hobson's choice.' He is said to have been the first man in England to let out horses for hire, and though his livery stables were large and well stocked, no horse was allowed to be taken out except in its proper turn. If a client objected to the one offered, which was in the stall nearest the door, he received a curt 'This or none.' *Spectator* 509 has a reference to Hobson and his proverb, 'which by vulgar error is taken and used when a man is reduced to an extremity, whereas the propriety of the maxim is to use it when you would say, there is plenty, but you must make such a choice, as not to hurt another who is to come after you.'

Hobson was a loyal churchman. In 1626 he gave a large bible to St. Bene't's, and in his will left five shillings annually for a learned preacher to deliver a special sermon. He was equally loyal to the town, as well he might be, for it had brought him a lifetime of prosperity. In 1628 he conveyed to trustees on behalf of the university and town the ground on which was erected a building called the Spinning House, or Hobson's Workhouse. In a sense Hobson was yet another victim of the plague, for it brought his business to a standstill, and it was at the end of the period of enforced idleness that he died. It is sometimes said that he founded alms-houses

for six poor widows in St. Bene't's Street, an institution Fuller would know well. This, however, is incorrect.
These almshouses were a much older foundation. On the
12th January 1631 he was buried in the chancel of St.
Benedict's church, and Fuller, who admired a man of
character, and thought no worse of him for having gained
some honest profit for himself, must have preached a capital
sermon on the occasion.

This grand old man, Thomas Hobson, was even able to
draw humour out of Milton, and it took more than the
common run of character to bring a smile to the poet's cold
though seraphic lips. Milton, in fact, is our authority for
counting Hobson among the victims of the plague. In a
prefatory note to his two poems on the old carrier he says his
subject 'sickened in the time of his vacancy, being forbid to
go to London by reason of the plague.'

> His leisure told him that his time was come,
> And lack of load made his life burdensome.

Though mediocre as poetry, there is nothing else in Milton
that has so much warm humanity in it as the first of the two
poems on Hobson:

> Here lies old Hobson; Death hath broke his girt,
> And here, alas! hath laid him in the dirt;
> Or else, the ways being foule, twenty to one,
> He 's here stuck in a slough, and overthrown.
> 'Twas such a shifter that, if truth were known,
> Death was half glad when he had got him down;
> For he had any time this ten years full
> Dodged with him betwixt Cambridge and *The Bull*.
> And surely Death could never have prevailed,
> Had not his weekly course of carriage failed;
> But lately, finding him so long at home,
> And thinking now his journey's end was come,
> And that he had ta'en up his latest inn,
> In the kind office of a chamberlin
> Showed him his room where he must lodge that night,
> Pulled off his boots, and took away the light:
> If any ask for him, it shall be said,
> 'Hobson has supped, and 's newly gone to bed.'

Hobson was one of the men about whom legends grow and
ripen like apples on a gnarled old tree. One of the best of the

true stories relates how he used to tell the young bucks who
hired horses from him that they would come time enough to
London if they did not ride too fast, which taught them a
valuable lesson in life and at the same time reduced the wear
and tear on the horses.   In London he usually put up at the
Bull Inn, Bishopsgate Street, and long after his death this
old house still had the well-known portrait of him grasping
the bag of money, with the inscription:

> Laugh not to see so plaine a Man in print,
> The shadows homely, yet there 's something in 't,
> Witness the Bagg he wears (though seeming poore)
> The fertile Mother of a thousand more:
> He was a thriving Man, through lawful gain,
> And wealthy grew by warrantable fame,
> Then laugh at them that spend, not them that gather,
> Like thriving Sonnes of such a thrifty Father.

Several inns had the old man's name and head on their
signs—there was formerly an inn called 'The Old Hobson'
in Mill Lane, Cambridge.   He must have been known far and
wide long before his death, for as early as 1617 a quarto
pamphlet was published with the title *Hobson's Horseload of
Letters, or Precedent for Epistles of Business*, etc., a reminder
that he carried the Cambridge mail, which, no doubt, accounted for much of his popularity and importance.

Fuller must have enjoyed drawing out this shrewd
man, and it is possible that some of the carrier's witty
saws are incorporated in various parts of his parson's works.
Besides being a carrier, Hobson was farmer, maltster, and
innkeeper, and by his industry and enterprise he turned all
to profit.   The entry in St. Bene't's parish register recording
his burial shows beyond doubt that Fuller conducted the
service, so when we read in *The Holy State* that 'dumbness is
oratory to a conscientious man; and he that will not be
merciful to his beast is a beast himself,' we may well wonder
if the words were first used in Hobson's funeral sermon, or,
better still, by the old man himself.

Fuller's last years at Cambridge seem to have been years of
reform.   In a former chapter we mentioned the tightening of
discipline.   According to Fuller's *History of Cambridge*, the

college fabrics also received attention at this time. He says: 'Now began the University to be much beautified in buildings, every college either casting its skin with the snake, or renewing its bill with the eagle, having their courts, or at leastwise their fronts and gate-houses repaired and adorned. But the greatest alteration was in their chapels, most of them being graced with the accession of organs. And, seeing music is one of the liberal arts, how could it be quarrelled at in an university, if they sang with understanding both of the matter and the manner thereof? Yet some took great distaste thereat as attendancy to superstition.'[1]

In the fifth section of the *History of Cambridge* a matter of prime importance to the university, the draining of the fens, is discussed. Negotiations with Cornelius Vermuyden, a Dutchman, were begun in 1630; but opposition to a foreigner having charge of the enterprise soon stopped them, and the work was not done until 1635–8. Throughout the preliminary discussions there was the most astonishing prejudice against this desirable project, much of it coming from learned members of the university who ought to have known better. Earlier attempts to drain the fens had been defeated by the 'Bailiff of Bedford,' as the Ouse in flood was called by the country people. This worthy, according to Fuller, was 'attended like a person of quality, with many servants,' in the form of tributary streams. After dealing with the many objections to draining the fens on the ground of its impossibility, Fuller says with his usual common sense, 'But the best argument to prove that a thing may be done, is actually to do it.'

It was natural that Fuller should have a lively interest in this question, because he had been born on the edge of the fens and so far had spent his entire life either in or near them. How amused he must have been by the opposition of the Church! Sir Christopher Wren's uncle, Dr. Matthew Wren, afterwards Bishop of Ely, preaching an assize sermon on the text 'Let judgment run down as the waters, and righteousness as a mighty stream,' thought it his duty to issue a warning against tampering with Creation. The learned doctors of the university pointed out that Athens stood in a

[1] *History of Cambridge*, ix. 27.

fen, as also did Pisa, and they declared that a damp air quickened the wits and stimulated the memory. Fuller thought little of the argument, though he humorously referred to it in both the *History of Cambridge* and *The Holy State*: 'Some say a pure and subtle air is best; another commends a thick and foggy air. For the Pisans, sited in the fens and marsh of Arnus, have excellent memories, as if the foggy air were a cap for their heads.' Of the attitude of the fenmen themselves we have a valuable report in the *Worthies*, where, after remarking that the land has been much improved by draining, he says, 'though the poorest sort of people will not be sensible thereof. Tell them of the great benefit to the public, because where a pike or duck fed formerly, now a bullock or sheep is fatted; they will be ready to return, that if they be taken in taking that bullock or sheep, the rich owner inditeth them for felons; whereas that pike or duck were their own goods only for the pains of catching them.' [1]

With plague, famine—for the sermons on Ruth were preached during the famine that followed the plague—and such folly over so sensible a proposal as that to drain the fens, Fuller had no lack of practical illustrations for his wise and serviceable morality. And by trying out different methods of presenting a case he acquired skill in the effective use of words in the soundest way, which must surely be by trying them out on an audience. In particular he mastered the art of apt illustration.

His ministry—while still following his studies in order to qualify for his B.D.—kept him in touch with everyday life. On the other hand, his election in 1631 to a fellowship of Sidney-Sussex shows that he maintained his connection with scholarship. This early necessity of balancing his life nicely between the academic and the parochial must have helped to settle his mind and give it direction. It is true that he was only three years at St. Bene't's, but three years has been the term of more than a few historic ministries. Towards the end of March 1633 he signed the register of St. Bene't's for the last time, and in July of that year Edward Palgrave succeeded him.

---

[1] *Worthies* : Cambridgeshire.

Fuller's student days, his ministry at St. Bene't's, and his first efforts as an author are all interesting; but it was in the *History of Cambridge*, published more than twenty years after he left, that the best fruit of these years ripened. We have seen that his theology, taken from his father and his uncle of Sarum, belonged to the Reformation. In the *History of Cambridge* we see that whereas Dr. Davenant had brought the Reformation spirit into his lectures as Lady Margaret Professor, a position of great prominence in those theological days, Fuller brought it to the writing of history, in that where others had written principally in Latin he wrote principally in English. There had been three histories of Cambridge. First an important one by Dr. John Caius, from whom Fuller took most of his information about the early history of the university, and short sketches by Archbishop Parker and Richard Parker. But Fuller was the first to write a full-length history of Cambridge in English, and in giving the people the history of one of their two ancient seats of learning he must have had something of the spirit that inspired those who a few generations earlier gave them the Bible in English. And we have to remember that works of learning in English were almost unknown at the time of Fuller's birth. In the 1605 catalogue of the Bodleian Library only thirty-six of the six thousand volumes were in the vernacular.

To the information taken from Caius about the early history of the university, Fuller added much that he had gleaned from the Rolls of the Tower of London,[1] and valuable personal knowledge that had come to him from such friends and acquaintances as Archbishop Ussher, Drs. Ward and Butts, and Joseph Mede. To these went his own experiences and the many anecdotes current in the colleges of his day, which professional historians were later to dismiss as gossip, but which often tell us far more than statistics about student interests and the general social atmosphere of the period. It is worth while observing that for more than two hundred years

---

[1] 'He that may with as much ease go to the fountain, and yet will drink of the dirty river, deserveth no pity if choked.'—*History of Cambridge*, i. 54–6.

no attempt was made to replace Fuller's history with a more authoritative work.

Like everything Fuller wrote, it is full of his own personality, and has many shrewd digs at pomposity. Of those who pursue phantoms in argument he writes: 'For he that falls heavy on a ghost, or shadow, will in fine give the greatest blow or bruise unto himself.'[1] It is not surprising in one so loyal that his own colleges should be given more sparkling paragraphs than most. Thus when he writes of the two ancient guilds of Cambridge, 'The Guild of Corpus Christi, keeping their prayers in St. Benedict's Church, the Guild of the blessed Virgin, observing their offices in St. Mary's Church,' he says:

'Betwixt these there was a zealous emulation, which of them should amortize and settle best maintenance for such chaplains to pray for the souls of those of their brotherhood. Now though generally in those days the stars outshined the sun; I mean more honour (and consequently more wealth) was given to saints than to Christ himself; yet here the Guild of Corpus Christi so outstript that of the Virgin Mary in endowments, that the latter (leaving off any farther thoughts of contesting) desired an union, which being embraced, they both were incorporated together.

'Thus being happily married, they were not long issueless, but a small college was erected by their united interest, which, bearing the name of both parents, was called "the College of Corpus Christi and the blessed Mary." However, it hath another working-day name, commonly called (from the adjoining church) Bene't College; yet so, that on festival solemnities (when written in Latin, in public instruments) it is termed by the foundation name.'

Writing of the feast and procession of Corpus Christi started by the pope in 1246 and continued until about 1535, which was revived by Lord Queenborough in 1949 to strengthen the ties between town and gown, he says: 'Then in Corpus-Christi College was a dinner provided them, where, good stomachs meeting with good cheer and welcome, no wonder if mirth followed of course. Then out comes the cup

[1] *History of Cambridge*, i. 51.

of John Goldcorne (once alderman of the guild) made of an horn, with the cover and appurtenances of silver and gilt, which he gave this company, and all must drink therein.' [1]

The trouble in starting a quotation from Fuller is that it is so hard to stop, for there is scarcely a paragraph that has not some good thing in it. Never, surely, did learning walk with a lighter step or pause so often for a jest. Fuller is seldom more delightful than in his digressions, and even if it were proved that his scholarship has been superseded, he would still be a most profitable author for the savour of his asides. Thus, writing of Trinity Hall, he says:

'Henry Harvey the sixteenth master of this hall was he who out of a pious intent—as we are bound to believe, because profitable to others—with great expense did make a causeway on the south and other sides of Cambridge for the more convenience of passengers in those dirty ways. So that his bounty hath made summer unto them in the depth of winter, allowing a large annual revenue for the maintenance thereof.

'Here I cannot forbear one passage, which I may call a serious jest, which happened on this occasion. A noble person, but great anti-academic, met Dr. Harvey one morning overseeing his workmen, and bitterly reflecting on his causelessly suspected inclinations to popery:

'"Doctor," said he, "you think that this causeway is the highway to heaven."

'To whom the other as tartly replied: "Not so, sir, for then I should not have met you in this place."'

The human note is still there, and in writing of a place where so high a premium is set on brilliance, it is particularly gratifying to find our university historian saying in section iv, 'Yea, the general weight of God's work in the Church lieth on men of middle and moderate parts. That servant who improved his two talents into four, did more than the other who increased his five into ten. Tradesmen will tell you it's harder to double a little than treble a great deal.'

Whether in gown or surplice Fuller was always a man of the people, and there is more virtue in this than at first appears. We know that at this time there was a rising of the

---

[1] *History of Cambridge*, iii. 5–7.

national spirit against arbitrary and restrictive rule in the State, and that in the Church there was a similar movement, which Fuller supported. The king stood in the way of one, Laud in the way of the other, and eventually both were removed. It is true that later they proved more powerful in death than they had ever been in life, but nevertheless the popular movement of the day was against them. Fuller's position was complicated. He was a king's man, but not a Laudian. On the surface it may seem contradictory that so convinced a democrat as he was should have been so ardent a Royalist. As he himself saw the relationship between the king and his people this was not so. The king's England was everyman's England, because the king was everyman's ruler and guardian. Fuller's universe was authoritarian. He acknowledged his fealty. First, he served God; under God he served the king. Because his neighbours were God's people and the king's he honoured and respected them. They were not to him the common people, but God's children and the king's subjects.

As a writer Fuller became a pioneer in this movement for liberation. And the fruit of freedom that is to be gathered from his works sprang from the seed of freedom sown in his mind at Cambridge, of which the first show of blossom burst into the light while he was minister of St. Bene't's. This movement towards literary freedom as well as political and religious freedom was in the air in Fuller's day. Milton gave supreme expression to its grand philosophical aspect. But there was an aspect of it more widely felt and closer to the common mind of the people, which the warm-hearted Fuller could express far better than the austere and lofty Milton. The poet, while politically on the side of the people against the bishops, wrote much of his work in Latin, the language of the bishops, while the parson, who defended the bishops, was at pains to translate, and to write his history of Cambridge in English. In short, as democrats, Fuller was practical where Milton was theoretical. And while the latter was concerned to liberate literature from political control, the former, without making any fuss about it, was effectively liberating it from academic control.

CHAPTER V

A COUNTRY CURE

*The great and glorious masterpiece of man is to know how to
live to purpose; all other things, to reign, to lay up treasure, to
build, are, at most, but little appendices and props.*

MONTAIGNE.

THE death of his father early in 1632 brought new responsibilities to Fuller, who as eldest son, though only twenty-four,
was now charged with the care of his mother and her younger
children.   Fortunately Uncle Davenant was still a benevolent
figure in the background.   If parentage was no longer a
sheltering tree, the boughs of patronage were still laden with
ripe fruit.   Mr. Fuller senior had died poor; but Sarum was
rich.   By the timely passing of Dr. John Rawlinson on the
18th June 1631 the prebend of Netherbury-in-Ecclesia,
Beaminster, Dorsetshire, a stall in the cathedral of Salisbury,
and 'one of the best prebends in England,'[1] had become
vacant and Fuller had been appointed.   This had supplemented his income from the college living; but he must
gradually have come to feel that in order to fulfil his family
obligations he must sooner or later quit the academic courts
that were now so pleasant to him and undertake heavier, or at
least more remunerative, duties.

By this time Uncle Davenant was well advanced with his
task of finding husbands for his eight nieces—'our maidens,'
as he calls them in his letters—bequeathed to him, as it were,
along with their mother, by his brother-in-law, Dr. Townson.
By coupling a living with a niece he found no great difficulty
in coupling a niece with a husband.   As Aubrey put it, he
'married them all to clergymen; so he was at no expense for
their preferment.'   In State Papers Domestic there is a
letter dated 31st March 1633, in which the writer fears that
he will be unable to win a certain Mr. Chandler as a husband

---

[1] *The Appeal of Injured Innocence*, i. 286.   Fuller's composition for
£39 5s. 3d., dated 25th November 1631, is in the Public Record Office.

for one of his own sisters, because the said Mr. Chandler had
recently been made a prebendary of Sarum, which probably
meant that he was destined to become the husband of one of
the remaining Townson sisters.

If space allowed, it might be interesting to trace the off-
spring of these eight sisters through the rectories and
bishoprics of England in succeeding centuries.   We might
find that more than one, like Hobson's bag of gold, became

> the fertile mother of a thousand more

so prudently did the bishop invest them with

> thriving sons of such a thrifty father.

The moves in the diocese and patronage of Salisbury during
these years were rather like those in the old-fashioned parlour
game, family post.   Thus Margaret Townson's husband,
John Ryves, received a prebend in 1625, and became Arch-
deacon of Berkshire on Edward Davenant's resignation in
1634.   Ellen's husband, Humphrey Henchman, had the
prebend of South Grantham in Salisbury Cathedral given to
him in 1628.   In 1660 he succeeded his first patron by himself becoming Bishop of Salisbury in reward for his service in
helping Charles to escape from the country after the battle of
Worcester.   Mary's husband, Dr. Alexander Hyde, Clarendon's first cousin, was made Sub-dean of Sarum and later
Prebendary of South Grantham, as successor to Henchman.
Later he was Dean of Winchester and yet another Bishop of
Salisbury, which by this time must have become something
of a Townson or Davenant perquisite.   He succeeded Earle
in 1665.   And so we might go on.   The source of these many
streams of information is that most valuable of all the Fuller
and Townson family papers, the will of Bishop Davenant—
the well from which so many mercies flowed.

At the bishop's death in 1641, most of his property went to
Edward Davenant, his nephew, who had a large family to
support; and it was this particular legacy that moved
Aubrey to say (*Letters*, ii. 300–1) that Edward Davenant had
gained more profit from the see of Sarum that any man since
the Dissolution.

Fuller is not a safe guide to his own life.   He was too busy making notes about other people to have time for many about himself. Rarely has so illustrious a writer been less of an egoist. Even in writing of his association with Cambridge we find him confusing; but other records are available there, so we do not lose the thread of his life until the end of March 1633, the date of his surrender of the living of St. Bene't's. It seems likely that he spent the next few months at Salisbury, or in that neighbourhood. Then in the middle of the following year, 1634, he was presented to the valuable Dorset living of Broadwindsor, eight miles inland from Bridport, with a parish seven miles long and four miles wide close to the Somerset border. Its landmarks are two hills, Lewesdon and Pilsdon, which serve to guide sailors, who know them as the Cow and Calf. The village itself, with its grey stone cottages, its pastures, and orchards, is not unlike his native Aldwincle except that being built in the folds of the hills it is more compact. About it is a

> variegated scene, of hills
> And woods and fruitful vales, and villages
> Half hid in tufted orchards, and the sea
> Boundless, and studded thick with many a sail.

Instead of the one straggling street, the village has several roads, radiating like the spokes of a wheel from a small square in the centre. To the north is the church, with its fine embattled tower dominating the cottages. Near by is a cottage where Charles II spent one of the perilous nights after the battle of Worcester. As his cousin's husband had assisted in arranging the flight, it is possible that Fuller, no longer the parson, helped to the extent of recommending a loyal cottager who could be asked for shelter.

Broadwindsor responded to the addresses of its rector as eagerly as Cambridge had done, and there is still a tradition in the parish that he used to preach from the steps in summer to congregations so large that they could not find room in the church. His parsonage had become ruinous by the nineteenth century, and during the incumbency of Archdeacon Denison a new one was built on another site. For a time the old house served the curate. Later it was reconstructed to become the village school and schoolhouse.

Fuller seems to have settled down happily to life in the country. He had been born and bred in a village parsonage and was always at ease sitting with country folk in their cottage parlours. He knew how to talk the homely wisdom that went to their hearts, and knew also the value of liberality: 'This much takes the affections of country people, whose love is much warmed in a good kitchen and turneth much on the hinges of a buttery-door often open.' [1] Never can he have felt the least inclination to write of Dorset what his fellow clergyman, Robin Herrick of Dean Prior, wrote of Devon:

> More discontents I never had
> Since I was born than here;
> Where I have been, and still am sad,
> In this dull Devonshire.

The reply of Mrs. Thrale's mother to the country parson who complained of the dullness of rural society would apply equally well to Fuller.

'They talk of runts,' said the superior clergyman.

'Sir,' replied the old lady, 'Mr. Johnson would learn to talk of runts.'

Fuller certainly did. He was obviously excellent company. As Lamb said, 'his way of telling a story, for its eager liveliness, and the perpetual running commentary of the narrator happily blended with the narration, is perhaps unequalled.' How many of those stories, we may wonder, were first tried out on his village neighbours? The parson on his side was not slow to profit from the confidences of his parishioners and his own reflections on their ways. He observed, for example, how a farmer would stroke a skittish cow before milking her, and used the figure to make a point in an argument. As a collector of local proverbs he had fine sport. There was one,

> As much akin
> As Lewson Hill to Pilson Pen.

This meant no kin at all. He made use of it in the *Worthies*: 'It is spoken of such who have vicinity of habitation

[1] *The Holy State*, iv. 12.

or neighbourhood, without the least degree of consan-
guinity or affinity betwixt them: for these are two high hills,
the first wholly, the other partly, in the parish of Broadwindsor, whereof once I was minister.' Had he kept a diary
we might even have had an entry like that of Parson Josselin
of Earl's Colne, Essex, for 3rd April 1670: 'Cow calved;
administered the sacrament, only fourteen present.'

At Bridport and Charmouth he would see more of seamen
than he could have seen at Aldwincle and Cambridge. There
were even descendants of Sir Francis Drake among his
parishioners. In recording an anecdote about Drake at
Porto Rico he says he had it 'from the mouth of Henry
Drake, Esquire, there present, my dear and worthy parishioner, lately deceased.' Henry Drake, according to the
Broadwindsor register, married the widow of Sir Arthur
Champernoune. From another of his Dorset neighbours,
Gregory Gibbes, a stout church-and-king man with whom
Charles I lodged on the night of 3rd–4th September 1644, he
obtained information about the warfare of the Knights of
Malta with Tunis and Algiers, which he used in the *Holy War*,
just as Samuel Purchas picked up material for his *Pilgrims*
while vicar of Eastwood in Essex. So when our worthy
doctor came to write his sketch of 'The Good Sea Captain'
in *The Holy State* he was able to fly a brave flag:

'In taking a prize he most prizeth the men's lives whom he
takes; though some of them may chance to be Negroes or
savages. 'Tis the custom of some to cast them overboard,
and there's an end of them: for the dumb fishes will tell no
tales. But the murder is not so soon drowned as the men.
What, is a brother by the half blood no kin? A savage hath
God to his father by creation, though not the Church to his
mother, and God will revenge his innocent blood. But our
captain counts the image of God nevertheless his image cut
in ebony as if done in ivory, and in the blackest Moors he sees
the representation of the King of Heaven.'

Thus in his cottage vicarage, supported by his prebend,
his £70 a year from the living, his glebe, and his tithes of
wool and lamb, orchard fruits, and woven cloths, Fuller
developed new interests and gave the old a chance to mature.

The change from a brilliant university congregation to one of plain country folk was a test. He saw at once that the Saviour of all must be as readily understood by the farmer and his wife as by the masters and fellows of the Cambridge colleges, and he saw that what binds each to Him also binds them to each other. So it became a characteristic of his preaching, as of his writing, that he addressed himself to men as men and not as members of one particular calling. What was food for the man was food for the master. How well he would have understood Dr. Johnson's desire to omit 'civilization' from his *Dictionary* and substitute 'civility'!

We may find the ideal he set himself in his sketch of 'The Faithful Minister' in *The Holy State*, which, in his usual way, he divides into 'maxims.' The first is: 'He endeavours to get the general love and goodwill of his parish . . . otherwise he may preach his own heart out, before he preacheth anything into theirs. The good conceit of the physician is half a cure, and his practice will scarce be happy where his person is hated; yet he humours them not in his doctrine to get their love. . . . He shall sooner get their goodwill by walking uprightly than by crouching and creeping.'

The third maxim is Fuller to the life: 'His behaviour towards his people is grave and courteous. Not too austere and retired. . . . Specially he detesteth affected gravity.' And another might be said by many—and perhaps rightly— to be the public speaker's golden rule: 'Having brought his sermon into his head, he labours to bring it into his heart before he preaches it to his people.'

Though friendly and affable, Fuller was not incapable of anger. We have it on his own confession that he was 'choleric' by nature. He had no patience with humbug, and above all liked to square ideas with the practical affairs of life. Here we have him on that common village tragedy, the birth of a child out of wedlock: 'Some, perchance, will smile, though I am sure all should sigh, at the following story:

'A minister of these times sharply chid one of his parish for having a base child, and told him, he must take order for the keeping thereof.

'"Why, sir," answered the man, "I conceive it more

reasonable that you should maintain it.   For I am not book-
learned, and ken not a letter in the Bible; yea, I have been
your parishioner this seven years, present every Lord's day
at the church, yet did I never there hear you read the ten
commandments; I never heard that precept read, 'Thou
shalt not commit adultery.'   Probably, had you told me
my duty, I had not committed this folly."

'It is an abominable shame,' comments Fuller, 'and a crying
sin of this land, that poor people hear not in their churches
the sum of what they should pray for, believe, and practise;
many mock-ministers having banished out of divine service
the use of the Lord's prayer, creed, and ten commandments.'[1]

His books are full of reflections of village life used to point
a moral in this manner.   Thus, 'I have observed that
children,' he says in one place, 'when they first put on new
shoes, are very curious to keep them clean. . . .   Yea, rather
they will wipe the leather clean with their coats; and yet,
perchance, the next day they will trample with the same
shoes in the mire up to the ankles.   Alas, children's play is
our earnest.'   Or, having watched a servant girl make,
kindle, and blow a fire, and afterwards go about her work
while her mistress sat by the fire, he noticed that the servant
girl was warmer than the mistress, enjoying a 'more general,
kindly, and continuing heat.'   This he was able to use for a
homely moral.   And it must have been after listening to one
of the long-winded Calvinistic harangues of the day that he
wrote that gem: 'Grant that I may never rack a Scripture
simile beyond the true intent thereof, lest, instead of sucking
milk, I squeeze blood out of it.'

We might pick fruit of this kind from every chapter,
almost every page of Fuller, no matter what the subject,
and what is most engaging is his watchfulness over himself.
In *Good Thoughts in Worse Times* he confides: 'A person of
great quality was pleased to lodge a night in my house.   I
durst not invite him to my family prayer; and therefore for
that time omitted it; thereby making a breach in a good
custom. . . .   Bold bashfulness, which durst offend God
whilst it did fear man.   Especially considering, that though

---

[1] *Mixt Contemplations in Better Times*, part ii, xlv.

my guest was never so high, yet by the laws of hospitality, I was above him whilst he was under my roof.'

While, however, it is plain that at Broadwindsor he was still as interested as ever in the poor, then, as increasingly afterwards, it was desirable if not essential for the parson to be on the best of terms with the local gentry, whose noble mansions, set in their deer parks, stood out in the great tracts of heath and moor that made up most of the seventeenth-century landscape. So learned and sociable a divine as Fuller could not fail to be something of an adornment to rural society, and he soon found it necessary to be on his guard against facile popularity. His books have many warnings against its deceptive lure. Perhaps the best is in *Good Thoughts in Bad Times*, where he says: 'I perceive there is in the world a good-nature, falsely so called, as being nothing else but a facile and flexible disposition, wax for every impression. What others are so bold to beg, they are so bashful as not to deny. Such osiers can never make beams to bear stress in Church and State. If this be good-nature, let me always be a clown. If this be good fellowship, let me always be a churl. Give me to set a sturdy porter before my soul, who may not equally open to every comer. I cannot conceive how he can be a friend to any, who is a friend to all, and the worst foe to himself.' [1]

The great people in that part of the country were the Pouletts, connections of the Marquess of Winchester. Fuller was introduced to them by their relations, the Rolles. The Pouletts had their principal seat at Hinton St. George, Somerset, and of the head of the family Fuller says, he was 'a very accomplisht gentleman of quick and clear parts, a bountiful housekeeper.' One of the sections of the *Church History*, published in 1656, was dedicated to Lady Poulett, a relation of Bishop Ken. Though not published until so long after he had left his country cure, the *Church History* was planned at Broadwindsor, and other sections were dedicated to notable persons in the neighbourhood. One was to Gerard Napier of Middlemarsh Hall and More Crichel, who entertained Charles II and his queen when they visited Salisbury

[1] Mixt Contemplations,' xiii.

during the 1665 plague.   His chief parishioners, Sir Hugh
Windham of Pilsdon Court and John FitzJames of Lewesdon,
also had dedications, one in *A Pisgah Sight of Palestine*, the
other in the *Church History*.

The great advantage of a country retreat to Fuller at this
time was that it allowed him to sit back, as it were, and take
stock of his talents.   Just as we can only see our faces as they
are reflected in mirrors, we can only see our minds as they
are returned to us in correspondences from other minds.   A
present-day writer said recently that when he looked backwards through his life he felt that he had been overpraised
for what he had done with least effort, while what had cost
him most had remained unrecognized.   Fuller must have put
more concentrated work into *David's Heinous Sin* than into
anything else he did, and he must have been proportionately
disappointed when the judgment of competent critics went
against it.   On the other hand, he must have marvelled at
first that by merely being himself he could fascinate the
hearts out of men with either voice or pen.   Now that he had
time to reflect on his own distinctive gifts he was able to see
how to employ them most profitably.   He would, of course,
take into account the difference between quick and slow
returns, and he may have wondered whether he was getting
his effects too easily—producing plants that would soon
wither because they were without roots.   But he seems to
have recognized that the first essential for success is to accept
natural facilities, which meant that he took the image that
had come back to him from his friends and worked from that.
Even his weaknesses, or supposed weaknesses, he accepted.
He had, he says, a poor voice, one that was 'harsh and
untunable.'   Leaving aside the point that his opinion on his
own voice was quite worthless, since he could not hear it, the
comment was characteristic.   He simply said that if God had
given him a better voice he would have praised Him with a
better voice.   As it was, he would ask instead for a better
heart.   As he was always aware of the value of effort and
discipline, he may have come to a conclusion similar to the
wise reflection of Joubert, that a good writer 'must have a
natural facility and an acquired difficulty.'

At Broadwindsor, then, he learned to know himself, and we find that his entire career as a writer, excluding his early experiments at Cambridge, was the patient fulfilment of his Dorset projects. For the rest of his life, which was to be harassed and frustrated to an extent he could not then have believed possible, he quietly pursued his purpose, which, whatever the disturbances of his outward life, was as plain in 1660 as in 1640, and unchanged. May not his equanimity throughout the civil wars be due to this? Surely there is no peace on earth to surpass that of a settled creative occupation. Fuller's good counsel to himself and every one else was the same as Chaucer's:

> That thee is sent, receyve in buxumnesse,
> The wrastling for this worlde axeth a fal.
> Her nis non hoom, her nis but wildernesse:
> Forth, pilgrim, forth! Forth, beste, out of thy stal!
> Know thy contree, look up, thank God of al;
> Hold the hye wey, and lat thy gost thee lede:
> And trouthè shal delivere, hit is no drede.

The other side to Fuller's success might be taken for granted if it were not so pronounced and reiterated in him that it ought to be stated, if only for the emphasis he gave it. This was his easy acceptance of others. Obviously a man who accepts his own image as it comes to him from others must accept the good faith of those who present it. There was never any difficulty about this for Fuller. His weakness is towards over-confidence. It must be a matter of opinion with his readers whether, or to what extent, he was too easy an acceptor. Certainly he did accept people easily, and sinners, apparently, as easily as saints. For a man who enjoyed good company as much as Fuller did this may not be surprising. There is much to be said for the motto: 'Pray with the saints; but play with the sinners.' Fuller's prayer was simply 'Let not the smoke of their badness put out mine eyes, but the shining of my innocency lighten theirs. Let me give physic to them, and not take infection from them. Yea, make me the better for their badness. Then shall their bad company be to me like the dirt of oysters, whose mud hath soap in it, and doth rather scour than defile.'

So much for the manner; for the matter—particularly the antiquarian and historical—Dorset was a fine soil to be planted out in.   These studies were to assist his natural temperament and help him to build up steadfastness in the troubled years ahead.   He had already had a foretaste of the vain disputations that were to divide both Church and nation. Such glimpses as he had seen of the dawn of modern science had made him more than doubtful of the value of theological positions supported only by claims of personal inspiration, which often seemed to him nothing but the shifting sands of personal opinion.   And so, as he went deeper into his favourite study of history, with his dogmatic contemporaries in mind, he became more than ever convinced that doctrines may vary but historical facts are sacrosanct.   It was an important attitude just then, when the leaders of the Church were inclined to emphasize the doctrinal rather than the historical foundations of Christianity, and by so doing to prepare the way for the progressive stages that eventually led to nineteenth-century atheism.

With these broad general interests went also his inborn delight in human nature.   Stories told in books written many years later were gathered while he was parson of Broad-windsor.   Thus in *A Pisgah Sight of Palestine*, published in 1650, while he was at Waltham Abbey in Essex, he says: 'I remember whilst I lived in the West of England and confines of Somersetshire hearing a labourer speak much of his long living in the Low Countries.   I demanded of him whether he had ever been in Amsterdam?   He answered that he had never been there, but often at Taunton.   Whereby I plainly perceived what low countries he meant; namely, the flat and level of Somersetshire under Quantock Hills, according to the language of the people in those parts.'   In his final work, the *Worthies*, while writing of the Dorset Sir Thomas More, he has a note of historical value that was evidently picked up from his friends, no doubt retainers of the Pouletts of Hinton St. George: 'Aged folks have informed me, whilst I lived in those parts, by report from their fathers, that this Sir Thomas, whilst sheriff, did, in a wild frolic, set open the prison, and let loose many malefactors.   Afterwards,

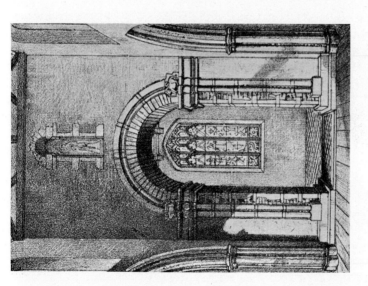

ST. BENE'T'S CHURCH, CAMBRIDGE

Mr Hobſon

obyt año 1630,
vixit annos 86.

Laugh not to ſee ſo plaine a Man in print,
The ſhadow's homely, yet ther's ſomething in't,
Witnes the Bagg he wear's though ſeeming poore)
The fertile Mother of a thouſand more :
He was a thriueing Man, through lawfull Gaine,
And wealthy grew by warrantable paine ;
Then laugh at them that ſpend, not them y^t gather,
Like thriueing Sonnes of ſuch a thriſty Father.

Cum priuileg: Are to be ſoud by P. Stent I Payne fecit

HOBSON, THE CAMBRIDGE CARRIER

considering his own obnoxiousness for so rash an act, he seasonably procured his pardon at court, by the mediation of William Paulet, lord treasurer, and afterwards Marquess of Winchester; and a match was made betwixt Mary, this sheriff's daughter and co-heir, and Sir Thomas Paulet, second son to the said lord, by whom he had numerous issue.'

Such casual collection of data was pleasant and sociable, if often unreliable. With their more exacting standards, later professional historians and biographers were to discredit such delightful amateurs as Fuller and the less scholarly but no less delightful John Aubrey. But while professional historians have been able to obtain for us the facts about any given period better than the early amateurs could, they have all too often had to do so by sacrificing the life. Fuller's instincts were more scholarly than they are sometimes supposed to have been. He consulted authorities and verified facts as well as he could under the circumstances of his life. He was far more conscientious than Aubrey in this. But he never lost sight of the personal background. And if the personal is fallible, it is also organic. There is no life without it.

Meanwhile Fuller was being missed by his old friends at Cambridge, where learning was common but genial wisdom rare. Nominally his residence at the university continued after he left in order to qualify for his degrees in divinity. It continued also for social reasons. There is a brief account in the anonymous biography of a visit to Cambridge attended by some of his Dorset parishioners which has a veritable Parson Adams quality. It was when he went to take his B.D.:

'Having taken care therefore to supply his place for the time of his absence, at his setting forth he was acquainted that four of his chief parishioners, with his good leave, were ready to wait on him to Cambridge, to testify their exceeding engagements, it being the sense and request of his whole parish. This kindness was so present and so resolutely pressed, that the doctor, with many thanks for that and other demonstrations of their love towards him, gladly accepted of

D

their company, and with his customary innate pleasantness entertained their time to the journey's end.'

We can imagine the feelings of these good countrymen when they found their parson as highly esteemed among the learned of Cambridge as he was among the farmers of Broadwindsor or the seamen of Bridport. The anonymous biographer records that while at Cambridge he was in fact visited 'almost by all considerable persons of the university and town; especially of his parishioners of St. Bennet; fame and love vying which should render him most addresses, to the great delight and satisfaction of his fellow travellers and neighbours in having a minister who was so highly and yet no less deservedly honoured, but to the trouble of the modest doctor, who was then forced to busy his invention with compliments, to which he was most naturally averse.' Just how true this last statement was at that time we cannot know; but it is a surprising one, for in later life, at all events, there can seldom have been even a clergyman who was a a better hand at paying compliments than Tom Fuller, though even he never produced anything to match the tribute of Anthony Walker of Fyfield to Mary Rich, Countess of Warwick: 'Oh, for a Chrysostom's mouth, for an angel's tongue to describe this terrestrial seraphine; or a ray of light condensed into a pencil, and made tactile, to give you this glorious child of light *in vivâ effigie*.' [1]

But he was not entirely cut off from Cambridge associations when at home, because Edward Davenant, his old tutor and kinsman, was now vicar of Gillingham, five miles northwest of Shaftesbury, where his seven sons and five daughters were born. Edward Davenant held this vicarage for fifty-three years, and one of his daughters married Thomas Lamplugh, who became Bishop of Exeter and afterwards Archbishop of York. Between Broadwindsor and Gillingham there was frequent coming and going, and in 1637 the link, already close, was strengthened when Fuller married Mrs. Davenant's sister, Eleanor, or Ellen, Grove of Chisenbury in the parish of Enford, which lies to the north of Salisbury Plain. Her father was M.P. for Shaftesbury.

---

[1] *Funeral Sermon*, p. vii.

In his will Bishop Davenant refers to old Mr. Grove as a 'loving friend.' The will was, in fact, deposited with him.

Fuller's first marriage remained a mystery until 1918. Then two correspondents to *Notes and Queries*,[1] one correcting the other, disclosed it. That so normal a match should have been hidden at all requires an explanation, and this is not difficult to find. Mrs. Fuller's half-brother, Captain Hugh Grove, was a Royalist hero, and while Cromwell remained in power Fuller did not wish to imperil his son's career by making the relationship public. If he had survived the Restoration long enough to see his *Worthies* through the press himself, no doubt the curtain would have been lifted. As it is, Hugh Grove is not mentioned among the worthies of Wiltshire, and his only notice in the work appears in an apparently casual reference in the Exeter section: 'Yea, in the very worst of times, a depressed party therein were so true to their principles, that I met with this epitaph in the chancel of St. Sidwell's: "Hic jacet Hugo Grove, in comitatu Wilts. armiger, in restituendo Ecclesiam, in asserendo Regem, in propugnando Legem ac Libertatem Anglicanam, captus et decollatus 6 Maii, 1655."'

Hugh Grove lost his life for his share in the rising of March 1655, when Colonel Penruddock, along with Grove and Sir Joseph Wagstaffe, entered Salisbury at the head of a hundred and fifty horsemen and took possession of the city. Colonel Dove, the sheriff, had refused to proclaim Charles II king, and he and two judges, Rolle and Nicholas, who were then on circuit, were seized in their beds at four o'clock one morning. The judges were there and then made to robe and surrender their commissions. After Penruddock had read the proclamation, the three prisoners were tried. Penruddock would have taken severe measures with them, but Wagstaffe persuaded him to dismiss the judges, and to reserve judgment on the sheriff, whom they carried away with them when they rode out of the city later in the day. Of the two judges, Rolle had the better reputation in his own profession. All who knew him agreed that he was a

[1] Captain A. W. F. Fuller and John T. Hammond in *Notes and Queries*, 12th series, vol. iv., May and July 1918.

remarkably fair-minded man.   There are conflicting opinions about Nicholas.   Anthony Wood says that he had 'in his pleadings some sense, but was extream, virulent, and had foul language at his command.'   All these powers he seems to have exhibited as prosecuting counsel at Laud's trial.   On the other hand, John Aubrey, who was one of his cronies after he had settled down to the life of a Wiltshire country gentle-man, said 'Judge Nicholas was the greatest Antiquary as to Evidences that this Country hath had in the memory of man.'   For that, if for nothing else, we may be glad that he was spared at Salisbury when he came so near to being hanged.   The sheriff also escaped.   He was placed 'on parole,' but broke and returned to Salisbury.

Meanwhile the fortunes of the armies had changed, and when the Royalists were pursued and routed at South Molton only one of the three leaders, Sir Joseph Wagstaffe, escaped.   Penruddock and Grove were carried to Exeter and beheaded by Cromwell's orders.

But while there were good and sufficient reasons for suppressing the name of his first wife's family, we can find none for suppressing all knowledge of her personal character. It is unlikely that so shrewd a judge of human nature as Fuller would choose other than wisely, so we may assume that he took his own admirable advice, which was to 'take the daughter of a good mother.'   But, alas, the marriage was brief.   In 1641 Eleanor Fuller died, leaving an infant son, named John after the bishop, who died shortly before his great-nephew's birth.

As the first subject in Fuller's *Holy State*, published in the year after his wife's death, is 'The Good Wife,' we can-not help connecting the portrait with the lady.   The lines may not resemble Mrs. Fuller's in all particulars, but she must have been in her husband's mind while he sketched. For all that, there is little personality in the study, and when we come to the end of it we may well recall Dr. Johnson's reply to Boswell's question:

'Pray, sir, do you not suppose that there are fifty women in the world, with any one of whom a man may be as happy as with any one woman in particular?'

'Aye, sir,' replied the doctor, 'fifty thousand.'

To-day it might be difficult to find fifty such women as Fuller describes. In his day, as in Johnson's, it would be easy enough to find fifty or even a hundred thousand.

The good wife was a popular subject with seventeenth-century character writers, and in general effect Fuller's conception differs little from the rest. The good wife is thought of as a prudent housewife and good mother rather than as a companion. She is meek and tractable, and 'never crosseth her husband in the spring-tide of his anger.' She conceals her husband's infirmities and never gives away his secrets, if, indeed, she is entrusted with them, for Fuller says 'He knows little who will tell his wife all he knows.' Her clothes are comely rather than costly, and this, perhaps, was the most common note of all. The divines of the day preached much against female vanity—no doubt, because they found it a safer subject than masculine arrogance.

It is disappointing to find Fuller as conventional as his contemporaries; but he is kinder than most, if no more encouraging towards independence. We have it on the authority of the anonymous biographer that he was a most desirable husband—'certainly, no man was more a tender, more indulgent a husband and father: his conjugal love in both matches being equally blest with the same issue, kept a constant tenor in both marriages, which he so improved, that the harmony of his affections stilled all discord and charmed the noise of passion.' If that is accepted, perhaps even the emancipated woman of the twentieth century, though critical of his idea of the good wife, will hear him on the good husband and the good parent. In the second of these two characters he may even be thought liberal. In the first, however, he is still conventional. There is to be no question of equality between husband and wife in authority and responsibility: 'Excellently doth the Apostle argue the doctrine and dignity of men above women from the end and intent of their creation.' What he calls 'fondness' is to be deplored—'a sick love, to be praised in none, and pardoned only in the newly married.' But his second maxim will not be disputed: 'He is constant to his wife, and confident of her.

And sure where jealousy is the gaoler, many break the prison, it opening more ways to wickedness than it stoppeth; so that where it findeth one, it maketh ten dishonest.' He allows the wife freedom in her own affairs: 'Yea, therein he follows her advice: for the soul of man is planted so high, that he overshoots such low matters as lie level to a woman's eye, and therefore her counsel therein may better hit the mark.'

The good parent as Fuller sees him is much nearer the modern conception. He relies on example rather than counsel, and respects the natural aptitudes of his children, 'yet he humours not his child when he makes an unworthy choice beneath himself, or rather for ease than use, pleasure than profit.' A note on the best way to treat wild and unruly sons is interesting. The good parent, says Fuller, 'is careful whilst he quencheth his luxury, not withal to put out his life. The rather because their souls who have broken and run out in their youth, have proved the more health-ful for it afterwards.' On the question whether elderly parents should pass on some of their estates before they die he has a shrewd remark: 'He doth not give away his loaf to his children, and then come to them for a piece of bread. He holds the reins—though loosely—in his own hands, and keeps to reward duty, and punish undutifulness; yet on good occasion for his children's advancement he will depart from part of his means. Base is their nature who will not have their branches lopped till their body be felled; and will let go none of their goods, as if it presaged their speedy death: whereas it doth not follow that he that puts off his cloak must presently [i.e. forthwith] go to bed.'

There is no romantic nonsense about Fuller, no false 'idealism.' Though only thirty-three at the time and newly married, he had no extravagant ideas about the felicity of the wedded state: 'Deceive not thyself by over-expecting happi-ness in the married estate. Look not therein for content-ment greater than God will give or a creature in this world can receive.' Yet, when everything has been taken into account, he is willing to allow that 'all the molestations of marriage are abundantly recompensed with other comforts which God bestoweth on them who make a wise choice of a wife.' But if Fuller had no illusions about marriage, he had the temperament to make a success of it. As for himself as father, two short notes in *The Holy State* tell us more than all his precepts: 'That may be done privately,' he says, 'which may not be done publicly; as when a father makes himself a child's rattle, sporting with him till the father hath devoured the wise man in him.' And the second: 'A gentleman having led a company of children beyond their usual journey, they began to be weary, and jointly cried to him to carry them, which, because of their multitude, he could not do, but told them he would provide them horses to ride on. Then cutting little wands out of the hedge as nags for them, and a great stake as a gelding for himself, thus mounted, fancy put mettle into their legs, and they came cheerfully home.' Such a man had not much to learn in the art of parenthood.

CHAPTER VI

THE GOOD LIFE

*A fine life is a thought conceived
in youth and realized in maturity.*

ALFRED DE VIGNY.

In 1641, as we have seen, Fuller lost both his wife and the bishop, his uncle. The brightness of his life's morning had proved deceptive. The following year brought further clouds, which, if not darker to him personally, were more widespread and lowering, until, on the 22nd August 1642, the royal standard was raised at Nottingham and the nation divided itself into two armed camps. During the spring and early summer of that year the parson of Broadwindsor must have been impressed, as all are impressed who live in the country when war breaks, by the contrast between the rocketing course of politics and the genial rhythm of the seasons. As he watched the seed being sown and the harvest reaped that year he may well have felt that though man cannot live by bread alone, the homely diet is none the less necessary, and that man can, in fact, make a better show of living by bread alone than he can by ideas alone. But Broadwindsor was not so remote from national politics as we might suppose. Lyme was only a few miles away, and already the people of that brisk little port, heavily taxed and disaffected, were ready to take up arms against the king, while everywhere there was the Church controversy. Though Fuller was a Royalist, he was in sympathy with the moderate Puritans on the other side in their concern about the prevailing laxity in morals. Whatever his thoughts on the national aspect of the quarrel he would, we may be sure, continue to exhort the people to look first to their personal integrity: 'Whatsoever it is which hence may be collected, sure I am, those are the best Christians who least censure others and most reform themselves.'[1]

[1] *Church History*, xi 148–9.

In this faith, at a time when his family life was broken and the nation's life divided, he quietly followed his studies and brought out the most popular of his books, *The Holy State*.

Before considering this, however, we ought to glance at his first historical study, *The History of the Holy War*, which came from the press in 1639 and was so successful that it was reprinted the following year. Like most of Fuller's works it was published by John Williams, then of the 'Crane,' St. Paul's Churchyard, afterwards of the 'Greyhound,' and later again of the 'Crown,' who prospered greatly by the sale of Fuller's books, and at the same time did well for the author.

In dedicating *The Holy War* to Edward Montagu and Sir John Poulett, Fuller makes a neat apology for 'lavishing two noble patrons on one book,' explaining that being so much indebted to both he thought it only fair to share his estate between them, and after pointing out that 'none can go far in our English chronicles but they must meet with a Montagu and a Poulett, either in peace in their gowns, or in war in their armour,' he introduces the much quoted passage: 'Now know, next religion, there is nothing accomplishes a man more than learning. Learning in a lord is as a diamond in gold. And if you fear to hurt your tender hands with thorny school-questions, there is no danger in meddling with history, which is velvet-study, and recreation-work. What a pity it is to see a proper gentleman have such a crick in his neck that he cannot look backward! Yet no better is he who cannot see behind him the actions which long since were performed. History maketh a young man to be old, without either wrinkles or grey hairs; privileging him with the experience of age, without either the infirmities or inconveniences.'

History as Fuller writes it is certainly recreation-work, though perhaps too brisk and lively to be described as velvet-study. Though suave he was not plushy. There is something of the sportsman in his headlong race after facts and his verve in rousing the game of wit and fancy from every historical and theological convert. He did so enjoy himself.

The Holy War is a history of the Crusades in five books, of which four deal with the actual progress of events. At the

*D

end of these Fuller was honest enough to admit that his task
was done; but he was a five-book man, so could no more send
the work to the printer with four books only than a five-pint
man can go home without the fifth, even though he has completed the festivities of the evening in four. And with both,
the last tends to be the merriest. Fuller wrote about the
East well enough; but he was at his best while drawing his
conclusions quietly in his own parlour, or, as he himself puts
it, adding a hem to his history to prevent it ravelling.

There are some excellent Fullerisms in the work:

'Mariners' vows end with the tempest.'
'Modesty being the case of chastity, it is to be feared that
where the case is broken the jewel is lost.'
'It is charity to lend a crutch to a lame conceit.'
'No doubt the Christians' army had been greater if it had
been less, for the belly was too big for the head.'
'The best way to keep great princes together is to keep
them asunder.'

There were shrewd digs at those 'who had more sail of valour
than ballast of judgment,' and naturally so stout a Protestant
as Fuller had to score off the pope where possible. So we
have: 'England, the pope's packhorse in that age, which
seldom rested in the stable when there was any work to be
done,' or, 'And thus scraped he a mass of coin from such silly
people as thought themselves cleansed of their sins when they
were wiped of their money.'

It is clear that in collecting material for this history of the
Crusades, Fuller knew how to work his sources. Though no
more than thirty, he could not only find his way through the
heavy folios of his age, but could carry them in his mind as if
they were no heavier than our modern octavos. He had his
favourites, of course. Though he could keep in step with the
old chroniclers, Matthew Paris was a more congenial companion: 'A moderate man whom we follow most.'

In writing of these far-off events and legendary heroes he is
notably unimpressed by the romance and mystery of it all.
The proudest potentate was no more than human to him,
and he could write of a queen in as homely a vein as if she

had been the wife of a neighbouring rector. Thus when he tells the story of Eleanor of Castile's alleged sucking of the poison from the wounds of her king, Edward I, he says: 'So sovereign a medicine is a woman's tongue, anointed with the virtue of loving affection,' then adds teasingly—and we must remember that Eleanor was his wife's name—'Pity it is so pretty a story should not be true . . . and sure he shall get himself no credit, who undertaketh to confute a passage so sounding to the honour of the sex.' But the truth was that Eleanor was kept away from the king while the surgeon did what was necessary. This failure to be suitably impressed by greatness, which is so characteristic of Fuller, while it produces the friendly atmosphere that is one of his special charms, was also part and parcel of his chief deficiency as historian and biographer, his almost complete lack of dramatic sense.

Fuller's candour and sincerity win us to his side on every occasion. If the problem before him is more than commonly difficult he does not knit his brows and assume a solemn judicial pose. He merely smiles and wags his wise head as he looks up his authorities, then chuckles to see so many grave and ponderous scholars come to grief like clumsy riders at an awkward ditch. Thus of Frederick I he says: 'Little hope have I to content the reader in this king's life, who cannot satisfy myself; writers of that age are so possessed with partiality.' The Guelphs and the Ghibellines had so confused the chronicles between them, that as Fuller examined the figure of Frederick as they had left it, he said it reminded him of the fable of the man who had two wives. While his old wife plucked out the black hairs of his head, the evidence of his youth, his young wife plucked out the grey hairs, the evidence of his age, so that between them they made him as bald as an egg. 'So amongst our late writers,' says Fuller, 'whilst Protestants cut off the authority from all papized writers of that age, and Romanists cast away the witness of all imperialized authors then living . . . betwixt them they draw all history of that time very slender, and make it almost quite nothing.' Then comes the authentic Fullerian note: 'We will not engage ourselves in their quarrels; but may safely believe that Frederick was neither saint nor devil, but man.' As man he is therefore examined, and found to be 'very learned, according to the rate of that age, especially for a prince, who only baiteth at learning, and maketh not his profession to lodge in. . . . But this gold had an alloy of cruelty. . . . His pride was excessive, and so was his wantonness: a nun's veil was but a slender shield against his lust.' Then comes that superb Fullerism: 'This sin he was given to, which was besides the custom of the Dutch, saith one, who, though great friends to Bacchus, are no favourites of Venus; which is strange, that they should heap up so much fuel, and have no more fire.'

From the fifth book of *The Holy War*, Fuller would pass naturally, almost inevitably, to *The Holy State*, which is also in five books, each divided into numbered divisions called maxims, an arrangement that suited his terse, epigrammatic style and popular treatment. It could be adapated with equal effect to the three literary forms he used in it, the character, or brief sketch of a type, the thumb-nail portrait, and the essay. In all three he was more successful than may at first be apparent. The character was a popular literary form of the day, and on a first reading there may seem to be nothing remarkable about Fuller's treatment of it except in his peculiar turns of expression, his 'quaintness' as it is called. His debt to Breton, Heywood, Richard Brathwaite, and John Earle, Bishop of Salisbury—whose *Microcosmographie* is the best of all these collections of characters—will be noticed. We may think much of the matter derivative, and suspect that he is merely paraphrasing, though very skilfully, what he has read. To some extent he is doing this—we should never claim for Fuller that he was an original thinker—but when we attempt to trace passages to their source we discover that it is not so simple as we thought. We can find parallels of thought, and authorities for information; but there is nearly always a new element, and that is the essential characteristic of our worthy doctor: the note that he was to strike in all his best work, and that gives him a permanent and not unimportant place in the development of English biography. It is only when we read a number of his sketches together that we see what this was. Biography is an ancient art, and Fuller did not start with any new theories about it. He learned it from the Bible, Foxe's *Book of Martyrs*, and the classics. But he brought to these his own personality, and his instinct for seeing everything in personal terms. And so, where other character writers had set out the attributes of types, Fuller described the characteristics of persons. He wrote with sympathy as well as understanding; always with shrewd common sense, and always with an arrestingly acute perception of human motives. Possibly without knowing it he was feeling his way into the art of biography as it was to be practised most successfully in England in later centuries. There may be different views on the merit of Fuller's biographies. Each man may take them for what they are worth to him. It is no part of the argument here to claim for him any great mastery. No one who has sat at the feet of Fuller for long ought to try to force his own meat on to another man's plate. But there can be no question of his importance as a forerunner. In other words, whether we do or do not believe that he produced the flower and the fruit, we cannot deny that he had the root in him. As the *Dictionary of National Biography* is implicit in *The Worthies of England*, the seed of the *Worthies* is in *The Holy State*.

Before looking further into this, we might pause for a moment to think of the background to this fashion for describing the supposed virtues and vices of various types, such as 'The Good Wife,' 'The Good Husband,' 'The Good Soldier,' and so forth. The instinct which produced them was that which produced so many family portraits at this time. The new families brought to the fore at the Dissolution were now sufficiently settled to be ripening into a new culture. Their position was not to become assured until the revolution of 1688 gave them such immense power through their control of parliamentary and local government; but they were already aware of having become a society, though still self-conscious and not quite sure of themselves. They were very youthful about their newly acquired importance, like the man who on buying a new and superior car pins up a plan of its mechanism on the wall of his garage. Like him again they, and the character writers with them, were inclined to see the new acquisition in terms of an elaborate lay-out of attributes and principles. Fuller, instead of all this gimcrackery, did see a person, and that person an Englishman; yet even he, in setting up house, as we saw in the last chapter, found it helpful to pin up before himself a sketch of the ideal husband and father as he understood them. It was a usual thing to do. George Herbert at Bemerton did the same in *The Country Parson*.

Thus it came about that in Fuller's day there were many books dealing with the virtues, or supposed virtues, of the English gentleman in a manner that would have been improbable, to say the least of it, later. In the early seventeenth century there was still enough difference between one esquire and another to make those who eventually lined up behind Cromwell widely different in the popular mind, if not actually, from those who lined up behind the king. Both, when seen as types, still had on them many sharp corners that were rubbed off between their day and ours.

The Holy State may be described as Fuller's conception of the good life. The ladies' side of it, as became apparent when we glanced at the portrait of 'The Good Wife' for the last chapter, was conventional. There are other aspects to be noticed presently; but its great interest in relation to the literature of the age is in its outline of the virtues to which the gentleman of the day ought to aspire. In effect, it finally becomes a composite portrait of the English gentleman as Fuller saw him. Fuller himself, of course, was a fine example of the scholar-gentleman, of whom there were more than a few among the Cavaliers. So his gentleman, as we should expect, is a scholar. What is most notable, however, is that he was so authentically an Englishman, and in this he differed from the portraits drawn by most of the courtesy and character writers of the day. There was however one essential difference between the English gentleman of Fuller's day and his counterpart of ours. The touchstone of manners to the seventeenth-century gentleman who did not reach the level of the court was the university, where to the twentieth-century gentleman it would be the capital. So the difference between them is the difference between Oxford or Cambridge and London.

Having noted that, we may consider the differences between the various ideas of the gentleman current then. Most of them, we find, were foreign importations. We saw in the sermons on *Ruth* delivered at Cambridge how early Fuller set himself against this hankering after alien attractions. He would have nothing to do with the Italianate creatures, then especially popular; nor would he accept the priggishly Puritan, who also was imported. His instinct here was as right as that of Shakespeare himself, who like him—being another soundly nurtured provincial—kept true to the English idiom. Whether Fuller was fully aware of the distinction or not we do not know. Though it does seem to have been a matter of principle with him, it sprang from his nature, and was simply part of the happy and contented Tom Fuller who had found his way into the hearts and cottages of the poor of Aldwincle and Broadwindsor and, with equal ease, into the college chambers at Cambridge. And simple as it seems, it is that which keeps his work alive when most of the character and courtesy writing of his day is dead. Whenever in reading him we feel like throwing up our caps and cheering —as men in every generation have done—it is not for literary merit or marked originality of thought, but because something in the sentiment or phrasing calls up the image of Tom Fuller, large as life, gay and garrulous as ever.

If we read Fuller impersonally we get little from him. He refuses to slip easily into either the square or the round hole that those who study him academically try to find for him. Often, it must be admitted, he seems to be running with the hare and hunting with the hounds. He supports one party theologically, the other politically. Then as suddenly he rounds on both—the Catholics in 'The Heretick,' the Puritans in 'The Donatists.'

The first of the five books in *The Holy State and the Profane State* is concerned with family life and the domestic virtues that make it. The second is given to the professional virtues—those making for sound and honourable conduct in daily work. The third sets out the social virtues, and the fourth those desirable in public life; while the last book, *The Profane State*, sketches the types to be avoided. The composition of the book is admirable. Fuller is so bland and unhurried in manner that the orderly character of his mind is not always apparent; but if we study his works with the architecture in mind we see that he always knew perfectly well what he was about, even if he was in no haste to accomplish it. Here in *The Holy State* the order is in keeping with his general conception of the good life. First, home; secondly, preparation for a profession; that mastered, there is leisure for cultivating the social virtues. So when firmly and honourably established in life, the gentleman ought to play his part in public life, and see that the national heritage is passed on unimpaired and, if possible, enriched. Fuller is, of course, writing for the educated and well-to-do. This was inevitable in his day. He would preach for the poor; but there was no point in writing for them, for the very good reason that they were unable to read.

There are thirty short biographies in *The Holy State*, used to point morals which the superior modern reader may at times find rather too obtrusive. As we read the first book we may well be reminded of the speech of Polonius to Laertes in *Hamlet*, and be inclined to dismiss Fuller as a prosy old parson. We are all familiar with this criticism of the didactic; but surely if we are honest we shall have to acknowledge that the lines given to Polonius:

> Give thy thoughts no tongue,
> Nor any unproportioned thought his act.
> Be thou familiar, but by no means vulgar;
> The friends thou hast, and their adoption tried,
> Grapple them to thy soul with hoops of steel,

and so on, are among the most popular in Shakespeare.

The enormous sales of Tupper's *Proverbial Philosophy*, the classic of platitudinous didacticism, showed that Victorian England was as prone to this kind of moral indulgence as Stuart England was. And if we in the emancipated twentieth century are tempted to feel superior to both, need we do more than remind ourselves of the extraordinary vogue in our own day of 'Brains Trusts'?

Most of the best examples of Fuller's wit and wisdom in condensed form are found in the third book. Here are a few:

OF HOSPITALITY

'Measure not thy entertainment of a guest by his estate, but thine own. Because he is a lord, forget not that thou art but a gentleman: otherwise if with feasting him thou breakest thyself, he will not cure thy rupture, and (perchance) rather deride than pity thee.'

OF JESTING

'The Earl of Leicester, knowing that Queen Elizabeth was much delighted to see a gentleman dance well, brought the master of a dancing-school to dance before her:

'"Pish," said the queen, "'tis his profession, I will not see him."

'She liked it not when it was a Master-quality, but where it attended on other perfections. The same may we say of jesting. . . . Wanton jests make fools laugh, and wise men frown. . . . Such rotten speeches are worst in withered age, when men run after that sin in their words which flieth from them in the deed.'

OF SCORN

'Scoff not at the natural defects of any which are not in their power to amend. Oh, 'tis cruelty to beat a cripple with his own crutches. Neither flout any for his profession, if honest, though poor and painful. Mock not a cobbler for his black thumbs.'

An aphorism on sinning, 'He that falls into sin is a man; that grieves at it, is a saint; that boasteth of it, is a devil,' reminds us of Longfellow's lines translated from von Logau, who was a contemporary of Fuller:

> Man-like is it to fall into sin,
> Fiend-like is it to dwell therein,
> Christ-like is it for sin to grieve,
> God-like is it all sin to leave.

In this kind of moralizing Fuller was as dull as the rest of them, and like the rest of them he cribbed. But as often as not he introduced an illuminating anecdote that was all his own, or an apt simile. Thus:

Of Apparel

'A great man, who himself was very plain in apparel, checked a gentleman for being over fine: who modestly answered: "Your lordship hath better clothes at home, and I have worse."'   And 'True there is a state sometimes in decent plainness.   When a wealthy lord at a great solemnity had the plainest apparel, "Oh," said one, "if you had marked it well, his suit had the richest pockets."'

In all of them we have Fuller's unfailing common sense and wisdom: 'When our hopes break let our patience hold,' is worth remembering.   So is 'Fancy runs most furiously when a guilty conscience drives it,' and 'To clothe low-creeping matter with high-flown language is not fine fancy but flat fooling.'   Such terse expression of plain truth would be as acceptable from the pulpit at Broadwindsor as from the pulpit at St. Bene't's, and would stick in the minds of those who heard.   It may well be that some of the homely and pithy maxims of Parson Fuller have been handed down in Dorset for generations and are still there.   Country folk cling to such sayings.

Two of the longer ones are so typically Fuller that they must be quoted:

Of Contentment

'He that at first thought ten thousand pounds too much for any one man, will afterwards think ten millions too little for himself. . . .

'I have heard how a gentleman travelling in a misty morning asked of a shepherd, such men being generally skilled in the physiognomy of the heavens, what weather it would be.

'"It will be," said the shepherd, "what weather shall please me."   And being courteously requested to express his meaning, "Sir," saith he, "it shall be what weather pleaseth God, and what weather pleaseth God, pleaseth me."'

This may remind us of Dean Ramsay's shepherd, who,

when someone found fault with the mist, exclaimed: 'What ails ye at the mist, sir? it weets the sod, it slockens the yowes, and'—adding with much solemnity—'it's God's wull.'

OF MODERATION

'Moderation is not a halting betwixt two opinions, when the thorough-believing of one of them is necessary to salvation. . . . Nor is it lukewarmness in those things wherein God's glory is concerned. . . . But it is a mixture of discretion and charity in one's judgment. . . . Pride is the greatest enemy to moderation. . . . Proud men having deeply studied some additional point in Divinity, will strive to make the same necessary to salvation to enhance the value of their own worth and pains.'

As we read this section of the book we begin to wonder whether this man was not as important in the development of the English essay as he was in the development of English biography. Indeed he was. In his day the essay was still an undeveloped form. Before him it had been practised with the greatest success by Bacon, in many ways his master, though so different in character. One of Fuller's best critics, Leslie Stephen, in the *Cornhill Magazine* for January 1872, brings out Fuller's general character as a writer by contrasting his style with Bacon's when both were dealing with the same matter. 'Bacon's sentences,' he says, 'are heavy with thought, as though compressed in a kind of intellectual hydraulic machine. Like Lord Thurlow, they look wiser than any sentence ever really was. . . . Bacon speaks of kings and criminals like a shrewd lawyer and statesman; Fuller like a good-humoured country clergyman, who expects everybody to be as good and happy as himself. In fact, when we endeavour to sum up Fuller's character, that is, perhaps, the last impression that remains with us.'

Plainly he had not Bacon's intellect or command of language any more than he had Milton's. He was not sufficiently selfish to be as ruthless as the great artist or scholar must be. There was nothing of the Olympian about Fuller. But in the very easing and moderating of the strict form used

---

[1] *Reminiscences*, 11th ed., 1864, p. 19.

by Bacon he was showing his 'Englishness,' and steering the essay into channels more congenial to the national temperament. No wonder Charles Lamb, the master of the very form introduced by Fuller, was so delighted when he discovered him. Fuller had not enough of the artist in him to bring this easy, humane kind of writing to perfection in the way Bacon brought his own incisive kind to perfection; but in his sweet reasonableness and detached yet warm-hearted manner he was the ancestor of several masters of this form in England. Here again he knew what he was about, for in his address to the reader at the front of the book he says that essays for the most part are not fare for a feast, but for an ordinary. That also was where Tom Fuller showed up at his best.

It is in this temperate spirit that he approaches this question of the gentleman. The background to the English gentleman in Fuller's mind was the English countryside. He came from the soil, and began in the honest heart of 'The Good Yeoman,' who was 'a gentleman in ore, whom the next age may see refined; and is the wax capable of a gentle impression, when the Prince shall stamp it. Wise Solon, who accounted Tellus the Athenian the most happy man for living privately on his own lands, would surely have pronounced the English yeomanry a fortunate condition, living in the temperate zone, betwixt greatness and want, an estate of people almost peculiar to England.' Fuller's joy in the yeoman glows in every line, and most heartily when he thinks of the bountiful fare at his table where 'you shall have as many joints as dishes: no meat disguised with strange sauces; no straggling joint of a sheep in the midst of a pasture of grass, beset with salads on every side, but solid substantial food; no servitors, more nimble with their hands than the guests with their teeth, take away meat before stomachs are taken away. Here you have that which in itself is good, made better by the store of it, and best by the welcome to it.'

This is a different approach to the conception of the gentleman from that of Peacham, whose *Compleat Gentleman* was one of the most popular of these courtesy books, or

manuals of polite behaviour. Peacham's gentleman is a
courtier, Fuller's a countryman. His line may not go back
as far as the Heveninghams of Suffolk or the Tilneys of Norfolk, or the Nauntons—again of East Anglia—whose ancestors were worth seven hundred pounds a year at the Conquest; but if he has virtue and valour he may take his place
with the best, for 'In England the Temple of Honour is
bolted against none, who have passed through the Temple of
Virtue.' Among other qualities, 'He is courteous and
affable to his neighbours. As the sword of the best tempered
metal is most flexible, so the truly generous are most pliant
and courteous in their behaviour to their inferiors. He
delights to see himself and his servants well mounted: therefore he loveth good horsemanship. . . . If the Commission
of the Peace finds him out, he faithfully discharges it. I say,
finds him out, for a public office is a guest which receives the
best usage from them who never invited it. . . . If chosen a
Member of Parliament he is willing to do his country service.
If he be no rhetorician to raise affections . . . he counts it
great wisdom to be the good manager of Yea and Nay. The
slow pace of his judgment is recompensed by the swift following of his affections, when his judgment is once soundly
informed. And there we leave him in consultation, wishing
him with the rest of his honourable society all happy
success.'

Fuller was well aware that all who attained high positions
in the land had not passed through the Temple of Virtue.
In reading him on the professions we are reminded that the
standards of public morality were much lower then than they
are now. He hints at sharp practices in his humorous way,
at the same time pointing out with all the gravity of his calling
that each man holds his station in life under God, to whom he
must render his account. And if we feel like saying with
Queen Elizabeth, 'Pish, 'tis his profession,' we are quickly
pulled up by maxims as shrewd as any in Bacon. Could
there, for example, be sounder advice to men in business or
public life than these?

'Having attained to a competent height, he had rather
grow a buttress broader than a storey higher,' and 'He

preserves all inferior officers in the full rights and privileges of their places.'

As Fuller was so ardent a Royalist, it is worth remarking that it is more than probable that one of the reasons for this interest in the cultured and godfearing gentleman, was that England had for nearly forty years been ruled by two kings who patronized learning more generously than any of their successors have done. So it was natural that the good life should be seen by Fuller as being lived under the sovereignty of a good king. Consequently the king is the final topic in *The Holy State*, which concludes with a prayer for His Majesty's safety: 'Smite through the loins of those that rise up against His Majesty, but upon him and his let the Crown flourish.' They were bold words to utter at such a time, and that Fuller knew their daring is shown in the book's appearance without a dedication. Clearly he did not wish to involve any one else in what he feared might be the consequences of his loyalty.

CHAPTER VII

KING'S MAN

That stout Church-and-King man, Tom Fuller.

COLERIDGE.

Doubtless there were many among Fuller's acquaintances who felt, to use the doctor's own figure, that it was a great pity so large a candle should be burning in the kitchen when light was needed in the hall. Contented as he was among the orchards of Dorset, a man so active and so well qualified for eminence could not remain in a remote and rural parish for ever. As a writer on subjects where research was necessary he would feel the need to be within reach of records. As a preacher of note he would long for opportunity to raise his voice in a more influential pulpit. There were also personal reasons for desiring a change. Since the death of his wife and uncle he had been lonely in his country parsonage. There is nothing to suggest that he was unhappy in Dorset. How could he be? But as the anonymous biographer has it, 'his spirit was framed by nature for converse and general intelligence, not to be smothered in such an obscurity.' Only in London, the 'quick forge and working-house of thought,' could his faculties have full play.

In 1640 he had attended the historic convocation of that year as proctor for the diocese of Bristol, elected by his fellow clergy after only six years' residence among them. His colleague had been Gilbert Ironside, afterwards Bishop of Bristol. The upshot of this episode in his life will be dealt with in a later chapter, but it is mentioned here because it was probably while attending convocation that he caught the ropes which eventually drew him to London. They were literary as well as theological, for when he went up to town he carried in his pocket the manuscript of the first of his many volumes of sermons, *Joseph's Parti-coloured Coat*, dedicated to Lady Jane Covert of Pepper-Harrow, near Godalming, Surrey, and that, if not flatteringly, at least with no lack of complimentary grace!

The date of his removal from Dorset cannot be given accurately because he did not resign the living until later. Years afterwards, in controversy with Peter Heylyn, when he said that for the sake of 'his lord and master, King Charles,' he had lost 'none of the worst livings and one of the best prebends in England,' and was therefore a fellow sufferer with Heylyn in the royal cause, Heylyn retorted that 'a sufferer he could not be, because he willingly relinquished both his cure and prebend.' What happened, apparently, was that he left the parish in charge of the curate, Henry Sanders, who with Fuller and all the two hundred and forty-two adults in the parish took the protestation ordered by the Long Parliament in 1641, until the Puritan John Pinney, who succeeded Fuller as vicar, was appointed to the charge of the parish during the interregnum. According to Calamy, Pinney, whose family still flourishes in the neighbourhood, was 'much of a gentleman, a considerable scholar, a very facetious, yet grave and serious companion, and an eloquent charming preacher.' Fuller and he were probably on good terms, and by an act of characteristic generosity the doctor did not reclaim his living as he might have done at the Restoration, but resigned in Pinney's favour. The document giving effect to this assignment is still at Racedown, the Dorset seat of the Pinney family. More than a century later—in 1795—one of John Pinney's descendants made a gesture of a similarly generous kind when he offered the Wordsworths the use of Racedown, with results so happily recorded in Dorothy's *Journal*.

The resignation is in these terms: 'These are to Certifie that Whereas John Pinney hath for severall yeares last past lived in & supplied the Cure of the Vicaridge of Broadwindsor in ye County of Dorset & hath exhibeted to me the unanim^s desire of the Parishion^s for his Continuance therein I Thomas ffuller Dr. in Divinity, the late true and Lawfull Incumbent thereof doe hereby declare and signifie my consent and allowance that the said John Pinney shall bee & continue in the cure and Vicaridge of Broadwindsor afores^d. To whome I doe hereby resigne & yeeld up my right title & claime to it for ever And all dues demandes fifths w^tsoever I doe hereby acquit release & descharge the said John Pinney his heires executours & Administrat^{rs} forever wch haue bin or shall be due or payable by him or them out of the sayd Vicaridge to me my heires execut^{rs} Administrat^{rs} or Assignes In testimony whereof I haue hereunto set my hand this 18th day of October 1660.'

The anonymous biographer tells us that on removing to the capital, Fuller preached 'in most of the voiced pulpits of London, being cried up for one of the most excellent preachers of his age, but most usually in the inns of court.' Then in the early summer of 1642 the master and brotherhood of the King's Chapel of the Savoy invited him to become their minister. The precise nature of the appointment is uncertain. The original Chapel Royal stood within the precincts of the ancient palace where John of Gaunt, 'time-honoured Lancaster,' lived so bravely. Henry VII converted its ruins into a hospital for the poor, which, when completed by Henry VIII, was placed in the charge of a master and four chaplains. In Edward VI's reign it ceased to fulfil its intended purpose; but was re-established by Mary. Under Elizabeth it found yet another use. Favourites were allowed to live in the hospital apartments rent free, while the church was granted to a new parish created by detaching part of St. Clement Danes and adding it to the royal precinct. So when the hospital was officially dissolved in 1702 it was declared that the statutes for the reception of the poor had not been observed in living memory. The master and his chaplains, however, who received £26 a year with other allowances, continued to enjoy the emoluments of office, though beneficed elsewhere. In other words: the poor came, the poor went; but the parsons continued for ever.

The master at the time of Fuller's appointment was Dr. Balcanquhall, king's chaplain and dean of both Rochester and Durham, who had held office since 1617. He and his chaplains appointed a curate whom they paid £20 a year, but who also received an allowance from the parishioners. It is by virtue of this voluntary support from the parish that the office may be regarded as a lectureship. Such particulars as we possess in authentic records are to be found in the *Journals of the House of Commons*, where we learn that on the 30th May 1642 fourteen or fifteen parishioners of St. Mary Savoy petitioned for one Thomas Gibbs, a Puritan, to be appointed lecturer.   The following month this petition was again presented.   But this time another, signed by one hundred and twenty parishioners, was brought in favour of Thomas Fuller.   Thus Fuller received the appointment at the request of a majority of the parishioners.   But whatever the precise nature of the office may have been, his own understanding of it is fairly clear.   When in January of the following year *An Innocents' Day Sermon*, preached from his new pulpit, was published, he was described on the title-page as 'Thomas Fuller, B.D., Minister of the Savoy,' and elsewhere he referred to his 'dear parish, St. Mary Savoy.' It was evidently one of those many complex and peculiar appointments that only the Church of England has the ingenuity to contrive.

It is unlikely that Fuller would lose much time in entering upon his new duties, so we may say with reasonable assurance of accuracy that he became minister or lecturer of the Savoy in midsummer 1642, at the time when the nation, as it were, stared in helpless terror towards the storm clouds of war that each succeeding day loomed darker.   At such a time we can imagine how eagerly the people of London would be listening for any new voice that would give them hope and confidence, and this voice they expected to hear from a pulpit, not a platform.   There have been times when we have forgotten how influential the spoken word can be—that Socrates was a talker, not a writer, and that Our Lord Himself transformed men through speech, not writing.   It is the written word that has brought the records of such influence down to us; but it was the spoken word that first caught men's ears and fastened on their hearts.   During the literary eighteenth and nineteenth centuries the written word might appear to have eclipsed the spoken; yet even then we have only to remember Dr. Johnson to see that the old potency of speech was by no means lost.   The radio of the twentieth century has brought it into full play again.   So it might be argued that it has never failed, and has only varied in that in one age it has been heard in the market-place, in another in crowded hall or church, in yet another at the dinner-table, and finally at the fireside.   Each of these different places has demanded its own technique; but the trend, seen across the centuries, has been for force to give place to persuasion.

In the seventeenth century the pulpit was undoubtedly the place of power.   Bishop Hacket referred to those who 'rang the pan in the pulpit, and the bees swarmed to rebellion.'   Clarendon complained that it was not the politicians but the clergy—'ambassadors of peace by their function,' who were the chief 'incendiaries towards rebellion.'   While Fuller himself, in the *Church History*, was to give the same complaint a humorous turn by saying that such preachers reversed 'the silver trumpets of the sanctuary,' and 'putting the wrong end into their mouths, make what was appointed to sound Religion, to signify Rebellion.'

The outward scene, as Fuller saw it, would in one respect be similar to that which Sir Roger de Coverley saw: 'The old Knight turning about his head twice or thrice to take a survey of this great Metropolis, bid me observe how thick the City was set with churches, and that there was scarce a single steeple on this side Temple Bar.'

The presence of a pretty French queen, with her dwarfs, her dogs, and her Negro servants, had done something to brighten the sombre, theological background of the city. There had been plays and Twelfth Night masques, and the ladies of the court had been resplendent in satin and pearls. Yet even at court there had been the long-drawn-out battle between the king's chaplains and the queen's confessors, which sometimes produced such vulgar exhibitions as the one at Titchfield when chaplain and confessor tried to shout each other down in a ludicrous altercation to decide which should say grace.   To the poets and artists of London, Charles and Henrietta were the handsomest royal couple in Europe.   To themselves they were the happiest.   But to the Puritan ministers they were the Man of Sin and the Popish Brat of France.

So we may think of Fuller entering an arena rather than a

parish, and in its lists he must have been tempted as at no other time in his life—tempted, not in his weakness but in his strength. When he took up his ministry at the Savoy he probably had it in his power to be the most popular London preacher of the day. Indeed, he was popular. The anonymous biographer says that 'He had in his narrow chapel two audiences, one without the pale, the other within; the windows of that little church, and the sextonry so crowded as if bees had swarmed to his mellifluous discourse.' In a sermon preached at Cambridge, Fuller had already made his own conception of a minister's function plain: 'Well it is said of Socrates, that he was the first of the Grecians which humbled speculative into moral philosophy. How well would the pains of that minister be employed who should endeavour to bring down and abate many superfluous contemplative queries into practical divinity.' It were liberty enough if the sermons of all preachers were bound to keep residence only on such subjects which all Christians are bound to believe and practise for their soul's health.'[1]

He was not a show preacher; but in spite of that he had such gifts and qualities that it was plain for him to see that London was offered in a nut, and that he had only to crack the shell to enjoy the kernel. But the lesson of the Temptation in the Wilderness had not been lost on him. He refused the laurel and kept his soul. Fuller has been dubbed a time-server. There could not be an emptier charge. He yielded nothing to popular applause. On the contrary, he saw how easy it was to win popularity, and how worthless the prize when won. He would never allow himself to become one of those who set 'lungs before brains, and the sounding of a voice before soundness of matter.' 'Yea,' he declared in *Faction Confuted*, one of his sermons, 'when pastors perceive people transported with an immoderate admiration of them, let them labour to confute them in their groundless humours. . . . Christ went into the wilderness when the people would have made him a king. Let us shun, yea fly such dangerous honour, and tear off our heads such wreaths as people would tie on them; striving rather to throw

---

[1] *Collected Sermons*, ed. Bailey and Axon (1891), i, 469.

mists and clouds of privacy on ourselves, than to affect a shining appearance.'

The King's Chapel of the Savoy, which to this day is a place of peace and refreshing modesty between the bustling Strand and the noisy embankment, still symbolizes the spirit of Fuller's churchmanship. It is now the chapel of the Royal Victorian Order, after serving as a royal chapel until 1925. Nothing, however, remains inside the church to remind us of Fuller. In 1864 the furnishings were destroyed by fire; but the fabric was restored by Queen Victoria, and as we look at it from the quiet churchyard we can still imagine the scene in Fuller's day when the bell called his fashionable congregation to worship. The Savoy of the seventeenth century was the Mayfair of the twentieth. Somerset House near by, which had been renamed Denmark House in honour of the consort of James I, was the queen's residence. She had landed on its steps after sailing up the river from Gravesend on the evening of the 16th June 1625, entering the gardens by the water-gate built—or rebuilt— by Inigo Jones two years earlier.

About the queen's house and the doctor's church lay a scene that still belonged to Merry England, though the Puritan ministers were quickly changing it with their passion for Hebrew fervour. There was no embankment then; but between the crowded Strand, cobbled and noisy, with its wooden houses hung with gaily painted signs, and the river, still the great highway of London, were the wharves of the merchants alongside the landing stages of the important houses. All the nobles of the day had their barges of state, each 'bravely pavilioned.' Houses, wharves, streets, and gardens were thronged with shouting, jostling, and often ribald crowds, cuffing and saluting each other as the humour took them. The king, with his sense of order and decency, was making some effort to improve the aspect, though not always successfully. In 1630 he stopped the erection of fish-stalls opposite Denmark House, 'lest in short space they might grow from stalls to sheddes and then to dwelling-houses, as the like was in former time in Old Fish Street and in St. Nicholas Shambles.'

Fuller enjoyed it all, and found some of his new parish-ioners mines of information.   James, Lord Compton, after-wards third Earl of Northampton, whose father, the second earl, was a favourite of the king and with him at York in 1642, lived near.   It was probably from him that Fuller obtained some of the information about the early stages of the war used in various works.   In the Staffordshire section of the *Worthies* he has the story of the second earl's heroic death at Hopton Heath in 1643.   When offered quarter the earl bravely declared that he would not owe his life to those who had forfeited all right to their own.   And there were still for Fuller those happy associations with the Montagu family that had been with him all his life.   The Countess of Rutland, who attended his church and befriended him later, was the Frances Montagu of Boughton who at Barnwell Castle, near Aldwincle, in 1628 married the John Manners who in 1641 became eighth Earl of Rutland.   And the queen was now doubly endeared to Fuller because she, too, loved Northamp-tonshire.   She had stayed at Wellingborough more than once in order to take the waters.   On her first visit, tradition asserts, she and her attendants encamped round a well on the north-west side of the town.   On her next visit she stayed with the king at the 'White Swan.'   She loved the quaint old town, and not least, perhaps, for its lace-makers.

It has sometimes been suggested that Fuller was over-assiduous in cultivating the acquaintance of the great.   His many complimentary dedications are produced as evidence of this, and indeed it is obvious to any one who glances at these that he was exceptionally fortunate in his social con-nections.   It is no less obvious that he lost few opportunities of profiting by them.   But there is no reason to think that those who conferred on him the favour of their patronage were not as happy to give as he was to receive.   His patrons were probably proud and delighted to be associated with him in his work, while he, like all sensible men, realized how little he could achieve in life unaided, and gladly availed himself of all the help offered.   Fuller was not such an egoist as to believe he could do everything off his own bat. And to balance the account we may observe that no English

author ever conferred immortality on a greater number of his
personal friends. At St. Mary Savoy, then, he became acquainted with many of the families he was later to celebrate
in the *Worthies*, and found them as friendly as the villagers
of Broadwindsor and the dons of Cambridge. In short, he
was a social success. But he was not overawed by grandeur,
and was still able to take an independent line when his
conscience required it.

From the beginning of 1642, by an order of the king, the
last Wednesday in every month was to be kept as a day of
fasting. This was to go on so long as the country continued
to show by its ungodly division that the Divine displeasure
was upon it. Fuller observed these fasts and took them
seriously. Some of his best sermons were preached on them.
One of the most remarkable, that preached on the last fast
day of 1642, which happened to be Holy Innocents' Day, had
more practical results than might be foreseen when he took
his place in the pulpit and announced his text. It was yet
another sermon counselling peace. Nothing could be expected from civil war, he said, but ruin and desolation. He
must have started many sermons in a similar strain; but this
time he was more than usually plain in his speech. He did
not advocate peace at any price. There must be no mistake
about that. Truth and honour were always to be set before
other considerations, and it was sometimes necessary to
'second our posture of piety with martial provisions,' yet
withal to realize that 'the sword cannot discern betwixt
truth, error, and falsehood. It may have two edges, but it
hath never an eye.' The root of the trouble, he preached—
in common, no doubt, with every other preacher of the day—
was the nation's sin. But unlike many, who were content to
tickle the ears of their own particular congregations, Roundhead or Cavalier, he added that the sin was not all on one
side: 'Think not that the king's army is like Sodom—not ten
righteous men in it; and the other army like Zion—consisting
all of saints. No, there be drunkards on both sides, and
swearers on both sides, and whoremongers on both sides,
pious on both sides, and profane on both sides. Like
Jeremy's figs, those that are good are very good, and those

that are bad are very bad, in both parties.' He was careful to avoid party politics; but he did advocate—and strongly—petitions to both king and Parliament for one last effort to reach an understanding.

By this time London was already fortified by Parliament and Oxford by the king. The sands were quickly running out, and within two or three days of preaching his sermon Fuller had given proof that he meant what he said and was ready to give it practical expression. On the second of the following month he appeared with five others: Sir Edward Wardour, clerk of the pells, John Castle, John Chichely, Laurence Lisle—formerly a bookseller, now a tax-collector—and Dr. Dukeson, rector of St. Clement Danes, before the House of Lords to seek permission to carry a prayer for peace to the king at Oxford. At the time there were bargaining factors on both sides, so their plea was successful. All six of them were granted passes to proceed on their journey with an equipage of two coaches, each with four to six horses, and attended by eight or ten mounted servants. These prepared, the party set out bearing what came to be known as the Westminster Petition. But at Uxbridge they were stopped by a Parliamentary outpost and searched. Their passes were in order, and there seemed to be no reason for alarm until out fell two 'scandalous books arraigning the proceedings of the House,' and with them letters in cipher addressed to Viscount Falkland and Lord Spencer. On the strength of these suspicious documents they were held in custody, and on the following day, the 5th January 1643, the House of Commons received a report of the incident and ordered the return of the six deputies to London. Two days later they were examined by a Parliamentary committee, which evidently reported to the House, but only to have its report 're-committed, upon information given that some of these ministers did in the churches publish a summons and notice for the parishioners to meet to subscribe the petition.' By some means, however, the Westminster Petition did reach the king, and was published on the 18th January with the royal reply.

The excitement caused by this petition must have brought

Fuller's name into still greater prominence in the city, and on the anniversary of the king's accession, the 27th March 1643, we find him preaching in Westminster Abbey, taking as his text: 'Yea, let him take all, forasmuch as my lord the king is come again in peace unto his own house.' It was another bold sermon, and the anonymous biographer says that it 'drew not only a suspicion from the moderate misled party of parliament, but an absolute odium on him from the grandees and principals in the rebellion.'

By this time he was almost the only Royalist left among the London ministers. That he had not already been compelled to abandon his church was probably due to a hope among parliamentarians that he might eventually be won over to their side. He would have been a prize worth winning at this time, and after all he had never flattered the Cavaliers. Perhaps his steadying influence was of value, too. And he must have added much to the cheerfulness of the city in these depressing times.

We should also remember that Fuller always had loyal friends on both sides. One of the most distressing results of war to a man so sociably inclined was that so many whose companionship he had enjoyed were now in the other camp. We know that he was considerably exercised in mind as to how he should conduct himself towards them. 'Must the new foe quite justle out the old friend?' he asked. Yet how could he be friendly towards his enemy without betraying the cause he believed just? He knew how easy it was to acquire that casual kind of tolerance which so many call good nature. This he referred to as 'a facile and flexible disposition, wax for every impression,' and he regarded those who cultivated it as friends to none and foes to themselves. In a word, they were dishonest. Fuller was a king's man by conviction, and felt that he was in honour bound to say so. 'Had I poised myself so politically betwixt both parties that I had suffered from neither,' he said in *Good Thoughts in Bad Times*, 'yet could I have taken no contentment in my safe escaping.' There came a time when he could no longer leave any one in doubt as to which side he stood for, and when that time came he found that the prominence of his isolation had clearly

E

become too great an offence to the stricter brethren of the other party. He found also that even the more tolerant were beginning to comment on his large congregations, and to suggest that though he had not so far said anything provocative to the point of being prejudicial to the cause of Parliament, it was unwise to leave so many London citizens under the influence of one who, though silent about the king's politics, had made no secret of his loyalty to the king's person. Moreover, he might be working in secret for the Royalist cause.

Suspicions came to a head in May 1643 when the plot designed by the witty, charming, but inconstant Edmund Waller, with the object of winning the city of London for the king, was discovered. Vigilance was redoubled immediately, and all who were under the least suspicion of having Royalist sympathies were closely watched. On the 17th June Parliament decided that the 13th July should be a day of thanksgiving for the discovery of the plot. On that day, it was decreed, every citizen of London must swear on oath that he was loyal to Parliament by declaring, vowing, and covenanting that he would 'not consent to the laying down of arms so long as the Papists, now in open war against the Parliament, shall by force of arms be protected from the justice thereof,' reciting this vow: 'I will not, directly or indirectly, adhere unto, nor shall willingly assist the forces raised by the king, without the consent of both Houses of Parliament.'

Fuller took this oath in the vestry of the Savoy chapel, but not without qualification. It was put to him in public, evidently by some who were anxious to catch him. His own account of the incident continues: 'This, not satisfying, was complained of, by some persons present, to the Parliament, where it was ordered that the next Lord's Day I should take the same oath *in terminis terminantibus* in the face of the Church, which not agreeing with my conscience, I withdrew myself into the King's parts.'

But before leaving he preached—on Wednesday the 26th July—his *Sermon of Reformation*, in which he spoke out boldly on the national position:

'O the miserable condition of our land at this time! God hath shewed the whole world that England hath enough in

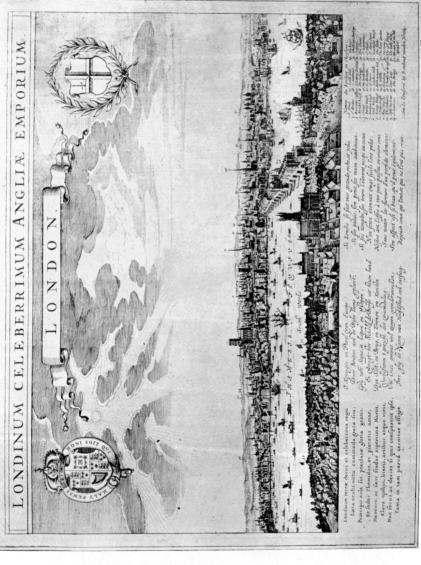

SEVENTEENTH CENTURY LONDON

itself to make itself happy or unhappy, as it useth or abuseth it. Her homebred wares enough to maintain her, and her homebred wars enough to destroy her, though no foreign nation contribute to her overthrow. Well, whilst others fight for peace, let us pray for peace; for peace on good terms, yea on God's terms, and in God's time, when He shall be pleased to give it, and we fitted to receive it. Let us wish both King and Parliament so well as to wish neither of them better, but both of them best—even a happy accommodation.'

Four days after the sermon was delivered, news reached London that Bristol had fallen to Prince Rupert, and with this second Royalist victory within a month—following so close upon Sir Ralph Hopton's victory at Devizes on the 13th—Parliament became nervous. Bristol at this time was the second city in the kingdom. Such a victory brought new hope to the would-be peacemakers, and on the 5th August the Lords and Commons even went so far as to decide by a majority of nineteen to treat with the king. But those champion warmongers, the city preachers, were not to be silenced so easily, and on the following day, the 6th August, they, supported by the Assembly of Divines, demanded the rejection of the proposed accommodation. Their influence was such that the lord mayor, the common council, and a great body of supporters, petitioned for a vigorous prosecution of the war. When this was carried to Westminster a large crowd gathered to demonstrate not for but against the peacemakers, and in view of this exhibition Parliament, by a majority of seven, rescinded the offending resolution.

If we look at Fuller's *Sermon of Reformation* in the light of this demonstration we see that it was an extremely bold performance. It amounted to a stern protest against the kind of reformation at that time being carried out by the Assembly of Divines, which was now shown to be strong enough to change the will of Parliament. Indeed, even Fuller could hardly have preached in such terms if he had not known that within a few days he would be inside the Royalist camp. Before going, however, he arranged for the sermon to be printed. It was entered at Stationers' Hall on the 2nd August and published the same day.

CHAPTER VIII

CAVALIER PARSON

Bold is the man that dares engage
For piety in such an age.

WALLER.

THERE can have been little left of the gay Tom Fuller of
Cambridge and Dorset, or even of the brilliant young
preacher of a few months earlier, in the heavy-hearted man
who left London on a day in August 1643 to join the king at
Oxford. His mission in London had failed. 'His exhor-
tations to peace and obedience were his constant subjects in
the church. All his sermons were such liturgies,' says the
anonymous biographer. They had achieved nothing. But
in one thing he still had cause for satisfaction: he had held
together his congregation. If he could have known it, in
friendship he was richer than ever.

On reaching Oxford he found the king at Christ Church.
Prince Rupert was at Magdalen. And as the queen and her
chattering ladies either swarmed in the streets or disported
themselves round the mulberry tree in the Fellows' Garden
at Merton, the university was sadly overcrowded with
Royalist refugees. It was also crowded with scholars. The
anonymous biographer says: 'Oxford was then the common
refuge and shelter of such persecuted persons, so that it never
was nor is like to be a more learned university. One breast
being dried up by Cromwell's visitation, the milk resorted to
the other. Nor did ever letters and arms so well consist
together, it being an accomplished academy of both.' The
bell-tower of Magdalen was full of stones ready for the heads
of rebel invaders. Both town and gown helped to dig
trenches.

The other breast, of course, was Cambridge, which had
fallen to Parliament at the beginning of the war and had
become the headquarters of the Eastern Association. The
heads of the colleges, alarmed by the plundering of Countess

Rivers's houses at St. Osyth and Long Melford at the outbreak of war, had sent their plate, or the money they had got
by melting it down, to the king while he was at York.   Parliament protested at once, arguing that the heads of the colleges
held the plate in trust, and had therefore no right to dispose
of it.   To this the heads replied that they had sent it to the
king for safety, and asked into whose hands the wealth of the
university and the bounty of its benefactors should be placed
if not into those of His Majesty.   Who better than he to
represent the founders and interpret their wishes, since he
was himself the heir of the most munificent among them?

Parliament had dismissed the university's plea, and Drs.
Beale, Martin, and Sterne, the masters of St. John's, Queen's,
and Jesus Colleges respectively, had been imprisoned in the
Tower.[1]   Rather more than a month after Fuller's flight to
Oxford the climax came when the masters and fellows of all
the colleges were required to take the Solemn League and
Covenant, which put many good scholars on the road.
Fuller himself tells us that it was difficult to know how these
maintained themselves, quoting the pathetic proverb, 'He
is either dead, or teacheth school,' to illustrate their plight.
And this, incidentally, shows how meanly teachers not
associated with universities were thought of in those days.

If Fuller had stayed in London he also would have been
caught in the net of the Solemn League and Covenant, the
agreement to adopt in only slightly modified form the Scot-
tish system of Church government, which was imposed by the
Scots on the English as the condition of their aid to Parliament, and taken in all the London churches on the last
Sunday of September 1643.   Fuller could never have subscribed to this in view of all he had said in his *Sermon of
Reformation* in denial of the right of 'mere private Christians'
to 'intermeddle with public reforming of a church.'   Safely
in Oxford, he avoided it and settled down to life at Lincoln
College, where he found new companions.   From one of
them, Sir Gervase Scroop, he heard the account of that gallant
soldier's preservation after the battle of Edgehill, which
finds a place in the Lincolnshire section of the *Worthies*: 'He

[1] *History of Cambridge*, ix. 28–34.

always after carried his arm in a scarf; and loss of blood made
him look very pale, as a messenger come from the grave to
advise the living to prepare for death.' It was but one more
instance of the delightfully friendly way in which Fuller
collected much of his knowledge of events in these times,
and it is more than likely that an older friend was present
when the story was told, for Sir Edward Wardour, associated
with Fuller in the Westminster Petition, was living in Lincoln
College at the same time.

As Fuller had so long cherished the idea of writing a history
of the Church, he must have sighed for the return of peace,
with all its opportunities for study, whenever he passed the
Bodleian library, which he was able to use only for *Truth
Maintained* and *Jacob's Vow*, two sermons printed at Oxford.
He had been unable to bring his books and papers from London. There they were confiscated. For the time being all
work on his major projects had to be abandoned, so his weeks
at Lincoln College were far from happy. In the *Church
History* he writes frankly of this period: 'I could much desire,
were it in my power, to express my service to this foundation,
acknowledging myself for a quarter of a year in these
troublesome times, though no member of, a dweller in it.
I will not complain of the dearness of this university, where
seventeen weeks cost me more than seventeen years in Cambridge, even all that I had; but shall pray that the students
therein be never hereafter disturbed upon the like occasion.'
This apparently inoffensive passage by the kindly doctor
stung Peter Heylyn, who was an Oxford man and extremely
jealous of her honour, to reply: 'He hath no reason to complain of the University, or the dearness of it; but rather of
himself for coming to a place so chargeable and destructive to
him. He might have tarried where he was, for I never heard
that he was sent for, and then this great complaint about the
dearness of that University would have found no place.'

Fuller's arrival did not pass unnoticed at court. His fame
had gone before him, and the king soon 'vouchsafed the
Doctor the honour of preaching before him.' Word went
round that the witty young clergyman of St. Mary Savoy was
to preach in St. Mary's, Oxford, before the king and his court,

and a brilliant assembly crowded to hear him. Again he had an apparently sovereign opportunity to place himself in the way of preferment and honour. Not only was the king himself there, but with him were many noblemen whose favour he might have courted. Unfortunately the sermon he preached is not extant, but we know its substance. It was the counterpart of the sermons he had recently preached at the Savoy. He quietly analysed the causes of the present discontents, showed where each shoe pinched, and pleaded with the court as he had pleaded with Parliament for renewed efforts to reach a peaceful agreement. 'He laid open,' says the anonymous biographer, 'the blessings of an accommodation.' Alas, such counsels were no more popular with one side than with the other. Both wanted to hear themselves justified. Fuller was not prepared to justify either, and the Royalists were even more rebellious than the Parliamentarians had been when he left London. At the moment, the king's men had proud stomachs. Recent successes of their arms had given them an illusory foretaste of victory. They hoped that the new preacher would cheer them forward, and instead he told them that the faults were not all on one side, and that the Cavaliers also must humble themselves before God and seek only righteousness. As for the king, it was well known that it was not in his nature either to compromise or to see a joke, so the sermon gave considerable offence, and we cannot believe that so shrewd a · judge of human nature as Fuller could be surprised by this. Nevertheless, he was grieved when those who had heard the sermon began to accuse him of being lukewarm in the royal cause. Certainly their conception of fervour was different from his. Tolerant as he was he could not feel easy about the tales that came in from the country of roistering Cavaliers who burst into the villages at midnight, singing blasphemous and ribald songs.

Unhappy as it was, there is no period in Fuller's life that his admirers can look upon with greater satisfaction than this. The man who counsels moderation and tolerance is so often accused of sitting on the fence. Sometimes it is difficult to refute the charge. But if Fuller took up a position on the fence that divided the two parties, it was that both might hear him.   There was nothing sensational about what he had to say.   It was the season he said it in that proved his courage.   It is easy to preach against the sin of gluttony when all have enough; it is not so easy when you know that you may be starved for your pains.   But he had his reward. Later in life, in *Mixt Contemplations*, he was to write of moderation, not as he had written of it in *The Holy State*, thinking only of its principles, but from the experience of long practice: 'Let not such hereby be disheartened, but know that, besides the reward in heaven, the very work of moderation is the wages of moderation.   For it carrieth with it a marvellous contentment in his conscience who hath endeavoured his utmost in order to unify, though unhappy in his success.' [1]

Such contentment may have been Fuller's at this time, but it cannot have been easy for a man who was used to being met with smiles wherever he went to find himself shunned. He saw clearly that what prevented his words finding root in the hearts of his hearers was the hard rock of pride on which they fell.   Both parties were puffed up with self-righteous-ness, and it is our great joy that Fuller, knowing that both sides were wrong while he was right, did not himself lose grace.   We cannot doubt that he understood perfectly what he had to deal with.   In *Mixt Contemplations* he wrote of this year: 'Had any endeavoured, some sixteen years since, to have advanced a firm peace betwixt the two opposite parties in our land, their success would not have answered their intentions, man's veins were then so full of blood, and purses of money.'   And the clergy, he knew, were not exceptions. They were never far behind the laity in desire for popular applause, and what easier way of winning it either then or now than to join in the general hue and cry after the hunted stag, always provided you could bay a little louder and run a little faster than others in the field?

Among these hounds in clerical collars was one, John Saltmarsh, a preacher 'full of poetical raptures, and highly conceited of himself and parts,' who could certainly both bay

---

[1] *Mixt Contemplations in Better Times*, part II, xviii.

louder and run faster than most of his fellows. Indeed he outran his quarry at times. Saltmarsh foolishly mistook Fuller for prey, fastening on the *Sermon of Reformation* and accusing the preacher of 'popish compliance.' The attack was airily described by its author as 'but the thoughts of an afternoon,' to which Fuller, in *Truth Maintained*, replied: 'You have almost converted me to be of your opinion, that some extraordinary light is peculiarly conferred on men in this age: seeing what cost me many days to make, you, in fewer hours, could make void and confute.' To appreciate the force of this we have to remember that many charlatans were then attributing their wrong-headed notions to the mysterious guidance of the Inner Light, much as their twentieth-century counterparts set them down to intuition. One of the best stories illustrating this superstition is told by Fuller himself in the *Worthies*, where John Ball is described as 'an excellent schoolman and schoolmaster—qualities seldom meeting in the same man—a painful preacher and profitable writer,' who hated 'all new lights and pretended inspirations besides Scripture: and when one asked him "Whether he at any time had experience thereof in his own heart?" "No," said he, "I bless God; and if I should ever have such phantasies, I hope God would give me grace to resist them."'

As the sermon criticized had been preached at St. Mary Savoy, Fuller in his reply took the opportunity of sending a greeting to his old friends there. In his jocular way he claimed the right to address them still as his parishioners, for 'although my calamities have divorced me from your bed and board, the matrimonial knot betwixt us is not yet rescinded. No, not although you have admitted another (for fear I hope rather than affection) into my place. I remember how David when forced to fly from his wife, yet calls her "my wife, Michal," even when at that time she was in the possession of Phaltiel the son of Laish, who had rather bedded than wedded her.' Then in more serious vein he wrote: 'The longer I see this war the less I like it, and the more I loathe it. Not so much because it threatens temporal ruin to our kingdom, as because it will bring a general spiritual hardness of hearts.'

* E

We wonder what Dr. John Bond, the intruded minister at the Savoy—the man 'who had rather bedded than wedded' the parish—thought of this. Bond was an out-and-out party man. He was so certain that the cause of the Parliamentarians was God's cause that he said: 'And if our God hath any cause this is it; and if this be not God's cause, then God is no God for me, but the devil is got up into heaven,' which is surely making God in one's own image with a vengeance. Of his death it was significantly recorded that 'he died 30th August 1658, the windiest day that had before happened for twenty years.' But perhaps we ought not to expect the God of the Parliamentarians to be more than a constitutional monarch!

After the letter to his own parishioners Fuller has one to 'the unpartial reader,' and in this he tells the delightful story, found in Selden's *Table Talk* and other places, which he says is now applicable to himself, about the gaoler who asked a new prisoner if he was a Roman Catholic.

'No,' answered he.

'What then?' said he. 'Are you an Anabaptist?'

'Neither,' replied the prisoner.

'What,' said the other. 'Are you a Brownist, or a Quaker?'

'Not so,' said the man. 'I am a Protestant, without welt or gard, or any addition, equally opposite to all heretics and sectaries.'

'Then,' said the gaoler, 'get you into the dungeon: I will afford no favour to you, who shall get no advantage by you. Had you been of any of the other religions, some hope I had to gain by the visits of such as are of your own persuasion, whereas now you will prove to me but an unprofitable prisoner.'

'I,' says Fuller, 'am likely to find no better usage in this age, who profess myself to be a plain Protestant, without welt or gard, or any addition; equally opposite to all heretics and sectaries.'

No man could enjoy such popularity as Fuller had enjoyed in Cambridge, Dorset, and London for so many years without provoking jealousy. Hitherto it had been tactful to hide this malice; but now that his light was flickering, the envious lips that had long been pursed in silence were pressed forward to blow out the flame. Perhaps he was thinking of his own experience at Oxford when he said in *Mixt Contemplations*, part II, xxiii), 'I have heard the royal party—would I could say without cause—complained of, that they have not charity enough for converts, who, came off unto them from the opposite side; who, though they express a sense of and sorrow for their mistakes, and have given testimony—though perhaps not so plain and public as others expected—of their sincerity, yet still they are suspected as unsound; and such as frown not on, look but asquint at them. This hath done much mischief, and retarded the return of many to their side.'

He suffered yet another discomfort at Oxford. For the first time in his life he felt the pinch of poverty. Salisbury was now in the hands of Parliament, so nothing came to him from his prebend; Savoy was filled by another. But he accepted these discomforts cheerfully, 'for why should I,' he said, 'equally engaged with others in sinning, be exempted above them from the punishment?' For all that, the heavy charges of Lincoln had to be met, and it was already clear that the Royalist party headquarters was no place for so active and forthright a mind as his. So he resolved to join the army as chaplain. That at least would put him in touch with reality again. It was a solution that several of the most eminent divines of the day were to light on. Two of these, John Pearson, the best theological scholar of his time, and Jeremy Taylor, whom Fuller called his 'respected friend,' were Cambridge men. A third—and as a chaplain the most interesting—William Chillingworth, described by Aubrey as 'a little man, blackish haire, of a saturnine complexion,' was to be in the same army as Fuller. And they must have been congenial companions. It was Chillingworth who made the often quoted remark, 'War is not the way of Jesus Christ.' He was a fine scholar, caught to the life by Aubrey, who says, 'he did walke much in the college grove, and there contemplate, and meet with some cod's head or other, and dispute with him and baffle him. He thus prepared himselfe beforehand.' When he resolved to become a chaplain, Fuller again, though he cannot then have known it, hitched his wagon to a star.   If he could no longer collect matter for his church history, he was now put in the way of even more valuable material, for as Jeremy Taylor's biographer says, he 'picked up stories of English worthies in the rear of a marching column.'

The man who made this possible was Sir Ralph Hopton, the one general in the king's army who enjoyed universal respect, a man as shrewd and kindly as Fuller himself.   In May 1643 Hopton had won a resounding victory at Stratton, which had opened up to him the whole of Devon and Cornwall.   In July he had defeated Sir William Waller at Lansdown, and when Fuller met him he was in Oxford to report to a grateful sovereign, who at the beginning of September made him Baron Hopton of Stratton.   This fine soldier was unique in the respect he enjoyed in both armies.   Waller wrote to him : 'Hostility itself cannot violate my friendship to your person,' and Fairfax that he was 'one whom we honour and esteem above any other of your party.'   These were not empty compliments.   Hopton was a man of honour as well as a brave general.   Moreover he, like Fuller, had no illusions about the character and disposition of both armies.   The anonymous biographer says that he was 'never averse to an amicable closure of the war upon fair and honourable terms, and did therefore well approve of the doctor and his desires and pursuit after peace.'   Like Fuller again, he had many friends in both parties, particularly among churchmen, for he was the most religious of the Royalist generals, strict in his observance of the Lord's Day and unfailing in his support of public worship.   To his chaplain he was the ideal soldier. His forces were relatively free from reproach because of his careful vigilance, and it was his constant concern that 'the scandal of his soldiers should neither draw the wrath of God upon his undertaking, nor enrage the country against his cause.' [1]

Hopton's engagements in Cornwall are described in the *Worthies* from the general's own accounts, and we can imagine the good relationship there must have been between the

---

[1] Lloyd's *Memoirs*, p. 344.

serious-minded general and his scholarly chaplains. Most of Hopton's interests were in the west. About the time of his meeting with Fuller, introduced, it seems likely, by the Marquess of Hertford, Hopton had been given the difficult task of forming a garrison at Bristol. As Prince Maurice had taken all the existing forces farther west it meant creating a new army, and Hopton succeeded in doing this. About December 1643 he reported to the king in Oxford, and as this would be about seventeen weeks after Fuller's flight from London, we may assume that it was on this December visit that the doctor joined the general as chaplain, probably accompanying him to Bristol, a city that both knew well. Chillingworth, who because born and educated at Oxford was said by Fuller to have dropped out of the lap of his mother into the arms of the muses, studied in other schools than those normally favoured by clerics. While with the king's army at Gloucester he invented engines for use in attacking fortifications, these he contrived after studying similar ones used by the Romans, called *testudines cum pluteis*. They were musket-proof boxes, like tortoise-shells, filled with marksmen and run out on cart-wheels,[1] and they gave him a great reputation among the common soldiers, who called him the King's Little Engineer, and the Black Art Man. He was also under suspicion of being a spy because, while making a serious examination of the Roman Catholic faith, he had studied for a time at Douai. Like Hopton and Fuller, he was a moderate Royalist and under suspicion for what was called his lukewarm preaching. Hobbes was sorely puzzled by him, and exclaimed to Aubrey: 'But by God, he is like some lusty fighters that will give a damnable back-blow now and then on their owne party.' Chillingworth was with Hopton at Arundel Castle in December 1643, and stayed there when the general marched away to meet Waller, who surprised the king's forces near Alton and put them to rout. When Arundel fell, Chillingworth was among the captured. According to Clarendon he was treated so barbarously that he died within a few days. However the soldiers treated him, he was certainly treated badly by

[1] Rushworth's *Historical Collections*, ed. 1692, part III, vol. ii, p. 290.

one of his own profession. A Presbyterian named Francis
Cheynell pestered him on his death-bed with arguments
against toleration. 'Why should men be more rigid than
God?' asked Chillingworth, reasonably enough. Cheynell
would have nothing to do with such latitude, and flung a
copy of Chillingworth's book *The Religion of Protestants* into
his grave, with these words: 'If they please to undertake the
burial of his corpse, I shall undertake to bury his errors,
which are published in this so much admired yet unworthy
book: and happy would it be for the Kingdom, if this book
and all its fellows could be so buried. Get thee gone, thou
cursed book, which has seduced so many precious souls!
Get thee gone, thou corrupt, rotten book! Earth to earth,
and dust to dust! Get thee gone into the place of rottenness,
that thou mayest rot with thy author, and see corruption.'

Fuller fared better. He was with the general at the end
of March when the Royalist forces were again defeated by
Waller in the battle of Cheriton Down. This time the
Royalists under Hopton's command had the initial advantage. They used it to such good effect that it was only when
action appeared to be over that a fresh charge altered the
position and allowed victory to be snatched from apparent
defeat by the wily Sir William, already known to his army as
William the Conqueror. Hopton was obliged to retreat in
haste, but, taking advantage of the darkness, he turned aside
to Basing House, leaving the enemy pursuing him, as they
thought, in the direction of Winchester.

According to the anonymous biographer, Hopton left
Fuller at Basing as he had previously left Chillingworth at
Arundel; but there is a doubt here, because on the 10th May
1644 Fuller preached before the king the sermon entitled
Jacob's Vow. Hopton may, of course, have hurried to
Oxford to report to His Majesty almost at once. Charles,
no doubt, became anxious about this time at the dangerous
turn in the fortunes of his armies and called for reports from
his generals. But whenever Fuller left Basing House, his
stay within it must have been one of the most memorable of
his wartime experiences. Basing House had come into the
possession of the Sir William Paulet—or Poulett, the name is

found in several spellings—who was created first Marquess of Winchester by Edward VI, and had been enlarged by him until, according to Fuller, it was 'the greatest of any subject's house in England, yea larger than most—eagles have not the biggest nests of all birds—of the king's palaces.' It was yet another of the great number of mansions built by the optimistic nobles of the Tudors and early Stuarts which embarrassed and often impoverished subsequent owners. The first marquess's son had difficulty in maintaining it; but at the beginning of the civil war the fifth marquess, by the exercise of extreme thrift, had succeeded in freeing it from debt. He was a Roman Catholic, and it is probable that his religion rather than his social position provoked the Puritans to show great bitterness towards him.

This gallant nobleman, so recently become master of his own possessions, at the very outbreak of war offered to turn Basing into a garrison for the king's use, and to place all he had at his sovereign's disposal. The situation of the mansion on the main road to the west made it of the utmost importance strategically, and consequently it figured in many plans of campaign, as did that other guardian of the western approaches, Donington Castle, near Newbury. At the beginning of the war the marquess himself was in command, with his family and retainers to form the garrison. Later these had to be reinforced; but they were the core of the defence throughout. To inspire the garrison with loyalty the marquess with his own hand scratched with a diamond the words 'AIMEZ LOYAUTÉ' on every window in the house, and it is recorded that when Sir William Waller, after storming the house three times in nine days, called upon the marquess to surrender, his lordship replied that 'if the king had no more ground in England than Basing House he would hold it out to the last extremity.'

The date of Fuller's arrival at Basing House is not recorded. It may have been either before or after Hopton's. The carrying of messages was one of the important functions of displaced clergymen during the civil wars, and if Hopton had an advance message Fuller would be an obvious choice of bearer on account of his friendship with the Pouletts, which dated, as we have seen, from the Broadwindsor days. He would be most curious to see the mansion, and not least because it was built by a lord treasurer, which, as Fuller discloses, 'was ever beheld as a place of great charge and profit,' continuing: ' One well skilled in the perquisites thereof, being demanded what he conceived the yearly value of the place was worth, made this return, " That it might be worth some thousands of pounds to him, who, after death, would go instantly to heaven; twice as much to him who would go to purgatory; and a *nemo scit*—nobody knows what—to him who would adventure to go to a worse place."' Fuller was not being cynical. The Earl of Suffolk, who in his Cambridge years had been chancellor of the university, was another lord treasurer who had built himself a mansion while holding that office, and one that provoked the shrewd Scot, James I, to say that it was too big for a king, but might do very well for a lord treasurer. Indeed, such was the general attitude then, that if asked for his views Fuller might simply have said: ' He that is a bad husband for himself will never be a good one for his sovereign; and therefore no wonder if they have advanced fair estates to themselves, whose office was so advantageous, and they so judicious and prudent persons, without any prejudice to their master, and, for aught I know, injury to his subjects.'

Apart from the mansion—and, indeed, far more than the mansion—the kindness of the Poulett family towards him would dispose him in favour of Basing, and when he met the marquess and the marchioness his joy must have been as great as the circumstances of war could possibly permit. The fifth marquess was a scholar and man of culture, the translator of Quare's *Devout Entertainments of a Christian Soul*, of *The Gallery of Heroic Women*, and of Talon's *Holy History*. When he died in 1674 the epitaph for his tomb in Englefield Church was written by Dryden, who said of him that he was ' a man of exemplary piety towards God, and of inviolable fidelity towards his sovereign.'

Another member of this gallant household was Dr. Thomas Johnson, the herbalist, who took part in the sallies and was eventually given a command as lieutenant-colonel.

Fuller could not fail to enjoy his brief stay in so congenial a household, and with his usual detachment from outside affairs he occupied the intervals between the actual fighting with notes for his *Worthies* and his *Church History*, disturbed only when the noise of the cannon interrupted his studies. Here we turn again to the anonymous biographer who, though it is to be feared with some exaggeration since no other account supports him, describes Fuller's part in the defence of Basing House the following November. 'Sir William Waller,' he says, 'having taken in Winchester, came to besiege the doctor's sanctuary. This no way amated or terrified him, but only the noise of the canon playing from the enemy's leaguer interrupted the prosecution of digesting his notes; which trouble he recompensed to them by an importunate spiriting of the defendants in their sallies; which they followed so close and so bravely, suffering the besiegers scarce to eat or sleep, that Sir William was compelled to raise his siege and march away, leaving above a thousand men slain behind him, and the doctor the pleasure of seeing that strong effort of rebellion in some way by his means repulsed and defeated, and in being free to proceed in his wonted intendments.'

Fuller tells us that he was choleric by nature, and if what the anonymous biographer says is true we have a delightful illustration of the character of the scholar. To understand Fuller's annoyance at having his studies in the library of Basing House interrupted by this barbarous soldiery, we have to remember that the ambition of his life was to write a history of the Church. The war had turned that dream into a haunting delusion. In his own account of the civil wars he says: 'For the first five years, during our actual civil wars, I had little list or leisure to write, fearing to be made a history, and shifting daily for my safety. All that time I could not live to study, who did only study to live.' His fellow chaplain, Chillingworth, would never write again. All gentle and civilized life seemed gone for ever, until, by this unexpected turn of fortune, he found himself in the home of the Marquess of Winchester, perhaps still the noblest mansion in the land, with a splendid library at his disposal. What wonder, then, that when Waller's cannons roared outside he lost his temper and, perhaps in less pastoral language than he normally employed, told the soldiers how to deal with those howling wolves that threatened his peace?

Whatever Fuller's part may have been, we have circumstantial evidence of Johnson's. Fuller himself says in the *Worthies* that when a risky adventure had to be undertaken, 'this doctor, who publicly pretended not to valour, undertook and performed it.   Yet afterwards he lost his life in the siege of the same house, and was, to my knowledge, generally lamented of those who were of an opposite judgment.'

Before it was finally reduced by Cromwell in October 1645, Basing House was to shelter other famous men, most notable among them Inigo Jones and Hollar, the engraver, who supplied some of the illustrations for Fuller's works. His 'Siege of Bazinge House' is reproduced opposite.

The Protector's wife got a magnificent collection of jewels from Basing House as her share of the spoils.   They had belonged to ladies whose charms and virtues had been celebrated by such poets as Milton and Ben Jonson.

The best of the stories told of the fall of Basing House relates how an actor named Robinson was killed by Major-General Harrison.   The player could not hope to fight the soldier successfully, so he laid down his arms and begged for mercy, whereupon the Puritan officer shot him through the head exclaiming: 'Cursed is he that doeth the work of the Lord negligently.'   It is said that when Cromwell attacked, the garrison was at cards, and that this gave rise to the local tag used when making a bid at whist or bridge: 'Clubs trump, as when Basing House was taken.'

On leaving Basing, Fuller joined Hopton, who was preparing for another excursion into the west country, where clearly the Royalist strength must be built up if their arms were finally to succeed.   The war was at its fiercest, and the issue still uncertain.   Wherever their marches took them, Fuller, in the anonymous biographer's words, 'preferred the duty of his holy function with as much solemn piety and devotion as he used before in places consecrated to God's worship, and according to the form used and appointed by

THE SIEGE OF BAZINGE HOVSE

A. THE OLDE HOVSE . B. THE MEW . C. THE TOWER THAT IS HALFE BATTERED DOWNE . D. THE KINGES BREAST WORKS . E. THE PARLIAMENTS BREAST WORKS.

the Church of England.' His movements at this time can only be assumed to be the same as those of Hopton. What matters is that wherever he went he made use of every opportunity to collect material for his projected works. Nowhere is the anonymous biographer's account more engaging than here:

'Indeed his business and study then was a kind of errantry, having proposed to himself a more exact collection of the worthies general of England, in which others had waded before, but he resolved to go through. In what place soever therefore he came, of remark especially, he spent frequently most of his time in views and researches of their antiquities and church monuments, insinuating himself into the acquaintance (which frequently ended in a lasting friendship) of the learnedest and gravest persons residing within the place, thereby to inform himself fully of those things he thought worthy the commendation of his labours. It is an incredible thing to think what a numerous correspondence the doctor maintained and enjoyed by this means.

'Nor did the good doctor ever refuse to light his candle in investigating truth from the meanest person's discovery. He would endure contentedly an hour's or more impertinence from any aged church officer or other superannuated people for the gleaning of two lines to his purpose. And though his spirit was quick and nimble, and all the faculties of his mind ready and answerable to that activity of dispatch, yet in these inquests he would stay and attend those circular rambles till they came to a point; so resolute was he bent to the sifting out of abstruse antiquity. Nor did he ever dismiss any such feeble adjutators or helpers (as he pleased to style them) without giving them money and cheerful thanks besides.'

In the course of these wanderings the doctor came again to Bristol, where Hopton had been charged with the task of securing the defences. Waller was known to have many friends there, and it was vital to the cause that Bristol should be a Royalist stronghold. Each day now increased the embarrassment of the king's party. His Majesty himself, according to Clarendon, had become alarmed by the course of events. The queen left Oxford for Exeter on the 12th April. The kingdom, it was thought, had no safer place, and if the worst happened she could escape from there to the Continent. By the end of the month, however, Exeter was threatened by both Essex and Waller. The king himself, therefore, resolved to withdraw into the west, and on the march to collect such loyal recruits as could still be attracted to his standard. Finally he hoped to link up with Prince Maurice and consolidate the Cavalier strength. At the same time Hopton was advised of the danger of the situation and ordered to draw into Bristol all the men he could collect from Monmouthshire and South Wales, then to join the king and Prince Maurice with as many as could be spared from the Bristol garrison.

On the 15th July news reached the king at Bath of Prince Rupert's defeat at Marston Moor, which meant that the northern armies, the right arm of Royalist defence, had been crushed. Hopton's forces joined the king's near Yeovil, and together they proceeded with all speed towards Exeter, reaching that city on the 26th July. But in the meantime they had received news of the queen's flight to France.

CHAPTER IX

CHAPLAIN TO THE PRINCESS HENRIETTA

I meant to make her fair, and free, and wise,
Of greatest blood, and yet more good than great.

BEN JONSON.

WHEN the queen reached Exeter on the 1st of May 1644 she was so ill that her life was despaired of. Sir John Wintour her physician-in-attendance—not to be confused with Sir John Winter her secretary—was at his wit's end. About the middle of June she was expected to bear her ninth child. The responsibility was too much for Sir John, and he sighed in relief when she announced her intention of sending for old Sir Theodore Mayerne, the fashionable London doctor who had attended the sick-beds of all the royalty and many of the nobility for the past twenty years. While writing of New Forest deer in the *Worthies*, Fuller says: 'Besides, there is a concave in the neck of a green-headed stag, when above his first crossing, wherein are many worms, some two inches in length, very useful in physic, and therefore carefully put up by Sir Theodore Mayerne and other skilful physicians.'

Sir Theodore was a Swiss. He was a brilliant man—one of the first to use chemicals in medicine—but above all he was a character. His bluntness in addressing his patients acted on them as a tonic. Old Lord Conway used to tell how once when he appealed to Mayerne for something to relieve his gout the doctor replied fiercely: 'The late King Henri [the Fourth of France], my master, used to define the gout which often tormented him by saying that sometimes he had the gout and sometimes the gout had him. This is not the time to be ill, my lord.' But the classic story of Mayerne's brusqueness concerned the queen herself. In 1641 Her Majesty had been ill and overwrought, and had called in Mayerne, who had first won her confidence by his skill in prescribing cosmetics.

'Good Mayerne,' she had said, 'I fear I shall go mad.'

'Do not fear that, madame,' Sir Theodore had replied, 'you are already so.'

Nevertheless there was no one else in whom she had such confidence, and because she could not be sure that even her best entreaties would move the grumpy old doctor, she wrote at the same time to the king, begging His Majesty to command Mayerne to come to her. Charles responded with a single line:

'Mayerne,' he wrote, 'for the love of me, go find my wife.' [1]

So towards the end of May, old Mayerne, in appearance a benign and venerably bearded gentleman in the early seventies, grumbling about the roads, the distractions of the country, and the inconvenience of the places chosen by royalty to be ill in, rattled across southern England with his friend, Sir Matthew Lister, to do what he could for the queen.

Her physical condition was bad enough, but she had far worse troubles than that to depress her. For a year she had lain under a charge of high treason on account of the money and arms she had brought from France. Sir John Berkeley, who was in charge of the Exeter defences, had prepared Bedford House, north-east of the cathedral, to receive her, and on the day after her arrival the mayor and corporation had granted two hundred pounds, 'as a testimonie of the respect of the city.' But nothing reassured Her Majesty. She knew only too well how much her enemies hated her, and believed that as soon as they knew that Exeter harboured a Catholic queen they would attack and blockade it. In these unhappy conditions the child was born on the 16th June 1644, and contrary to all expectations both babe and mother lived.

This royal birth was a unique event in the history of Exeter, and in consequence one to be remembered. The princess's portrait, painted by Sir Peter Lely years afterwards when she was Duchess of Orleans, and presented to the city by her brother, Charles II, still hangs in the medieval guildhall. At the birth there was no time for rejoicing. Fifteen days after the event the queen, though half paralysed, was obliged to flee. Her fears had been well founded. The

[1] Sloane MS. 1679 f. 72.

Earl of Essex, who was already advancing on the city, in
reply to her request for a safe-conduct to Bristol or Bath
while she recovered her strength, had made it plain that he
intended to take her prisoner, and himself to wait on her
until she was safely delivered to other, and not more friendly,
authorities in London.   When he reached the city, however,
the queen was no longer there, and he saw no point in
attempting to reduce it immediately.   Had he known it, she
was still in the neighbourhood.   Sir John Wintour, in his
own account of the flight, tells us that with a single servant,
her faithful priest, and Sir John himself, she lay for two days
in a wretched hut about three miles from the city walls, from
which she could hear the soldiers of the Parliamentary Army
—'lobsters' the Devon folk called them—as they marched
past swearing to each other and boasting of what they would
do with the fifty thousand crowns they would get if they
captured the queen.   Her misery seemed complete.   She
had already sent a 'last' message to her beloved Charles.
If she lived she could never hope to see England again, and
perhaps on this last journey she thought of the day nineteen
years ago when she came as a bride to this strange new
country that had given her such extremes of joy and sorrow.
There had been the scene on the bowling green at Barham
Downs, where a group of ladies recognized their future king
and queen and curtsied to them as they passed.   Charles had
ordered the coach to stop, and after helping her down had
led her on to the green to receive their compliments and loyal
services.   That had been the first time she had noticed with
a thrill of joy his graciousness and nobility of bearing.   And
what of the children?   What of Charles, her Prince of Wales,
already so full of wit, whose liveliness had done so much to
cheer her when the king had been a little too noble and
impatient of her French vivacity?   What of her dwarfs, her
dogs, and monkeys?   What of the babe?   Would Lady
Dalkeith, to whom she had entrusted it, be able to follow
her?   All these and many other questions went through her
mind.   It seemed that her life was now all questions and no
answers.   Or if there were answers they were too gloomy to
be borne.   If she had any consolation at all it was in the

loyalty of her servants. She had always been a kind, even an indulgent, mistress, delighting in the antics of her dwarfs and 'pretty, dimpled boys' who served as pages. She had taken an unaffected interest in every trivial circumstance of their lives, and lately she had found their devotion almost too much for her. They had wanted to stay with her when she could find nowhere to house them, and when she had nothing left to give them.

On the third night the queen and her three attendants left the hut and started on the journey to Pendennis Castle, near Falmouth, which they reached six days later. But meanwhile a party came out from Exeter with news of the young princess's safety. She was already said to have the same bright eyes—bright as stars, they said—as the queen, whom she bade fair to resemble in feature and sweetness of disposition. All this was pleasant hearing for the invalid Henrietta, still unable to walk and apparently blind in one eye, who was carried in a litter with Sir John Wintour and her priest walking alongside, trying their best to cheer her with such poor attempts at conversation as they could muster on so miserable a journey. They must have looked a dejected train most of the time, and it is little wonder that a Cornish gentleman who saw them wrote to his wife that they were the woefullest spectacle he had ever set eyes on.

In Falmouth Bay a Dutch vessel, kindly placed at the queen's command by the Prince of Orange, awaited them, and, when safely aboard, Her Majesty smiled again at the prospect of the safety and welcome awaiting her across the narrow channel. But her troubles were not yet over. Her boat was recognized and pursued as far as Jersey; but by this time she had regained some of her native high spirits, and when a shell from the Parliament ship hit the rigging of the queen's she told her servants not to be afraid, adding sardonically that queens of England never died at sea. After this the intentions of the Parliamentary captain were supported by a fierce gale, which scattered the French ships that had come to escort her, and the queen's boat was driven against the rocks near Brest, where she and her attendants landed and found shelter in the cottages of the fisher-folk near by. She was not yet thirty-five, but when she reached Paris her old friends had difficulty in recognizing the bent and haggard woman who greeted them as the woman who had once been their own lovely and vivacious Henrietta Maria.

Meanwhile, the care of the infant princess was a heavy responsibility for Sir John Berkeley, the governor, who had, however, made so favourable an impression on the queen in the short time he had been with her in the city that she wrote to Charles in one of several 'last' letters to him: 'Farewell my dear heart: Behold the mark which you desire to have to know when I desire anything in earnest (†). I pray begin to remember what I spoke to you concerning Jacke Berkeley for Master of the Wards.' The most delicate matter Berkeley had to arrange after the queen left was the princess's baptism, which was administered in the cathedral on the 21st July, with himself, Lady Dalkeith, and Lady Poulett of Hinton St. George as sponsors. A new font was placed in the nave for the sacrament, with a canopy of state above it, and the officiating clergyman was Dr. Lawrence Burnell, Dean of Exeter. By the king's wish she was christened Henrietta. Anne, her second name, was added later as a compliment to her aunt, Anne of Austria, who had sent over to her sister-in-law just before the birth a complete layette, and with it Madame Peronne, the best midwife in France, to attend to the birth.

The king saw the princess on the 26th July, when he arrived with Prince Charles from Honiton. Prince Maurice, the Earl of Bristol, Sir John Poulett, Sir John Berkeley, and all the distinguished citizens of Exeter received His Majesty outside the city gate and attended him to Bedford House, where the baby, dressed, like all French babies of high degree, in white satin, was laid in his arms.

Once again Exeter gave proof of its loyalty by voting substantial sums of money, though whether freely or under some form of persuasion seems to be in doubt. Anyhow, the gift was dutifully stated to be 'as a testimony of the citie's service and the joy of his Mat$^{tie's}$ presence here.' The amounts were £500 to the king, and £100 to the prince. In addition, £20 was voted to the king's servants, £12 to the queen's servants, and £200 to provide the troops with footwear. Charles was delighted, and promptly knighted the worthy mayor, Hugh Crocker, an Exeter merchant of good family. But in making the grants Exeter politely expressed the hope that the city might now be thought to have done its share for the Royalist cause.

Exeter had always been Royalist in sympathy, though disinclined to provoke either side unnecessarily. Described by Fuller in the *Church History* as 'a round city on a rising hill, most capable of fortification,' it had been a coveted prize throughout the war. Its four gates had opened first to Roundhead, then to Cavalier, and had been fiercely defended by both. In October 1642 the Parliament army under the Earl of Stamford had stormed them successfully; but eleven months later, after an eight months' siege—the ninth in its history—they opened to Prince Maurice. Since then Sir John Berkeley, whose forces had actually reduced the city, had been governor and had quickly turned his prize into the strongest garrison in the west.

Charles spent one night only in the city. On the 27th he rode out with Prince Maurice and Lord Hopton in pursuit of Essex, whom they engaged in Cornwall, and on the 1st September nearly the whole of the Parliamentary army in the west surrendered to the king. On the 17th His Majesty returned to Exeter, lodging as before at Bedford House, and it was on this visit that he made arrangements for his daughter's household, appointing Fuller to be her chaplain.

In making the appointment it is probable that Charles had something more than the bestowing of an honour upon a loyal clergyman in mind. By this time Fuller had gained a reputation for uncompromising adherence to principle. He had offended both Puritan and Catholic because he had refused to flatter either. The one thing he had been true to in the expression of his churchmanship was the Protestant faith. By making Fuller his daughter's chaplain the king would thus demonstrate his own loyalty to the reformed church in England, which some were inclined to doubt. Other favourite clergymen might tactfully hold the balance between the Roman Catholic queen and the supposedly Protestant king, adjusting their practice according to private instructions. Not so Fuller. So in view of this appointment, he may have thought, it would now be difficult for his enemies to charge him with papist sympathies.

When the king marched away he took with him a man who, if he had only remained in Exeter, would have been one of Fuller's dearest cronies, Richard Symonds, an Essex man, born in the same village as John Ray, the naturalist. Symonds, like Fuller, copied inscriptions and picked up antiquarian lore as he marched with the king's soldiers. While in Exeter he examined heraldic glass in the Mermaid Inn and rummaged through two chests there, which he found to contain papers belonging to the Earl of Bath. These he was told had been there for forty years unknown to his lordship.

Fuller's chaplaincy carried no remuneration. Charles was not then able to pay for such services; but he offered in lieu of wages the living of Dorchester, worth £400 a year, if his cause triumphed. As far as we can see, the man Fuller was intended to succeed there was John White, often called the 'Patriarch of Dorchester,' who had a leading part in founding Massachusetts, first settled by Dorchester men. He has a long notice in the *Worthies*. According to this he was 'a grave man, yet without moroseness, as who would willingly contribute his shot of facetiousness on any just occasion.' For upwards of forty years he had been a father to the old Dorset town, but 'Towards the end of his days factions and fond opinions crept in his flock; a new generation arose which either did not know or would not acknowledge this good man; disloyal persons, which would not pay the due respect to the crown of his old age, whereof he was sadly and silently sensible.' Such intimate information about White suggests that Fuller had been at pains to inquire into the relationship between parson and people at Dorchester. Whether this was done at the time of the king's offer or not we cannot know, but for some reason the living was declined. The anonymous biographer suggests that the doctor still had London in his eye, and no doubt he is right in this. No other place outside the two universities could afford him adequate facilities for research.

The king finally left Exeter about the 23rd September, and Fuller would then settle down happily to his duties in the princess's household, in which he continued to serve for two years. The duties cannot have been onerous, so once again he had leisure to write and to enjoy the good company his heart loved, which Exeter at the time was well able to supply. There were his old friends the Pouletts. Lady Poulett seems to have been living in the city, and Sir John and his son, both of whom had been with Prince Maurice at Lyme and in reconnoitring the country they knew so intimately, were there when the demands of the king's service permitted. Sir John Berkeley was a respected friend. He had all the attributes that appealed most strongly to Fuller, and was an efficient and conscientious governor who earned favours rather than bought them. In gaining his will he used persuasion instead of force, and was able to do this effectively because he could never be charged with neglecting his own duties. No one worked harder than Sir John, and no one was better informed about the condition of the city and its people. Herrick addressed him thus:

> Stand forth, brave man, since fate has made thee here
> The Hector over Aged Exeter;
> Who for a long sad time has weeping stood,
> Like a poor Lady lost in Widowhood:
> But fears not now to see her safety sold
> (As other Towns and Cities were) for gold,
> By those ignoble Births, which shame the stem
> That gave Progermination unto them:
> Whose restless Ghosts shall hear their children sing,
> *Our Sires betrayed their Country and their King.*
> True, if this City seven times rounded was
> With rock, and seven times circumflanked with brass,
> Yet if thou wert not, Berkeley, loyal proof,
> The Senators down tumbling with the roof,
> Would into praised (but pitied) ruins fall,
> Leaving no show, where stood the Capitol.
> But thou art just and itchless, and dost please
> Thy Genius with two strength'ning Buttresses,
> Faith, and Affection: which will never slip
> To weaken this thy great Dictatorship.

Such a man could not fail to call out all the loyalty and help

that Fuller could give him. The Earl of Carlisle, who was to
be his patron at Waltham Abbey, also became a close friend
at this time, and Lord Berkeley, his greatest patron, yet
another. Among local worthies, Dr. Vilvain, antiquary,
physician, theologian, who was perhaps the most respected
townsman of the day, was his greatest friend. William
Oldys must be our authority here. He says[1]: 'Old Dr.
Vilvain of that city was pleasantly rallied by the Governor of
Exeter for inviting him [Fuller] so often, or detaining him so
long from the society of others; as a cornholder that hoardeth
up the grain to enhance the market and make a dearth in the
neighbourhood.' He then goes on to point out that the
advantages of the friendship of these two cronies were
reciprocal. Vilvain had a good library and a remarkable
museum of natural curiosities, 'and being of a generous
disposition, as his benefactions in that city may testify,
notwithstanding his sufferings in those destructive times, as
also of courteous comportment and communicative conversation, they were mutually agreeable to each other.' The old
doctor lived to be eighty-seven, and at his death his library
went to the cathedral.

Dr. Vilvain enjoyed a certain notoriety in those superstitious days from being the possessor of a skull, 'no bigger
than a bean,' which was alleged to be that of one of the three
hundred and sixty-five children brought forth at a birth by
Margaret, Countess of Henneberg. Fuller mentions having
seen this in his *History of Cambridge*,[2] and Pepys has a reference to it in the *Diary*, under date 19th May 1660.

In this pleasant cathedral-city atmosphere, notwithstanding the annoyance of having troops quartered there,
Fuller was able to savour again the delights of civilized
life. He would relish, too, the humours of its breezy
humanity, and who better than old Dr. Vilvain to pass on
to him the local gossip? There was that capital story of
Dr. Turberville and the landlord's daughter, for example.
Turberville and a friend, during these hard times found themselves with £100 apiece chalked up behind the landlord's
door in their usual inn, and there seemed little prospect of

---

[1] Memoir of Fuller, *Biographia Britannica*.　　[2] ii. 21–2.

INTERIOR OF EXETER CATHEDRAL

either being able to pay. One day, as they sat over their tankards, the landlord entered the parlour leading by the hand his daughter. He had an offer to make. If either of them would marry her he should have his debt wiped out. The doctor resisted temptation, assisted perhaps by professional ethics; but the other fell, and had 'his scores wiped out with a wet dish-clout.' Fuller always had a ready ear for such tales. But he must also have gained much valuable historical information from the many gentlemen of affairs quartered in the city. Perhaps the Earl of Bristol was as useful as any one in this respect. It was he who had tried to negotiate the marriage of Charles with the infanta of Spain on which James I set his heart in 1619. Fuller, as we saw in reviewing that part of his life, had witnessed the public rejoicings in Cambridge when the negotiations failed. Here was the man who had conducted them, and Fuller tells us that he had actually seen and perused the patent given to him by James I. Like so many others at this time, the earl was accused of being a papist in secret. In the Warwickshire section of the *Worthies* the charge is indignantly rebutted in these words: 'The worst I wish such who causelessly suspect him of Popish inclinations is, that I may hear from them but half so many strong arguments for the Protestant religion as I have heard from him, who was, to his commendation, a cordial champion for the Church of England.'

So high did Fuller stand in the earl's esteem that he was invited to join the Royalist party when the leaders were at last obliged to seek a refuge on the Continent: 'May the reader be pleased to know, that, living in Exeter, I had many hours' private converse with the Right Honourable John Digby, Earl of Bristol, who favoured me so far—much above my desert—that, at his last going over into France, where he died, he was earnest with me to go with him, promising me, to use his own expression, "that I should have half a loaf with him, so long as he had a whole one to himself."'[1] But invitations to leave the country never had much appeal for Fuller, who was an Englishman through and through, with nothing of the cosmopolitan about him.

[1] *Appeal*, part. ii, p. 551.

With so many congenial friends to encourage him, he could not fail to take up his pen again.   First, no doubt, he put his notes for the *Worthies* in order, supplementing them with information he was able to gain from the many gentlemen of good family quartered in the city.   That done he turned again to the easy, conversational kind of writing that had proved so successful in *The Holy State*, this time using it for a series of reflections in brief, moralizing essays, to which he gave the title *Good Thoughts in Bad Times*.   When published they were to prove so popular that the book became one of the favourite devotional manuals of the day.   It was the first book printed in Exeter, or as Fuller put it, 'the first-fruits of the Exeter Press.'   The dedication was to Lady Dalkeith, one of the beautiful ladies of the Villiers family, now the Princess Henrietta's governess.   Her husband afterwards became Earl of Morton.   Fuller hints at the progress made by these ladies of the Villiers family and their husbands, though matched with 'little more portion than their uncle's smiles, 'their uncle being the handsome but dissolute Duke of Buckingham who had made the first three years of the queen's married life so miserable.   Nor were husbands the only ones to attend upon the Villiers ladies.   Poets vied with each other to do them honour, and we find Herrick, the laureate of Devon in that age, writing:

> To the Lady Mary Villiers,
> *Governess to the Princess Henrietta*
>
> When I of Villiers do but hear the name,
> It calls to mind that mighty Buckingham,
> Who was your brave exalted uncle here,
> Binding the wheel of fortune to his sphere,
> Who spurned at envy; and could bring, with ease,
> An end to all his stately purposes.
> For his love then, whose sacred relics show
> Their resurrection and their growth in you;
> And for my sake, who ever did prefer
> You above all those Sweets of Westminster:
> Permit my book to have a free access
> To kiss your hand, most dainty governess.

Fuller, of course, could not come up to that in his preface; but, considering that he had to continue to serve in the same household as the lady, he was fairly bold with his compliments.

Other books of the kind had already appeared, the best of them being John Donne's *Devotions upon Emergent Occasions*. Perhaps the most popular, and probably the one that gave Fuller the idea for his, was Bishop Hall's *Occasional Meditations*. Hall had been Bishop of Exeter from 1627 to 1641 and was a well remembered figure in the city. But what no other writer of the kind could have was Fuller's own personality, and it was this above everything else that sent the book through at least ten editions before the end of the century. In *Good Thoughts in Bad Times*, far more than in *The Holy State*, we hear the man speaking. Each of the four sections into which it is divided has twenty-five meditations. All are brief and of a kind that never ceases to appeal. Tagore's *Gitanjali* has, perhaps, been the most successful twentieth-century book of the type, though Fuller's is different in that it is devotional and human, where Tagore's is mystical and poetic. Here is the first of the Personal Meditations:

'Lord, how near was I to danger, yet escaped! I was upon the brink of it, yet fell not in; they are well kept who are kept by thee. Excellent archer! Thou didst hit thy mark in missing it, as meaning to fright, not hurt me. Let me not now be such a fool as to pay my thanks to blind Fortune for a favour which the eye of Providence hath bestowed upon me. Rather let the narrowness of my escape make my thankfulness to thy goodness the larger, lest my ingratitude justly cause, that, whereas this arrow but hit my hat, the next pierce my head.'

In the next he says that he is afraid that if he were visited with a sharp disease he would be impatient, because he is 'tender' by temper and has never yet known sickness. 'I cannot,' he says 'expect any kind usage from that which hath been a stranger unto me. I fear I shall rave and rage.' Many of the thoughts used in this book must have come from his sermon notes, and if they did we cannot wonder that his churches were always full. Who could resist such a preacher? Here are a few extracts from the first section:

'Lord, before I commit a sin, it seems to me so shallow,

F

that I may wade through it dryshod from any guiltiness: but when I have committed it, it often seems so deep that I cannot escape without drowning. Thus I am always in the extremities: either my sins are so small that they need not my repentance, or so great that they cannot obtain thy pardon. Lend me, O Lord, a reed out of thy sanctuary, truly to measure the dimension of my offences.'

'Lord, I saw one, whom I knew to be notoriously bad, in great extremity. It was hard to say whether his former wickedness or present want were the greater; if I could have made the distinction, I could willingly have fed his person, and starved his profaneness. This being impossible, I adventured to relieve him . . . count me not accessory to his badness, because I relieved him.'

'Lord, what faults I correct in my son, I commit myself: I beat him for dabbling in the dirt, whilst my own soul doth wallow in sin: I beat him for crying to cut his own meat, yet am not myself contented with that state thy providence hath carved unto me: I beat him for crying when he is to go to sleep,[1] and yet I fear I myself shall cry when thou callest me to sleep with my fathers. Alas! I am more childish than my child.'

'Lord, I perceive my soul deeply guilty of envy. By my good will, I would have none prophesy but mine own Moses.[2] I had rather thy work were undone, than done better by another than by myself. . . . Dispossess me, Lord, of this bad spirit, and turn my envy into holy emulation. Let me labour to exceed them in pains, who excel me in parts.'

'Lord, when I am to travel, I never use to provide myself till the very time; partly out of laziness, loth to be troubled till needs I must; partly out of pride, as presuming all necessaries for my journey will wait upon me at the instant. Some say this is scholar's fashion, and it seems by following it I hope to approve myself to be one.'

The book is full of such passages. Who except Fuller ever prayed God to 'pinch' him into a remembrance of his

---

[1] This 'beating' for small offences was, of course, the universal custom of the age.
[2] Numbers, xi. 28.

promises? Or made such a confession as this: 'Almost twenty years since I heard a profane jest, and still remember it. How many pious passages of far later date have I forgotten! It seems my soul is like a filthy pond, wherein fish die soon, and frogs live long.' And surely no other book of this character ever ended so frankly. 'How easy is pen and paper piety!' the concluding meditation begins. 'I will not say it costeth nothing, but it is far cheaper to work one's head than one's heart to goodness.'

Here indeed was an honest man, and it was this candour and common sense that worked so mightily on the hearts of the people he met. But there is something else. These meditations show again that this most sociable of men knew how to preserve inviolate the sanctuary of his soul. Only a very deep river could have flowed so calmly down the rapids of civil war, and we cannot doubt that the real strength of Fuller's character was in the depth of his devotional life.

The calm of these early days at Exeter was not to last. The tide of war again flowed westward in the spring of 1645. Early in March, Prince Charles, with the Marquess of Hertford and Archbishop Ussher in attendance, took up residence in Bristol in the house Lord Hopton had got ready for him. But almost at once the plague became so virulent in Bristol that the prince was compelled to move, and at the end of May we find him at Barnstaple. Naseby in June put the Royalist forces to confusion, and the leaders came into the west to make a final stand. On the 27th August Prince Charles reached Exeter, and remained until the 15th September. His presence inevitably increased the alarm already felt, for Waller and Fairfax were now in the neighbourhood and attack was to be expected. Lady Dalkeith tried to escape with the princess, but failed. She felt trapped. Still the Parliamentary forces came on, pushing Goring and his dissolute troopers back into the city, and by the end of October preparations were well advanced for the siege, which continued throughout the winter until on the 27th January 1646 Fairfax called for surrender. When Berkeley refused, Fairfax blocked up the western approaches, thus completing the land encirclement of the city, and settled down to await the unavoidable result. It must have been about this time that the incident recorded by Fuller in the *Worthies*—similar to those vouched for in other places—occurred:

'When the City of Exeter was besieged by the Parliament's forces, so that only the south side thereof towards the sea was open unto it, incredible numbers of larks were found in that open quarter, for multitude like quails in the wilderness. . . . They were as fat as plentiful; so that, being sold for twopence a dozen, and under, the poor (who could have no cheaper, as the rich no better meat) used to make pottage of them, boiling them down therein.'

In the middle of January an attempt had been made to rouse the Royalists by making Hopton commander-in-chief under the prince, but he seems to have had little stomach for the task. He did what he could, however, to bring some discipline to Goring's unruly cavaliers, reinforced with new levies from Cornwall, and Fairfax felt obliged to leave Sir Hardress Waller in charge of the siege while he went out to Torrington to destroy any hopes the Royalists might have of recovering their strength. His victory was decisive. Fuller said of the Royalist footmen on this occasion that they were well named, for they used their feet more than their hands, meaning that they were ready to run rather than to fight, and Clarendon described the rabble that escaped into Cornwall as 'a dissolute, undisciplined, wicked, beaten army . . . whom only their friends feared, and their enemies laughed at.' Hopton, however, still held the respect of both sides, and on the 14th March was offered honourable terms for surrender, which he wisely accepted.

Fairfax then returned to Exeter, which surrendered at the end of the month, and the treaty, begun on the 3rd April, was signed on the 9th. Fuller is said by Nichols, one of his editors, to have been useful in gaining favourable terms for the garrison and the inhabitants of the city; but his name does not appear in any document connected with the surrender. Possibly he advised the Exeter authorities, who by this time were his close personal friends; but any speculations as to his part must be without the support of documentary evidence. He had, however, recently been given further proof of the high regard in which the city fathers held him by being appointed, on the 21st March, to the important Bodley lectureship, though it must then have appeared extremely unlikely that he would hold it for long. As the lectureship was a civic appointment, and its founder the brother of the man who gave Oxford the Bodleian Library, it was one that he must have valued.

By the terms of the surrender the princess and her household, which, of course, included Fuller, were allowed to pass with their plate, money, and goods to any place in England or Wales selected by Lady Dalkeith. They thereupon went to Oatlands, the royal dower-house at Walton-on-Thames, where Lady Dalkeith at once tried to enter into negotiation with the Parliamentary generals, the Speaker of the House of Commons, and the Surrey authorities for a safe-conduct for herself and the princess to France. In reply she was told frankly that she would be dismissed, and that the child would be held in custody with her royal brothers and sisters. There was no time to lose, so, without informing the household, Lady Dalkeith stole out one night, her gown stuffed with rags to disguise her beautiful figure, bearing the princess, dressed as a boy, in her arms. When she reached Dover she found the authorities only too ready to bundle what they took to be French beggars on to the first boat to sail.

Across the channel the story is taken up by the queen's Capuchin, Father Cyprien de Gamache, who tells us how Her Majesty sent carriages to receive the heroic governess and 'her precious deposit which she had so happily preserved amidst so many awful dangers. Oh, the transports of joy! Oh, the excessive consolation to the heart of the queen! She embraced, she hugged, she kissed again and again, that royal infant. . . . Many thanksgivings did she render God for his mercy; and regarding the Princess as *un enfant de bénédiction*, she resolved with the grace of God to have her instructed in the Catholic and Roman religion, and to use her efforts to obtain the consent of the king her husband.'[1]

Waller, then an exile in Paris, took up the chorus of praise

[1] De Motteville; de Gamache; de la Fayette.

for Lady Dalkeith, still remembering her when on New Year's Eve 1649 he addressed to her an epistle which contained these lines:

> But thus to style you fair, your sex's praise,
> Gives you but myrtle, who may challenge bays;
> From armed foes to bring a royal prize,
> Shows your brave heart victorious as your eyes.

Fuller's work was done—or he may have thought, undone. The child of two with the pretty brown hair and quick eyes was already mercurial and precocious. Her brother was to give her the nickname Minette, little pussy, and she was to be brought up in her mother's country. She visited England at the Restoration, and on the 22nd November 1660 Exeter voted £200 to buy her a piece of plate. But it is unlikely that Fuller ever saw her again, though she did not forget him. When *Good Thoughts in Bad Times* was published he had a copy specially bound in blue morocco, embellished with the princess's own cipher and coronet, and this he solemnly presented to her as she sat up in the arms of her governess, with the loyal ladies of Exeter in attendance. Perhaps when she was old enough to understand, she was told by Lady Dalkeith about the kind and learned gentleman who had been her first chaplain, for the book was always treasured by the princess—who grew up to be one of the wittiest ladies in France—and long afterwards it was found with passages transcribed on the title-page in her own hand. In 1661, the year of Fuller's death, Henrietta married Philippe de Bourbon, Duke of Orleans and brother of the French king. After a short and tragic life she died in suspicious circumstances at the age of twenty-six.

Whatever others may have thought of the Exeter Articles of surrender, Fuller always regarded them as fair and just. He referred to them as 'the best-made and best-kept articles,' and when he became curate of Waltham Abbey by the favour of the Earl of Carlisle, one of the noblemen he came to know intimately at Exeter, he said: 'I must not forget the *Articles of Exeter*, whereof I had the benefit, living, and waiting there on the King's daughter.'

THE SAVOY CHAPEL, LONDON

CHAPTER X

WANDERING SCHOLAR

All confess there never was a more learned clergy.

SELDEN.

FULLER was again homeless and unemployed. What was worse, he was now without even the hope of finding parish or gainful employment. He was, in short, a redundant person. On his way from Exeter to London he would pass through the Dorset countryside, with its grey stone villages, its round hills, its valleys with their apple orchards just breaking into leaf; and he would remember how he had passed through them all with his wife not ten years ago, when it might have seemed to any one who knew him that nothing could hold from his hands a bishopric or, if he preferred it, the deanery of St. Paul's. The child of that marriage may have been with him as he travelled. There are several passages in *Good Thoughts in Bad Times* which suggest that the two were together in Exeter. But whether with him in the body or not, the father would have the child in mind as he thought of the future, for what future could there be for a Royalist parson's son? We have a reflection of his feelings at this time in the preface to the longer *Andronicus,* where he says: 'Wherefore, until such time as I shall by God's providence and the authority of my superiors be restored to the open exercise of my profession on terms consisting with my conscience (which welcome minute I do heartily wish and humbly wait for, and will greedily listen to the least whisper thereunto), it is my intent, God willing, to spend the remnant of my days in reading and writing such stories as my weak judgment shall commend unto me.' The passage is worth noting because it shows also that he intended neither to bemoan his lot nor to fight the oppressors. Arguments either way were only fuel for the flames that were already consuming both Church and State. Far better throw open a few windows, as it were, and bring down the temperature by writing tales and romances that would take the nation's mind off its troubles. That, it would seem, was how he felt when it became clear that his responsibilities for the princess had ended. As for the quarrel between King and Parliament, his attitude at this time was not unlike that of the countryman who wandered between the lines at Marston Moor, and when challenged to declare for 'King or Parliament,' replied: 'What, be they two at it again?'

The anonymous biographer tells us how Fuller returned to London and wandered despondently into his old parish: 'Upon his first arrival, he came to his own (the parish of Savoy), but they received him not, the face of things was so altered.' Incidentally, the Dr. John Bond who was still in charge—of the family that gave its name to Bond Street—was a Dorset man who must have been well known to Fuller by repute if not personally. He was of St. John's, Cambridge. Before the Civil War he had been a preacher in Exeter, and he was again to tread on the doctor's corns when, on the first anniversary of the surrender, he returned to that city to preach a sermon in celebration of the Parliamentary victory, receiving in acknowledgment a piece of plate worth £10. Eventually his loyalty to the Puritan cause was to gain him the appointment of Master of Trinity Hall.

But though Fuller returned as a stranger—and there is plenty of evidence to show that he felt like an alien at this time—he was far from friendless. Perhaps he did not wish to embarrass any of his former parishioners by asking them to take him into their homes, some of which may already have been full of ejected clergy, hundreds of whom were now destitute, or at least homeless. At all events, the man under whose roof he did find a breathing space was his publisher, John Williams, and it was from his house that he petitioned for composition in June 1646, describing himself as 'late of the Savoy in London, and since attendant in Exeter on the Princess Henrietta.'

Williams's house was a convenient place for seeing his new book, *Andronicus, or the Unfortunate Politician,* through the press. Most of it had been written in Exeter. Later, when the subject, Andronicus Comnenus, an emperor of Byzantium who reigned from 1163 to 1185, was supposed to represent Cromwell, the book was discussed as a remarkable example of prescience, and contributed greatly to Fuller's fame at the Restoration. Andronicus had first been used to illustrate the character of the tyrant in *The Profane State*. That was in 1642 when the sketch had run to little more than a thousand words. Since then Fuller had been able to study men of the type at close quarters, particularly while in Exeter, and he had gained a shrewd conception of the kind of man likely to usurp power if the king should be overthrown. So gradually his original sketch of the tyrant developed into a full-length book, and while we must be careful not to read into it more knowledge than Fuller could possibly have in 1646, it is clear enough that he could see farther ahead than most.

But though events developed along curiously parallel lines, it was not so much foreknowledge of action as shrewdness of insight into the mind of the man of power that was remarkable. Before the war Fuller had spent most of his time among scholars and country folk. Generals and politicians had been new to him when he took up his work in Exeter, and it is evident that in his quiet way he soon had the measure of them. By 1646 he had also seen cruelty and mob violence for himself. He knew the passions that war unleashes, and had seen the hard glint in the would-be tyrant's eye. Selfishness, hypocrisy, and all the old vices that he had preached about were still there, but in an older and more primitive form; a form that the shallow Utopians of the day thought of as belonging only to the past, for those who knew little of history or moral philosophy were confounded by the civil wars of the seventeenth century exactly as their counterparts were confounded by the world wars of the twentieth. But though *Andronicus* must have embarrassed the Roundheads, it was ostensibly, if not actually, about twelfth-century Byzantium. So Cromwell would have been a fool if he had allowed that the cap fitted. For all that, even in the short version there are shrewd digs, most of which are as apposite now as then, and likely to remain so. Take this, for example: 'Treason is so ugly in herself, that every one that sees it will cast stones at it, which makes her

* F

seldom appear but with a borrowed face, for the good of the Commonwealth; but especially when ambition hath caught hold on pretended religion, how fast will it climb.' Or, 'Besides, there were in the city many turbulent spirits, desirous of alterations, as profitable unto them . . . to whom rich fines and heriots would accrue upon every exchange, and all these took part with Andronicus.' Such have been found in every revolution, and it was of them and their gullible followers in the seventeenth century that Francis Quarles wrote:

> We 'll pull down Universities
>   Where learning is profest,
> Because they practise and maintain
>   The language of the beast;
> We 'll drive the doctors out of doors,
>   And all that learned be,
> We 'll cry all arts and learning down,
>   And hey, then up go we.

Then there was the trick that Fuller detested most of all: 'Many more did Andronicus win by his cunning behaviour, for he could speak both eloquently and religiously. He would ordinarily talk Scripture-language—often foully misapplied—as if his memory were a concordance of the whole Bible, but especially of St. Paul's Epistles, which he had by heart.'

When in 1659 the long *Andronicus* was translated into Dutch it proved a favourite with the exiled Royalists, and served to bring Fuller's name before them in a way that would have been much to his advantage if he had lived long enough to reap the harvest of his loyalty during the war years. But for the present we are in the London of 1646 with him, surrounded by the vociferous preachers who were now set up like rooks in a rookery in all the London pulpits. He would hardly have been human if he had not had the utmost contempt for them, 'spiritual clowns,' as he calls them, 'whose unreverend deportment bewrays their ignorance.' Most of this preaching was done out of vanity rather than grace. In *Abel Redevivus*,[1] Fuller deplores this courting of popularity

[1] p. 364.

by ministers of religion, yet there was so much of it that John Tombes was impelled to write his *Anthropolatria: Or, the Sinne of Glorying in Men, especially in Eminent Ministers of the Gospel*. As a high-spirited man Fuller must have longed to hold such beings up to ridicule, yet he never paid them back in their own currency of inflated rhetoric. Their effect on the Church was too serious to be used for mere gladiatorial contests. In 1660 he was to write: 'Our English pulpits, for these last eighteen years, have had in them too much caninal anger, vented by snapping and snarling spirits on both sides.'

Fuller was of a different kind. His restraint, no doubt, had its root in principle; but its soil was his temperament, which was never congenial to any kind of excess. His emotional range was small. Passionate feeling was beyond him, so his effectiveness in the pulpit sprang from the charm of his personality, his erudition, his wit, his sweet reasonableness, rather than from his eloquence. His sermons, like Jeremy Taylor's, were to all intents and purposes essays. Several of the best preachers of the age were of this order, and their performances depended for success upon skill in preparing and care in memorizing. Bishop Hall, for example, always committed the whole of his sermons to memory, though he preached on an average three times a week. Whitefoot, in his funeral sermon for Hall, said the bishop, accomplished preacher though he was, 'never durst climb up on the pulpit to preach any sermon whereof he had not before penned every word in the same order wherein he hoped to deliver it; although in his expression he was no slave to syllables, neither made use of his notes.'

By nature, perhaps, these men were writers rather than preachers. The Church was almost unavoidably their profession at such a time, and most of them were unquestionably sincere in entering it. Fuller, no doubt, wished it were possible to leave the world to wag as it pleased while he went off with his books to take his ease in some quiet retreat; but he never for a moment imagined that it would be consistent with his calling to do so. Nor had he, or most of the others, means for a life of studious retirement. In *Good Thoughts*

in Worse Times, published in the following year, and therefore
in course of writing during this depressing year of 1646, he
said: 'How shall God make my bed, who have no bed of mine
own to make?' replying: 'Thou fool, he can make thy not
having a bed to be a bed unto thee.'   And in another he
says: 'Small are my means on earth.   May I mount my soul
the higher in heavenly meditations, relying on Divine
Providence.'   Nevertheless, the thought of these learned
Caroline divines increasingly inclined to literary form and
expression, and their reading public grew in number and
increased in enthusiasm as the century proceeded.

Much of Fuller's second book of reflections just named was
written at Boughton, the old Northamptonshire home of the
Montagus, which he had known from childhood.   It is not a
cheerful book.   He was now in his fortieth year, and, in
spite of what has just been said, he did feel the lack of many
creature comforts.   If he had only had a hearth of his own,
his books, and the simple things necessary for a writing life
he would probably have been doing his best work.   It was
all very well practising Christian forbearance, exercising
patience, and all the rest of it; but he was by nature a home-
loving man, and homeless; a scholar, and bookless.   What
chance had he of doing good work under such uneasy conditions?

But the Montagus were kind, and the writing of meditations
helped to promote equanimity.   'I perceive controversial
writings,' he said, 'sounding somewhat of guns and trumpets,
do but make the wound the wider.   Meditations are like the
minstrel the prophet called for, to pacify his mind discom-
posed with passion.'   A refuge in the country, though tem-
porary and in another man's home, was a blessing at this
time.   The Articles of Exeter relieved him of obligation to
take the Solemn League and Covenant; but all ministers in
London who had come from Royalist garrisons were required
to register and accept supervision.   In Northamptonshire he
was free from this, and again with his own people.   Edward
Montagu, the second baron and present head of the family,
was a Sidney-Sussex man like himself, and as the eldest of the
three brothers to whom he had dedicated his first work,

David's Heinous Sin, had an even closer tie. But they were in different camps. Montagu was for Parliament, and had recently negotiated the surrender of Newark.

Like so many of the moderate families, the Montagus had connections in both armies. The first lord, or 'the old lord,' described by Clarendon as 'a person of great reverence, being about fourscore years of age, and of unblemished reputation.' was taken prisoner in his own house by the Parliamentarians 'for declaring himself unsatisfied with their disobedient and undutiful proceedings against the King, and more expressly against their ordinance for the militia; and notwithstanding that he had a brother in the House of Peers, the Lord Privy Seal, and a nephew, the Lord Kimbolton [second Earl of Manchester], who had as full a power in that council as any man, and a son in the House of Commons, very unlike his father, his lordship was committed to the Tower a close prisoner; and though he was afterwards remitted to more air, he continued a prisoner to his death.'[1]

The truth was not so discreditable to Parliament as Clarendon's account suggests. Old Lord Montagu still enjoyed the respect of the House, and to make his lot more bearable, as they thought, his judges offered to send him to the home of his daughter, the Countess of Rutland, who had been a member of Fuller's congregation at St. Mary Savoy, and was now on the side of Parliament. Thereupon the stout-hearted nobleman replied that if he deserved prison, to prison he would go. He would know in plain language what his position was to be. If he was to be a prisoner confined in his daughter's house, then let his daughter's house be described as what it would be, a prison. As Sir Philip Warwick has it, he 'would not be sent to her house until the warrant named her house his prison, which the lady was much disgruntled at.' So he was taken to the Savoy after a period in the Tower, and remained there until at his death in 1644 he found a last resting place next to his 'second sweet faithful companion,' Frances, a sister of Sir Robert Cotton, in Weekley church.

The children of such a character as old Lord Montagu

---

[1] *History of the Rebellion*, vi. 297.

might be expected to inherit their full share of their father's contentious spirit before they inherited their fair share of his large and fruitful estate. So, indeed, they did. The second lord was on the Parliament side, and married to a Puritan lady, a daughter of Sir Ralph Winwood, author of *State Memorials*. This lady disparaged the liturgy, which his lordship was in the habit of having read to his household daily.

'Daughter,' said the old man when she criticized the custom, 'if you come to visit me, I will never ask you why you come not to prayers; but if you come to cohabit with me, pray with me, or live not with me.'

To enjoy the patronage of this distinguished family was a great advantage to Fuller, and one that he acknowledged in whatever way he could. When a few years later he was again in possession of a living, and as comfortably established in a parsonage of his own as he could hope to be, he dedicated one of the illustrations in *A Pisgah Sight of Palestine* to a son of the second lord, 'who, when I was feeble, an exile, a nobody (i.e. undone, or good for nothing), was the first to take care of me, to receive me under his roof, to restore me by his munificence to my former self, and (as the sum of all) to provide generously for the education of my darling boy, the solitary hope of my old age.'

It is from another dedication of the time that we derive most of the information we have about Fuller's present condition. On the 25th January 1647, in dedicating his *Cause and Cure of a Wounded Conscience* to Lady Rutland, he describes himself as a servant of her noble family living in her brother's house, where, he says, he has of late 'been wedded to the pleasant embraces of a private life, the fittest wife and meetest helper that can be provided for a student in troublesome times.' This is, in fact, the first intimation we have of Fuller's removal to Boughton, and as the term 'of late' is used, and the work is described as the first issue of his mind since he came, we may assume that he had then been living under the Montagu roof for several weeks, if not months. We trust, however, that his sense of obligation to this family did not reduce him to the subservience of Lady Falkland's chaplain, who left it on record that his pious mistress 'was accustomed to hint unto them [her chaplains] what virtues it would be proper to commend in their sermons.'[1]

The Cause and Cure of a Wounded Conscience was written with less vivacity than most of Fuller's work. In a prefatory note he says that he has purposely avoided 'all light and luxurious expressions' as unsuitable for the subject; but there is a more personal reason than that for its sombre tone. The wounded conscience, we can hardly doubt, was his own. Read in the light of modern psychology the book has considerable interest. Fuller in the seventeenth century, at the prompting of his native sagacity, does what the twentieth-century psychologist does. He quietly brings his fears and troubles to the surface of his mind and faces them squarely. The book is in dialogues. In the first Timotheus asks Philologus what he means by a wounded conscience, and is told that 'It is a conscience frighted at the sight of sin, and weight of God's wrath, even unto the despair of all pardon during the present agony . . . a miserable malady of the mind.' Both the godly and the ungodly suffer from it, he says, but in different ways. Philologus suggests that the wicked are made to suffer out of justice, the godly out of love, as a surgeon might inflict pain on a patient in the course of curing him. Timotheus on his side says that the two can easily be distinguished 'because the godly, when wounded, complain most of their sins, and the wicked of their sufferings.'

When Philologus has given an account of the sad condition of a good man suffering from this depression, Timotheus suggests that merry company might help. But Philologus says:

'Alas! a man shall no longer be welcome in merry company than he is able to sing his part in their jovial concert. When a hunted deer runs for safeguard amongst the rest of the herd, they will not admit him into their company, but beat him off with their horns, out of principles of self-preservation.'

When a man is suffering from this malady he looks in vain to the things a healthy man finds pleasure in:

[1] J. Duncan, *Lady Lettice, Viscountess Falkland,* p. 91.

'When Adam had eaten the forbidden fruit, he tarried a time in paradise, but took no contentment therein. The sun did shine as bright, the rivers as clear, as ever before, birds sang as sweetly, beasts played as pleasantly, flowers smelt as fragrant, herbs grew as fresh, fruits flourished as fair, no punctilio of pleasure was either altered or abated. The objects were the same, but Adam's eyes were otherwise, his nakedness stood in his light; a thorn of guiltiness grew in his heart before any thistles sprang out of the ground; which made him not to seek for the fairest fruits to fill his hunger, but the biggest leaves to cover his nakedness.   Thus a wounded conscience is able to unparadise paradise itself.'[1]

Even Christ, he reminds his companion, felt deserted on the Cross, and Himself suffered this agony of being cut off from the source of life and peace, crying out 'My God, my God, why hast thou forsaken me?'

The effect of the mind on the body is discussed, and Philologus agrees that Luke, the physician-Evangelist, may be called upon to exercise both his professions together. Nevertheless the malady is acknowledged to be spiritual, and one that only spiritual means can cure.   Should spiritual reassurance be tried? asks Timotheus.   And Philologus replies that it will be of little use, 'for comfort daubed on a foul soul will not stick long upon it.'   The evil must be cut away before any soothing influences are used.

There is much in the discussion that will seem old-fashioned to a modern reader, but the main argument is remarkably sound.   And there are many flashes of Fuller's own refreshing sanity.   For example, when Philologus, after affirming the necessity of reinforcing broken vows, 'if of moment and material,' is asked by Timotheus what he means by the last clause, he says:

'To deal plainly, I dislike many vows men make, as of reading just so much, and praying so often every day, of confining themselves to such a strict proportion of meat, drink, sleep, recreation, etc.   Many things may be well done, which are ill vowed.   Such particular vows men must be very sparing how they make.   First, because they savour

[1] Dialogue iv.

somewhat of will-worship. Secondly, small glory accrues to God thereby. Thirdly, the dignity of vows is disgraced by descending to too trivial particulars. Fourthly, Satan hath ground given to throw at us with a more steady aim. Lastly, such vows, instead of being cords to tie us faster to God, prove knots to entangle our consciences.' [1]

He recommends work rather than rest—'A good way to divert or assuage their pain within, is, to take pains without in their vocation.' Briefly, his advice is to pray, to read, to keep good company, to be diligent in one's calling, and to observe Sunday. At the end he removes any doubts we might have had that he was prescribing for himself by asking for the prayers of all well-disposed readers until by God's grace and the service of 'some pious minister' his 'maimed soul' is restored to its former soundness.

Perhaps, however, in the intervals of such melancholy brooding Fuller knew something of the happiness that Jeremy Taylor was experiencing at Golden Grove, amid Nature's

> woods, where Echo talks,
> Her gardens trim, her terrace-walks,
> Her wilderness, her fragrant brakes,
> Her glooming bowers and shining lakes.
>
> DYER.

There, as Edmund Gosse so happily expressed it, Taylor—and why not Fuller also?—was 'nourished by the muses . . . as the goat-herd Comatas was fed with honey by the bees while he lay imprisoned in his master's cedarn chest.'

While at Boughton he would renew many of his childhood associations and memories. On the 16th February, in particular, he would remember one of the earliest and most vivid of them all—the arrival of James I at Boughton in 1603, when the Montagus gave the new king so worthy, and so profitable, a reception. The reason for remembering this event so vividly was that on that day in 1647 James's nobler but less canny son came into Northamptonshire as a prisoner of war;[2] but the part played by the head of the Montagus was somewhat different in 1647 from what it had been in 1603.

---

[1] Dialogue x.
[2] Rushworth, *Historical Collections*, vi. 396–8.

On the 13th January 1647, Lord Montagu, along with the Earls of Pembroke and Denbigh, had left London under commission to receive the king's person from the Scots. One month later they brought His Majesty to Holdenby House, of which to-day only two gateways and a broken wall remain, attended by a cavalcade of country gentlemen already aware that they must now look to the nephew of the Oliver Cromwell who had been knighted at Hinchingbrooke twenty-four years ago, as their fathers had looked to the man who knighted him. But the country folk had not yet forgotten their king. The lanes of Northamptonshire were thronged with villagers who had come out to pay homage to their sovereign, and who thought little of their upstart neighbour Master Cromwell.

Fuller witnessed this demonstration of loyalty, and was moved to write that His Majesty daily 'grows greater in men's hearts, pregnant with the love and affection of his subjects.'[1] The king was detained at Holdenby for about four months. He knew the house well. It had been rebuilt by John of Padua for Sir Christopher Hatton, and had been bought by James I in 1607. Since then it had been a royal palace, and it had been there, eleven years earlier, that his queen, as he well remembered, had received from the papal nuncio a picture of St. Catherine. She had caused it to be hung on the curtains of her bed, so that it might be the last thing she saw before sleeping, and the first thing on waking. Perhaps it was still there.

His Majesty did not pass his time unpleasantly in Northamptonshire. He was allowed to hawk regularly, and occasionally to drive over to Lord Spencer's house at Althorp for a rubber of bowls. Lord Montagu was in attendance throughout, and left his own account of the circumstances in which he and his fellow commissioners were called upon to hand over the king to Cornet Joyce, by trade a tailor, who arrived at Holmby with five hundred horse on the 2nd June. When the king asked to see his commission, Joyce pointed to the troopers. Charles smiled. It was, he said, as fair a commission as he had seen in his life.

[1] *Good Thoughts in Worse Times:* 'Meditations on the Times,' xii.

The Countess of Rutland may have been Fuller's closest companion while he was at Boughton. She would find her brother's house a safer retreat than her own home, Belvoir Castle, which had been garrisoned for Parliament at the beginning of the war. Though a Parliamentarian and moderate Puritan she was well disposed towards the Royalist clergy, whom, perhaps for her father's sake, she seems to have felt it her duty to protect.

Fuller's movements during the next two years cannot be traced in detail. He was simply one of those of whom he wrote: 'How do many, exiles in their own country, subsist now-a-days of nothing; and wandering in a wilderness of want (except they have manna miraculously from heaven) they have no meat on earth from their own means. At what ordinary, or rather extraordinary, do they diet, that for all this have cheerful faces, light hearts, and merry countenances? Surely some secret comfort supports their souls.' Our only clue to his benefactors during these years is to be found in the dedications to his later works, which are so full of kindly addresses. Sometimes the seemingly extravagantly large number of these bouquets has provoked cynical comment. There are said to be one hundred and sixty-six of them in the *Church History* alone. Bailey, in his careful way, followed up every reference of this kind, and compiled a list, useful for tracing the movements of other eminent divines of the day besides Fuller. The help of the Montagus was personal. They had known him all his life. But another patron, Thomas Rich of Sunning, Berkshire, is described as 'the Entertainer-general of all good men.' This son of a Gloucester alderman had made a fortune in the turkey trade, and seems to have been as comfortably built and as genially minded as Fuller himself. His benevolence in the Stuart cause earned him a baronetcy at the Restoration. Thomas Adams, Lord Mayor of London in 1646 and founder of the Arabic professorship at Cambridge, was another benefactor of the Royalist clergy. In acknowledging his liberality Fuller says he was 'one who had drunk of the bitter waters of Meribah without making a face thereat.'

Incidentally, we have a side-light on the difference in

wealth between the Church dignitaries of our own day and
their counterparts of Fuller's in the number of bishops who
were able to help their inferior brethren with money.　Among
these was Dr. John Warner, Bishop of Rochester, who helped
Jeremy Taylor's family generously, and William Chappell,
Milton's old tutor at Cambridge, now Bishop of Cork, who at
his death left his estate to be divided between his family and
distressed ministers.　Some of these superior clergy were
distributing money given to them for the purpose by wealthy
Royalists, and were, therefore, not always dipping into their
own pockets—Dr. Warmestry, Dean of Worcester, for
example, was well known as a Royalist almoner.　Nevertheless the well-to-do clergy were commendably generous and
set a fine example of Christian charity.

In the early spring of 1647 Fuller was again heard in a London pulpit, and in April–May of that year he preached four
sermons at St. Clement's, Eastcheap—not to be confused with
St. Clement Danes—a pulpit he was to occupy as lecturer
during the three succeeding years and at intervals later.
This was the first ray of light in his new day as a London
preacher.　It spread so quickly that Bailey believed Fuller
to have been the first of the great Cavalier parsons to win
the patronage of their political opponents.　Another of the
pulpits he occupied at this time was that of St. Dunstan's
East, where an amusing incident, recorded in *The Appeal of
Injured Innocence*, occurred.　After one of his sermons there,
a gentleman, perhaps Henry Herdson, came into the vestry
and claimed that he had taught Fuller the art of memory
while at Sidney-Sussex.　Fuller at once replied that this
could hardly be possible because he did not even remember
the gentleman's face, 'which I conceive,' he says archly,
'was a real refutation.'

But though the light had broken through, the clouds were
still there.　At the end of 1647 complaints were made in the
House of Commons about the 'countenancing of malignant
ministers in some parts of London, where they preach and use
the Common Prayer Book contrary to the ordinance of
Parliament.'　Fuller was one of these offenders, and for a
short time his preaching was again forbidden.　He was

obliged, therefore, to fall back on the private chapels of his patrons, where it was the custom throughout the Civil War for the Royalists to assemble to hear one of their own divines.

Fuller's position was complicated at this time because he was not a Laudian like most of the Royalists. He was a Prayer Book man; but in points of doctrine he tended towards a moderate Puritanism—though always a firm upholder of the constitution of the Church of England. It has sometimes been said that he was an early champion of what came to be called the Low Church party, but his churchmanship would be described more accurately as broad. This brought him into friendship with two eminent patrons who were politically opposed to him. Lord Montagu was one; the other was Sir John Danvers, the regicide. His friendship with the Montagus seems natural enough; but how shall we defend, or even explain, the friendship of so ardent a Royalist as Fuller with the man who was regarded by many, including Clarendon, as one of the most infamous of those who signed His Majesty's death warrant? The anonymous biographer is silent on the association; Bailey is puzzled.

Such facts as have come to light about Danvers since Bailey wrote, tend to dishonour him still further. Impoverished by vanity and extravagance he was guilty in later life of scheming to upset his brother's will in order to gain for himself some of the money bequeathed to his sisters. Indeed, he succeeded to the extent of being awarded a portion of the fine imposed upon one of them, Lady Gargrave, for her loyalty to the king. At the end of his life, despised by his family and cast off by Cromwell, he was obliged to fly the country under suspicion of having plotted against the Protector's life. He did, however, return, and died at Chelsea in April 1655. Fuller did not desert him. Bates, the historian of the Regicides, goes so far as to say that under Fuller's influence Danvers repented of his past and made a death-bed confession of guilt. However that may be, his estates were forfeited to the Crown at the Restoration.

In considering the relationship of these two contrasting characters we have to remember that it was no uncommon thing for families to be divided to the death on the political issue, yet to retain their family loyalties. We saw it with the Montagus, and indeed there were so many instances that it is impossible to avoid the suspicion that with many it was not entirely disinterested, but was done to ensure having friends in both camps. With others, of course, it was altogether sincere; and it was because each could respect the other's honour that they could remain on terms of trust and affection, as did the Montagus. Danvers, however, was a weak, vain character who may have been the tool of others stronger in mind than himself. For all that, he had his attractive side, and if we glance at this we have no difficulty in seeing what Fuller and he had in common.

At twenty, or thereabouts, Danvers married Magdalen Herbert, friend of John Donne, who wrote of her:

> No Spring, nor Summer Beauty hath such grace
> As I have seen in one Autumnal face.

She was at least twice as old as Danvers, and the mother of ten children, all living, of whom George Herbert, Lord Herbert of Cherbury, and Sir Henry Herbert, Master of Revels, were three. All who knew her agree that she was still a captivating companion. Danvers said frankly that he married her 'for love of her wit.' If we cannot explain the friendship of a Cavalier parson with a Regicide, we have no difficulty in explaining that of the man who married a widow with ten children, solely for the brilliance of her conversation, with the witty and genial friend of the Montagus. What would we not give for an hour in their company, Cromwell and all his kind forgotten, as they sat together in the Danvers home at Chelsea? Moreover, Danvers, like Fuller, had been entrusted with the care of the royal children. In July 1644, the Princess Elizabeth and the infant Duke of Gloucester had been sent to him at Chelsea. Alas, that he should have been a party to their father's death five years later!

The home of Sir John Danvers, when Fuller knew him, was near the river, close to Chelsea old church and Sir Thomas More's house. With its hall adorned with fine marbles, its gardens laid out in the best Italian style, it was one of the show places of London, and the most brilliant of the age were to be met there, whether statesmen, wits, divines, or philosophers. Magdalen Herbert died at this house in 1627. There was no shadow about Sir John's name then. The following year he married Elizabeth, daughter and heiress of Ambrose Dauntsey of West Lavington, bringing another mansion with ample grounds for him to expend his wealth and taste on. As for his own person, he was so handsome that townsfolk as well as country folk came out of their houses to see him pass. Aubrey, who was a great crony of 'my cos, Sir John,' had capital stories about him. He tells us that he had been a friend of Bacon—a strong recommendation to Fuller—and that the philosopher's life of Henry VII—'that learned and curious book'—was submitted to him for an opinion before it was sent to the printer:

'Qd. Sir John, "Your lordship knows that I am no scholar."

'"'Tis no matter," says my lord; "I know what a scholar can say; I would know what you can say.'

'Sir John read it, and gave his opinion what he misliked (which I am sorry I have forgotten), which my lord acknowledged to be true, and mended it.

'"Why," said he, "a scholar would never have told me this." '[1]

Fuller also was a man who valued the things that no scholar could tell him. Politics aside, there is no great mystery about their association, and certainly no reason for thinking that Fuller viewed lightly Sir John's misdeeds, which appear to have been prompted in the first place as an escape from the embarrassment caused by his reckless extravagance. He came to need money so desperately that he sold his honour to gain it.

When the king faced his judges it is said that Jack Danvers was the first man among them he recognized. His grief to see an old friend in such company must have been as great as Fuller's. Everything in Sir John's background was Royalist and gentle. There was no question of his burning with the fire of the reformers, whether of Church or State. He was

---

[1] *Miscellanies*, p. 222.

obviously a traitor, and what could either Charles or Fuller think but that he was selling his king for gold?

Of the king's death, which he called the 'midnight of misery,' Fuller wrote in *Mixt Contemplations in Better Times* (xxv): 'It was questionable whether the law should first draw up the will and testament of dying divinity, or divinity first make a funeral sermon for expiring law.   Violence stood ready to invade our property, heresies and schisms to oppress religion.'   The anonymous biographer tells us that 'such an amazement struck the loyal pious doctor, when he first heard of that execrable design intended against the king's person, and saw the villainy proceed so uncontrollably, that he not only surceased, but resolved to abandon that luckless work (as he was then pleased to call it).   For what shall I write, said he, of the worthies of England, when this horrid act will bring such an infamy upon the whole nation, as will ever cloud and darken all its former and suppress its future rising glories?'

It was at this time, the blackest hour of his life, that from James Hay, second Earl of Carlisle and son of one of the two ambassadors extraordinary who had treated for the marriage of Charles and Henrietta Maria, Fuller received the living of Waltham Abbey, or Waltham Holy Cross, in Essex, and entered upon the most productive decade of his life.

CHAPTER XI

A HOME AT WALTHAM ABBEY

Still did the notions throng
About his eloquent tongue;
Nor could his ink flow faster than his wit.

ABRAHAM COWLEY.

THE old Essex town of Waltham Abbey, or Waltham Holy
Cross, with its market square, its painted wooden houses,
quaint inns, and quiet riverside scenery dominated by
Harold's noble church, was an ideal setting for so genial a
scholar as Fuller.   About it lay a parish rich in history, while
the abbey church, the work of Norman builders brought to
England by Edward the Confessor—who was present at the
consecration in 1060—enshrined a tradition that went back to
a miraculous cross discovered at Montacute in Somerset and
brought to Waltham by one Tovi, standard-bearer to King
Canute.   It was, as Fuller described it, a low-lying town,
'seated on the east side of the River Lea, which not only
parteth Hertfordshire from Essex, but also seven times
parteth from itself, whose septemfluous stream in coming to
the town is crossed again by so many bridges.'   To a hill man
it might have seemed damp and unhealthy; to a fen man it
was home.   When others complained of its marshes, Fuller
was quick to point out that if the town itself was low there
were in the parish 'as many pleasant hills and prospects as
any place in England doth afford,' an exaggeration that
affection might be held to justify, and that without affection
could hardly have been made by a man who had seen Dorset
and Devon.

At Waltham his spirits were completely restored.   He was
always happiest in the kind of country he had been born and
bred in, and in the first book he wrote in his new parsonage,
A Pisgah Sight of Palestine, he expressed again a sentiment
never far from his heart: 'how good it is (especially in sad
times) to keep home, and not to be gadding abroad, without

great occasion.'   Fuller would have subscribed to the sentiment,

> Home-keeping hearts are happiest,
> To stay at home is best.

And he would have greeted with a loud guffaw of approbation
Johnson's reply to Boswell's confession that Captain Cook's
tales of adventure had made him wish to go himself on the next
voyage. 'Why, sir,' exclaimed Johnson, 'a man *does* feel so,
till he considers how very little he can learn from such voyages.'

The atmosphere of the town was as congenial to him
spiritually and intellectually as it was physically. As a son
of the Reformation he was fortified by the knowledge that it
was in a conversation at Mr. Cressy's house in the Romeland
near his church, between Thomas Cranmer, Edward Fox,
afterwards Bishop of Hereford, and Stephen Gardiner, that a
way was discovered to liberate the English Church from papal
control. 'In this house,' he says in his history of the parish,
'did Waltham give Rome the first deadly blow in England,
occasioning the pope's primacy to totter therein till it
tumbled down at last.'   John Foxe, author of the book he
had known from childhood, and that he still knew better than
any other book except the Bible, had lived in the town at the
height of his fame, and had worshipped in the abbey church.
Joseph Hall, whose writings had influenced his own, and
whom he venerated above most, had held the living for more
than twenty years before him, and still owned property in the
parish. 'When I consider,' wrote Fuller, 'how many worthy
words which had their first being within the bounds of this
our Parish, I may justly be ashamed that my weak endeavours should be born in the same place.'

Hall attended the Synod of Dort, and when Fuller, in
writing his account of this for the *Church History*, required
confirmation of what he had learned from John Goodwin's
Redemption Redeemed, he wrote to one of Hall's sons, not
knowing whether the father, who had been scandalously
treated as Bishop of Norwich, was still alive.   In the letter
he asked: 'Is your father well, the old man of whom ye spake,
is he yet alive?'[1]   On being informed that the bishop was

[1] *Church History*, book x, section v, 7.

WALTHAM ABBEY

still in good trim, Fuller wrote to him direct, and received a
reply couched in the most friendly terms, concluding—
'Your much devoted friend, precessor, and fellow-labourer,
Jos. Hall, B.N.'

John Foxe's family still flourished in Waltham, as they
continued to do for two centuries more. The husband of
Foxe's grand-daughter, Henry Wollaston, was the local
justice of the peace, and a man of great consequence in the
neighbourhood. In 1653 the custody of parish registers was
transferred from the Church to the civil authority, and from
1654 to the Restoration the magistrate, not the minister, had
the privilege of conducting marriages, after banns had been
published in the market place. It cannot invariably have
been a dignified proceeding. When the familiar question
about just cause or impediment why the two should not be
joined together was asked, we can hardly believe that in those
coarser days ribald comments would not sometimes be called
out from the open windows of the 'Welsh Harp' or the
'Cock.' There is a poem in Flecknoe's *Diarium*, 1656, 'On
the Justices of Peace's making Marriages and the Crying of
them in the Market':

> Amongst the rest, we have cause to be glad,
> Now marriages aie in the markets made;
> Since justice we hope will take order there,
> We may not be cousened no more in our ware.

> Let parson and vicar then say what they will,
> The custom is good (God continue it still),
> For marriage being a new trafique and trade,
> Pray where but in markets should it be made?

Fuller, as a law-abiding citizen, submitted to the Act,
though he cannot have regarded it with favour. Others,
among whom was Stephen Marshall, were less scrupulous.
Peter Heylyn tells us that Marshall, whom he describes as
'that great bell-wether, for a time, of the Presbyterians,'
actually defied the law by conducting the marriage of his
own daughter, though he had been one of the principal
compilers of the Puritan Directory. It is an astonishing

example of inconsistency, because Marshall even went so far as to use the Prayer Book service for the ceremony, instead of the one prescribed by the Directory, and at the end acknowledged the offence by promptly handing to the churchwarden present the £5 fine to which he had made himself liable. When Fuller was told of this he merely remarked discreetly that he could not answer for the actions of others, but in *The Worthies* he said of Marshall: 'He was of so supple a soul, that he brake not a joint, yea, sprained not a sinew, in all the alteration of times.'

Henry Wollaston, the magistrate, was the son of another Henry, a draper and alderman of London, who lived at Fishers, Waltham, where he is said to have died in his chair while singing a psalm. The second Henry married a daughter of Samuel Foxe of Warlies, and succeeded his father at Fishers' Green, still one of the most pleasant and secluded retreats in the parish. Did Izaak Walton's *Compleat Angler*, we wonder, lie on Henry Wollaston's table? It ought to have done. Indeed, the very name of Fishers' Green suggests that Izaak himself may have known the spot. He may also have known the worthy Henry, who, when he died in February 1670, was buried near his own pew in the abbey church, in which he is still commemorated by a marble bust.

Another prominent local gentleman connected with the Foxe family was Sir Richard Willys, whose wife was the martyrologist's great-grand-daughter. Willys had been Royalist colonel-general of the counties of Lincoln, Nottingham, Rutland, as well as governor of the town and castle of Newark, where he figures in an odd incident recorded by Sir Richard Bulstrode. It appears that after the battle of Naseby the king was so pleased with Sir Richard's conduct as governor of Newark that he promised to promote him to a higher command. Sir Richard, however, demurred. He said he lacked the means to support a superior station and begged to be excused. But Charles assured him that he would furnish means equal to the office, and with this promise left to attend church.

While the king was at worship Sir Richard heard in the

town a rumour that he had been removed from office, and hastened to report this to His Majesty during dinner, with Prince Rupert, Prince Maurice, Lord Gerard, and other officers present. The officers of the garrison, says Bulstrode, immediately fell to quarrelling among themselves as to who could have put out such a report, and before they could be stopped the table was in an uproar. The king, incensed at this undignified behaviour in his presence, retired to his chamber, with a haughty command to Sir Richard and one or two others, requiring them to follow. Unfortunately, Sir Richard was so angry by this time that instead of humbly waiting till he heard His Majesty's pleasure, he indignantly declared that he had received a public injury and had a right to demand a public satisfaction. Charles cut him short, and, says Bulstrode, 'with greater indignation than ever he was seen possessed with, he commanded them to depart his presence, and to come no more into it.'[1] Sir Richard then realized that far from hoping to receive further expressions of His Majesty's favour, he could no longer expect to enjoy his confidence. Flight was the only solution.

Waltham Abbey parish registers for the seventeenth century are full of distinguished names, many of which are of more than local interest. There were the Etheriges, related to Sir George Etherege. In Dr. Howard's *Miscellanea Genealogica et Heraldica* we find: 'My Grandfather dyed Saturday Aprill ye 10th 1652, att London and on Moonday following was carried to Waltham Holy Crosse in a hearse and on Wensday following was buried there in ye middle Isle above the pulpit by my Uncle William and Aunt Judith Etheredge. Mr Thomas Fuller preached his funerall sermon on ye 116 Psalm ye 15 verse. . . .' This was a William Etherege. Then there were the Bassanos, or Bassanios, who were of Italian origin and famous musicians. Indeed, members of this family were employed as musicians-royal in the courts of every sovereign from Henry VIII to Charles II. Anthony Bassano, musician to Henry VIII, was a Waltham resident. His son, we find, was married in the abbey church on the 4th February 1584, and when Fuller saw this entry,

[1] *Memoirs and Reflections*, i, p. 129.

as he would see it, he may have recalled Gratiano's lines in the *Merchant of Venice* (Act v, sc. i):

> My Lord Bassanio gave his ring away
> Unto the judge that begg'd it, and, indeed,
> Deserv'd it too; and then the boy, his clerk,
> That took some pains in writing, he begg'd mine:
> And neither man nor master would take aught
> But the two rings.

That is by no means the only Shakespearean echo in this noble abbey church.   Sir Anthony Denny, of:

> Where is he, Denny?
> He attends your highness' pleasure

lies here.   He acquired the abbey lands at the Dissolution, and was the ancestor of Fuller's patron, the second Earl of Carlisle.   Sir Anthony's son, the first Sir Edward, cousin of Sir Walter Raleigh, has a fine tomb in the abbey church. Anne Vavasour, now accepted as at least a not improbable 'Dark Lady' of the Sonnets,

> A whitely wanton with a velvet brow
> And two pitch-balls stuck in her face for eyes,

appears to have been related to, if not one of, the Vavasours of Waltham Abbey.[1]

But are these echoes of William of Stratford, or echoes of Edward de Vere, seventeenth Earl of Oxford, one of the claimants to Shakespearian laurels?   In 1562 the sixteenth Earl of Oxford died, and Edward de Vere, his son and heir, then a boy of twelve, became a royal ward entrusted to the care of the great Cecil, whose daughter he married.   In 1561 Cecil bought Theobalds,[2] the great house in the neighbouring parish of Cheshunt which later became the favourite palace of James I.   Edward de Vere would spend much of his youth there, and frequently visit his relations, the Golding family, who lived in Waltham Abbey.   His mother, the wife of the sixteenth earl, was Margaret Golding, and his uncle, who was also his tutor, was Arthur Golding, translator of Ovid's *Metamorphoses*, of Justin, and of Caesar.   Another member

---

[1] Harl. MSS. 4944 and 6065.
[2] Cecil was already associated with Waltham.   His daughter, Frances, was buried in the abbey church in 1599.

of the family, Sir Thomas Golding, was sheriff of Essex and Hertfordshire in 1561 and one of the commissioners for recording the chantry lands.   There was a grant of church property to Thomas Golding of Waltham in 1563, the first year for which we have entries in these abbey registers, with their long record of Dennys, Cecils, Goldings, Grevilles, and other noble families associated with this historic parish.

Another name that Fuller would note as he glanced through his well-kept registers was that of Fulke Greville. It would remind him of the Isaac Dorislaus case at Cambridge mentioned earlier.   This Waltham Fulke Greville, the son of Sir Edward Greville of Harold's Park, Waltham, was baptized on the 22nd January 1589.   He was to become one of James I's gentlemen pensioners, and here we may note the reason for so many courtiers being found in the abbey parish. In 1607 James I acquired Theobalds from Robert Cecil, Burleigh's son who became first Earl of Salisbury, and consequently many of his favourites bought or built houses in the neighbourhood.

In Fuller's time Theobalds was allowed to fall into decay until by Cromwell's order it was dismantled in 1651, in what Fuller ingeniously describes as its grand climacteric: 'Some sixty-three years from the finishing thereof, taken down to the ground, for the better partage among the soldiery.' Many of the old court families, however, remained, and among the most eminent were several with whom Fuller was on intimate terms.   His patron, the Earl of Carlisle— who had begun the war as a Royalist, but had changed sides in 1644, compounding for his estate—was the son of one of the gay and profligate young men who came to England with James in 1603.   Unlike Carr and Villiers he did not owe his rise to his good looks.   Elizabeth of Bohemia, James's daughter, called him 'Camel-face.'   But he had a special claim to favour.   He was said to have saved His Majesty's life by standing, knife in hand, to defend him against the Gowries.   According to report he was a somewhat ridiculous figure; but his son, the second earl, by his dignified bearing and courtly address, brought honour to the family name.[1]

[1] Lloyd's *Memoirs*, p. 676.

His mother was the heiress of Sir Edward Denny, first Earl of Norwich, who had been responsible for greatly improving the value of the abbey living, which in Fuller's case was further supplemented by the earl's chaplaincy.

On moving into his Waltham parsonage in the early spring of 1649 Fuller at once settled down to work on *A Pisgah Sight of Palestine*, which, however, may have been started in London. One of the illustrations is dated 1648. Several are the work of Robert Vaughan, an engraver who lived at Waltham, and by noting the number of plates dedicated to Essex gentlemen or members of their families we see how quickly and how happily Fuller settled down among his new neighbours. But however great his pleasure in local society may have been, it cannot have equalled his joy in knowing that he was writing in the room in which Joseph Hall had spent such fruitful hours with his ink-horn at his side and his candle and paper before him.

The church registers and churchwardens' account books do not help us as much as we might expect in building up a picture of Fuller's life at Waltham; but it is a happy circumstance that the first reference to the new parson in the churchwardens' book runs: 'Item to a poore minister sent to me by Mr. ffullers derection 2s. 6d.,' an entry which is followed by many of the same kind in succeeding years. It is obvious that a great number of homeless parsons and scholars—some of them, no doubt, from Cambridge—passed through the parish and called on the kindly doctor for a meal, or a few minutes' conversation, and were sent on their way with a crown or half-crown from the churchwardens' box.

But if the churchwardens' accounts tell us little about Fuller himself during these years, they tell us much about Waltham life, and there can have been few aspects of it in which he did not take a personal interest. Some of the improvements to the church during the ten years of his incumbency must have been made at his suggestion. Perhaps it was with the fires at Cambridge in mind that in 1651 he saw the parish provided with buckets, ladders, and firehooks. The list of contributors shows that of this, as of other public-spirited efforts in the town, he was a generous supporter. As one who always delighted in bells he must have done much to encourage their repairs carried out in his day, and such an item as the following seems to suggest his inspiration: '*Be it remembered* that in the yeare 1656 the Batchelers and Maides of the parish of Waltham Holy Crosse did by a volluntary contribution purchase a new treble to the other five bells.'

Bells in the seventeenth century provided a popular pastime, and at the 'Cock,' which was then the principal inn, there would doubtless be a gotch or ringers' jug such as may still be seen in other parts of Essex and Suffolk. The abbey bells, the 'wild bells' of Tennyson's *In Memoriam*, were rung every four hours in Fuller's day. At four in the morning they rang to rouse the apprentices, who listened still more intently for them at eight in the evening as the signal for release.

Fuller would discover at Waltham, if he had not already done so, that disputes between parishes could be as acrimonious as disputes between rival factions in the State. The 'septemfluous stream' dividing Essex from Hertfordshire was a bone—or channel—of contention from the thirteenth century to the nineteenth, and it was no uncommon thing for the parson and people of Waltham, in beating the bounds at Rogation, to come into conflict with the parson and people of Cheshunt. Such historic feuds as this would entertain rather than infuriate him, because he had read about all these traditional quarrels in a beautiful folio volume in his patron's library. The earl lived close to the church in the abbey house which his ancestor, Sir Anthony Denny, had bought at the Dissolution in 1540. Some of the possessions of the monks were still there, and among them was this *Registrum Cartarum Monasterii de Waltham*,[1] which proved to be a history of the foundation written by Robert Fuller, the last abbot. It had four hundred and thirty-six pages, three hundred and eighty-one of them written by the abbot himself, 'having,' says his namesake, 'as happy a hand in fair and fast writing, as some of his surname since have been defective therein.'

[1] British Museum, Harleian library 3739, Plut. lv. E.

G

After six years' residence in the town, Fuller published his own *History of Waltham Abbey*, amplifying the abbot's chronicle from his own observations and research. His work has been the basis of all subsequent histories of the abbey, which throughout the Middle Ages dominated West Essex and particularly what is now called Epping Forest, then known as Waltham Forest: 'On the one side, the town itself hath large and fruitful meadows, whose intrinsic value is much raised by the vicinity of London. . . . On the other side a spacious forest spreads itself, where, fourteen years since, one might have seen whole herds of red and fallow deer. But these late licentious years have been such a Nimrod, such an hunter, that all at this present are destroyed.' Of these Waltham deer he might have written what he wrote so delightfully of Oxfordshire deer in the *Worthies*, that they 'when living, raise the stomachs of gentlemen with their sport; and, when dead, allay them again with their flesh. The fat of venison is conceived to be (but I would not have deer-stealers hear it) of all flesh the most vigorous nourishment, especially if attended with that essential addition which Virgil coupleth therewith:

> *Implentur veteris Bacchi pinguisque ferinae.*
> "Old wine did their thirst allay, fat venison hunger."

But deer are daily diminished in England, since the Gentry are necessitated into thrift, and forced to turn their pleasure into profit: "Jam seges est ubi parcus erat"; and, since the sale of bucks hath become ordinary, I believe, in process of time, the best stored park will be found in a cook's shop in London.'

Most of the forest deer had been stolen by the gipsies, sometimes described in the registers as 'followers of the tent,' who frequented the forest region for centuries, and by a new class of outlaws, many of whom were ex-soldiers of the Civil War who had been unable to find employment since—principally because they had no trade in their hands. So with families connected with the gay, licentious, and sometimes scholarly court of the first James on one side of his parish, and outlaws on the other—both, however, lovers of the chase, and both predatory—he had as rich a varity of society in his parish as he had of scenery.

As for the town itself, the market, he tells us, was not very prosperous. 'We now have a market on Tuesday,' he says, 'but cannot boast of much trading therein. Indeed there is plenty of flesh, but little corn brought thither: and bread is the staff, as of a man so of a market. Nor let us impute the thinness of chapmen in summer to husbandmen's having no leisure, as busied in tillage, hay, or harvest: or in winter to their having no pleasure to repair thither in so deep and dirty ways, seeing the plain truth is, no underwood can thrive near the droppings of so great an oak, the vicinity of London. The golden market in Leadenhall, makes leaden markets in all the towns thereabouts.'

Then there were the powder mills. These are still in existence and are probably the oldest of their kind in England, for in 1561 we find John Tamworth of Waltham in treaty on behalf of Queen Elizabeth for the purchase of saltpetre, sulphur, and bow staves for barrels. This, however, was not an unmixed blessing to the town. 'It is questionable,' says Fuller, 'whether the making of gunpowder be more profitable or more dangerous; the mills in my parish having been five times blown up within seven years, but, blessed be God! without the loss of any one man's life.'

Though marriages were solemnized by the magistrate during the greater part of Fuller's incumbency, the parson still conducted the burial services, and as we cross the abbey churchyard, with its beautifully carved tombstones bearing inscriptions cut with the elegance of a more leisurely age than ours, we can imagine Fuller standing by the open graves of some of the old Waltham characters whose names and stations are preserved for us in the parish registers: 'Thomas Dickinson an ancient parish clerke, buried the 17 Aprill,' 1654, or 'Thomas Wright, Schoolmaister, Buried ye 2 June,' 1656. Such worthy townsmen as these were probably committed to their Maker by the parson himself, though it is quite evident that most of the parish work in Fuller's time was done by Nathaniel Hatley, who was assistant curate through the four incumbencies between 1633 and 1679.

Trollope, who lived at Waltham in the nineteenth century, and wrote many of his novels there, was in the habit of saying that he owed a great deal to the old servant who roused him with a cup of coffee each morning, and so helped him to be down betimes to his desk.   Fuller must have owed a similar debt, which doubtless he was no less ready to acknowledge, to Nathaniel Hatley, his right-hand man.   Without him he could hardly have done so much writing and preaching from London pulpits as he did during his ten years at Waltham, for though curate of the parish and chaplain to the earl, he was now a figure in society and an important man of letters.   As a chaplain he was not of the race described by John Taylor the Water Poet:

> His Worship's Chaplaine, twice (with double grace)
> In feare and trembling, takes and leaves his place,
> And (having read his Chapter) still must say,
> Thus ends your Worship's Lesson for the day.

He was certainly not like Eachard's servile attendant who left the table after one or two courses and stood by, 'picking his teeth, and sighing with his hat under his arm; whilst the Knight and my Lady eat up the tarts and the chickens.' He was a much invited guest, and one who was always welcome, being a fireside and expansive conversationalist, not like John Wesley, of whom Dr. Johnson said: ' John Wesley's conversation is good, but he is never at leisure.   He is always obliged to go at a certain hour.   This is very disagreeable to a man who loves to fold his legs and have out his talk, as I do.'

One of Fuller's most intimate friends at Waltham was Sir Henry Wroth of Ponders End.   The Wroths had been settled at Durrants, occupied later by the infamous Judge Jeffreys, since the end of the fourteenth century, and Fuller often entertained the company in that fine old moated manor house with his genial conversation.   Like so many other houses of its period it was destroyed by fire, started, it was said, by too many logs being piled on the hall fire at an annual banquet given to the tenants.   The scene may well recall Ben Jonson's lines written for a kinsman in a neighbouring parish, Sir Robert Wroth of Loughton Hall, describing a scene such as Fuller himself must have revelled in:

> The rout of rural folk come thronging in
> (Their rudeness then is thought no sin),
> Thy noblest Spouse affords them welcome grace;
> And the great heroes of her race
> Sit mixt with loss of state, or reverence;
> Freedom doth with degree dispense.
> The jolly wassail walks the often round,
> And in their cups their cares are drown'd:
> They think not then, which side the cause shall leese,
> Nor how to get the lawyer fees.

In short, at Waltham Abbey he was restored to that Merry England to which by nature he belonged, and from which Stuart dogmatism and Calvinist contention had exiled both him and the nation all too long.

This return to a normal society, and the possession of a parsonage, brought back to his mind the thought of marriage. The anonymous biographer says: 'The doctor having continued some twelve years a widower, the war finding him so, had the better relished the loss of his first wife by how much the freer it rendered him of care and trouble for her in those tumultuous times, so as by degrees it had almost settled in him a persuasion of keeping himself in that state. But now an honourable and advantageous match presenting itself, and being commended to him by the desires of his noble friends, he consented to the motion, taking to wife one of the sisters of the Viscount Baltinglas.'

Fuller was always an exceedingly obliging person, and we can almost believe that he married a second time for no other reasons than those set out by the anonymous biographer. In neither of his two marriages was there the least trace of romance, which perhaps explains their success. They were eminently sensible matches, and arranged, apparently, as much to the convenience of others as to his own pleasure. His first wife, Eleanor Grove, was the daughter of a friend of the family and the sister of his cousin's wife. In the second marriage, if the anonymous biographer is to be even half believed, he was equally obliging. The lady in question, Mary Roper, the younger of the two daughters of Sir Thomas Roper, who became Viscount Baltinglas, was related on her mother's side to the Harringtons, and through them to the Montagus of Boughton.   Incidentally, the anonymous biographer is mistaken in giving twelve years as the length of the doctor's widowerhood.   His first wife died in 1641 and his second wife bore him a son in 1652.

Obliging, however, as Fuller was in this respect, he cannot equal in that engaging attribute a still greater churchman, Richard Hooker, who, according to Walton, took the wife chosen for him by his landlady—who presented her own daughter!   But if less obliging than Hooker, he was more prudent.   He had, in fact, a wholesome scepticism in weighing the virtues of women, and this helped him to correct the bias in their favour so injudiciously planted in man's bosom by nature, and so assiduously exploited by themselves.   Indeed, it is difficult to avoid the conviction that he had been influenced by the apparent anti-feminism of St. Paul, for such phrases as the one about silly women in the third chapter of the second Epistle to Timothy find several echoes and spontaneous 'Amens' in the works of the worthy doctor.

But if happy again in his choice of a wife, his second marriage was not unclouded, as several entries in the parish register show.   The first-born, a son, who was tactfully given the name of his father's patron, James, was baptized on the 27th December 1652, and buried in the chancel on the 20th July 1654.   The second child of the marriage, Anne, born in November 1653, was buried in April 1655.   A third, more auspiciously named after his father and grandfather, lived, and at his father's death was described as being 'now six years old, a very hopeful youth.'   On the whole, however, his Waltham years were as bright as they were fruitful.

It is obvious that as a clergyman Fuller was more comfortably placed than most of his Royalist friends, and it is, therefore, not surprising that when some of the homeless clergy saw him so full of undisguised benefits they accused him of being something of a trimmer.   He was, as we have seen, more honourable than most men of his age, though he

never invited trouble.   Moreover, he was always so pleasant
a fellow that it would be hard to work up any strong indignation against him on any score.   As the Articles of Exeter
had relieved him of the necessity of taking the Solemn League
and Covenant, he was in little danger of sequestration; but
he did come before the Ecclesiastical Board soon after taking
up residence at Waltham, and there is a capital story told of
the occasion.   Fuller greeted the board genially, and presently one and another of them recalled tales about his
remarkable memory.

''Tis true, gentlemen, that fame has given me the report
of a memorist,' said the doctor, 'and if you please I will give
you an experiment of it.'

They readily accepted the motion, laid aside their papers,
and begged him to begin.   The old rogue saw that they were
in his power, so:

'Gentlemen,' he said, 'I will give you an instance of my
good memory,' then, pausing, he said that first he would pray
them to remember a friend of his.

'Your worships,' he continued, 'have thought fit to
sequester an honest, poor, but Cavalier parson, my neighbour, from his living, and committed him to prison.   He has
a great charge of children, and his circumstances are but
indifferent.   If you please to release him out of prison and
restore him to his living I will never forget the kindness while
I live.'

By this time they were in so good a mood that he had his
way with them.

But he was not always so successful.   Colonel Packer,
a prominent Anabaptist of the day, lived for a time in the old
palace at Theobalds and was a strong supporter of the
Waltham nonconformists, who were of the Anabaptist
persuasion.   Infant baptism, in which they did not believe,
was a prominent article in Fuller's faith, particularly after
losing the first child of his second marriage.   In 1653 he
published *The Infant's Advocate*, a statement of his belief,
bearing on its title-page the motto, 'Your little ones shall enter
into covenant with the Lord your God.'   Somewhat incon-
gruously the book was dedicated to the Earl of Carlisle, 'my

most bountiful patron,' and the Earl of Middlesex, who lived at Copt Hall, 'my noble parishioner,' one of whom was childless, the other not yet married. Nevertheless, the subject he thought might interest them, 'both of you being the sole surviving males of your families.' Not satisfied with two noble patrons, he followed this first dedication with another 'to the Right Worshipful Edward Palmer, Henry Wollaston, and Matthew Gilly, Esquires; John Vavasour, Francis Bointon, Gentlemen; with all the rest of my loving parishioners in Waltham Holy Cross.' Among the last named it is evident that he had the Anabaptists in mind no less than his own congregation, for on page thirty-seven he says to them: 'But as for difference in affection, seeing we conceive your error not such as intrencheth on Salvation (because not denying, but deferring baptism), and only in the out-limbs (not vitals) of religion, wherein a latitude may and must be allowed to dissenting brethren, we desire that herein the measure of our love may be without measure unto you.' Two pages later he adds: 'For mine own particular, because I have been challenged (how justly God and my own conscience knoweth) for some moroseness in my behaviour towards some dissenting brethren in my Parish; this I do promise, and God giving me grace I will perform it. Suppose there be one hundred paces betwixt me and them in point of affection, I will go ninety-nine of them on condition they will stir the one odd pace, to give them an amicable meeting.'

Towards the Quakers in Waltham he was much less friendly. George Fox visited the town and established a meeting there, which, it appears, caused Fuller continuous annoyance, and in the *Church History* this most tolerant of men makes it plain that he would be glad to see them suppressed. The attack provoked George Fox to reply, but not, unfortunately, until twelve years later, by which time Fuller had been dead six years.

But such troubles as came to him from his nonconforming neighbours were trivial in comparison with all that he and the nation had suffered a few years earlier. What counted most was that he now had a home, a parish, a parsonage, and leisure for writing.   The crowning happiness came from 'the noble parishioner' of *The Infant's Advocate*, Lionel Cranfield, third Earl of Middlesex, whose father, the first earl, had been lord treasurer to James I, and the possessor of a fine library. Fuller says that the first earl lost his office through falling foul of the Duke of Buckingham, 'the best of friends, and worst of foes.'   Afterwards, 'Retiring to his magnificent house at Copt-hall, he there enjoyed himself contentedly; entertained his friends bountifully, neighbours hospitably, poor charitably.   He was a proper person, of comely presence, cheerful yet grave countenance, and surely a solid and wise man.   And though their soul be the fattest who only suck the sweet milk, they are the healthfullest who (to use the Latin phrase) have tasted of both the breasts of fortune.'

When Fuller settled at Waltham Abbey the second earl was in residence at Copt Hall; but in 1651 he was succeeded by his younger brother, with whom Fuller appears to have been on terms of the warmest friendship.   Seeing how crippled the doctor was by the loss of his books, which had been confiscated when he joined the king at Oxford in 1643, the earl presented him with what remained of the Lord Treasurer's library, and in the neatly turned dedication to the fifth book of the *Church History* we see how much the gift was appreciated.   It is evident from an amusing passage in this dedication that part of the doctor's own library had been returned to him, but with volumes missing from sets and generally in such a state that it was of little use.   He now had a better than his own can ever have been, and promised to treasure it, 'not only to see your books dried and rubbed, to rout those moths which would quarter therein, but also to peruse, study, and digest them, so that I may present your honour with some choice collections out of the same. . . .'

By this time the Earl of Middlesex was married to a daughter of the Earl of Northumberland, a lady who had previously been married to the Earl of Bath, who also had a fine library, which his widow brought with her when she married again.   So Fuller had the use of yet another large collection of books, which we know he valued, because in *The Appeal of Injured Innocence* he says that he has seen the

*G

Earl of Bath's signature more than a thousand times on the
fly-leaf of books at Copt Hall.   What wonder, then, that after
his long term in the wilderness, and his bitter experience in
the treachery of Sir John Danvers, he created a new and
independent life for himself at Waltham Abbey in the spirit
of that pleasant passage: 'All men ought to have a public
spirit for the general good of our nation, the success whereof
we leave to the all-managing Providence of the God of heaven
and earth.   But I hope it will be no treason against our state
(and I am sure it will be safe for us who are but private
persons) to provide for the securing of our souls, and to build
a little cock-boat or small vessel of a quiet conscience in our
own hearts, thereby to escape to the haven of our own
happiness.   We wish well to the great ship of our whole
nation, and will never desert it so, but that our best prayers
and desires shall go with it.   But however Providence shall
dispose thereof, we will stick to the petty pinnace of peace in
our own consciences.   Sure I am, no soldiers will be able to
cut the cable.'

CHAPTER XII

CHURCH HISTORIAN

His talk was like a stream, which runs
   With rapid change from rocks to roses;
It slipped from politics to puns,
   It passed from Mahomet to Moses;
Beginning with the laws which keep
   The planets in their radiant courses,
And ending with some precept deep
   For dressing eels, or shoeing horses.

PRAED.

INCREDIBLE as it may appear, those lines from Praed's description of his vicar might pass as a fair summary of the thirteen hundred pages of Fuller's huge folio, *The Church History of Britain.* Soon after its appearance, Izaak Walton, as honest and kindly a critic as Fuller or any one else could desire, strolled into Waltham Abbey to ask a few questions about Richard Hooker, whose life he was then writing. What did he think of the *Church History*? he was asked.

'I think,' he replied, 'that it should be acceptable to all tempers, because there are shades in it for the warm, and sunshine for those of a cold constitution. With youthful readers, the facetious parts will be profitable to make the serious the more palatable, while reverend old readers will fancy themselves in a flower garden, or one full of evergreens.'

'And why not the Church history so decked?' asked Fuller, 'as well as the Church itself at a most Holy Season, or the Tabernacle of old at the Feast of Boughs?'

'That was but for a season,' Walton interposed. 'In your Feast of Boughs, we are so overshadowed that the parson is more seen than his congregation; who may wander till they are lost in the labyrinth.'

'Oh,' said Fuller, 'the very children of Israel may find their way out of this wilderness.'

181

'True,' replied Izaak, 'as indeed they have here such a Moses to conduct them.'[1]

From this we may gather that here was a history written as no history had ever been written before. Every one in the literary society of 1656 knew Tom Fuller and his way of writing; but they had expected him to show rather more gravity than usual in dealing with so lofty a subject. The book had been on the stocks for fifteen years or more, and had always been thought of as his great work. In comparison, the rest had been recreational. It was common knowledge that he had gone through the Tower records in collecting material for the earlier books, or chapters, that he had taken the middle part from sources as dependable as the registers of Canterbury, much of which he had transcribed, and, as later scholars discovered, with a high degree of accuracy. As Boswell's uncle said of Johnson, Fuller was 'a robust genius, born to grapple with whole libraries.' All the authorities in Sir Robert Cotton's collection had been consulted, together with 'walking libraries,' as he termed them, as reputable and varied as John Selden, Sir Roger Twysden, Elias Ashmole, Sir Symon Archer, Sir Thomas Hanson, Sir Thomas Barlow, and a host of others. In his own words: 'My pains have been scattered all over the land, by riding, writing, going, sending, chiding, begging, praying, and sometimes paying too, to procure manuscript materials.' And all these sources were acknowledged with exemplary courtesy, 'for,' said he, 'may my candle go out in a stench when I will not confess whence I have lighted it.' Bishop Nicolson, one of his severest critics, was ready to admit that 'If it were possible to refine it well, the work would be of good use: since there are in it some things of moment, hardly to be had elsewhere; which may often illustrate dark passages in more serious writers. These are not to be despised where his authorities are cited and appear credible.' But for the rest, said the same critic, the book was 'so interlaced with pun and quibble that it looks as if the man had designed to ridicule the annals of our Church into fable and romance.' This was not what the public had looked for. The Presbyterians, on

---

[1] William Oldys, *Biographia Britannica*, iii, p. 2061.

the one hand, were full of what Fuller referred to as 'causeless cavils'; the Laudians on the other were inclined to jeer at such material being passed off as history. Even his admirers were left gasping at his audacity.

The first disappointment was inevitable. A history of the Church was needed. Several had been planned, but none in recent times achieved. Bishop Montagu had designed such a work, and, says Fuller with characteristic generosity, 'had it been finished, we had had Church annals to put into the balance with those of Baronius; and which would have swayed with them for learning, and weighed them down for truth.'[1] That was the kind of work the public needed—a straight, authoritative history of the Church, not another of Tom Fuller's merry rambles; yet for better or worse they had to wait a long time for it, and in the meantime came to discover that there was more in Fuller's history than had at first been apparent.

Fuller himself cannot be charged with any breach of confidence. From the first book he made it plain that he did not intend to follow the accepted and approved course. He knew better than any one else both what he could and what he could not do. He was a good but not a great scholar. Others had more learning, more logic, and greater zest for battle. But the Kingdom of Heaven was more than these things. God's way with men through the Church, he believed, was simpler than the scholars supposed. He took and used them as they were; in particular he used them as persons, and since Christ became Man there had been a value in human personality that surpassed the glories of scholarship and the austerities of logic. Tom Fuller had proved to himself on countless occasions that for him there was only one way of writing, and that a highly personal one. So against all the advice of the authorities he wrote even his *Church History* in that way. Perhaps Sir Walter Scott, with whom Fuller has been compared, both as man and writer, said best what was in the doctor's mind. On the writing of history in general, and of his own life of Napoleon in particular, Scott said: 'Superficial it must be, but I do not disown the charge.

[1] *Worthies:* Buckinghamshire.

Better a superficial book which brings well and strikingly together the known and acknowledged facts, than a dull, boring narrative, pausing to see further into a millstone at every moment than the nature of the millstone admits. Nothing is so tiresome as walking through some beautiful scene with a minute philosopher, a botanist, or pebble-gatherer, who is eternally calling your attention from the grand features of the natural scenery to look at grasses and chucky-stones.'

We cannot believe that so shrewd and experienced a writer as Fuller did not know something of the criticism that his method would provoke. He had already had dealings with those ripe old antiquaries whose views on the writing of history were not dissimilar from those of Mrs. Battle on whist. They, like that estimable lady in the *Essays of Elia*, demanded 'a clear fire, a clean hearth, and the rigour of the game.' To Fuller, an interval between hands for an exchange of views on politics or religion, or merely to swop tales, would have improved rather than spoilt the game. And, most unforgivable of all, he would rather have yielded a trick than have started an argument. William Somner, 'my good friend and great antiquary of Canterbury,' who as registrar gave Fuller access to the records in his charge, and gave him also the benefit of his vast erudition, shook his head sorrowfully over the doctor's quips and cranks. In his life of Somner, Bishop Kennet says: 'Dr. Thomas Fuller, who laboured for the reputation of an historian and antiquary, courted the friendship of our author: and, had he been more guided by him, would never have defiled his writings with puns and tales.'[1] How little the bishop knew of the doctor's ambition! Never did he labour for the kind of reputation that belonged to those whose gifts were of a different order from his. Always his attitude was that for better or worse he was born Tom Fuller, and Tom Fuller he would remain.

There were others, and those no less learned than his critics, who saw and acclaimed his gifts. John Selden was one. 'The learned Mr. Selden,' says Fuller, '(on his own

---

[1] *A treatise of the Roman Ports and Forts in Kent, by Wm. Somner . . . To which is prefixt the Life of Mr. Somner.* Oxon. 1694.

desire) honoured my first four centuries with reading, and returned them unto me some weeks after, without any considerable alterations.' This was the man of whom Clarendon wrote: 'His Humanity, Courtesy, and Affability was such that he would have been thought to have been bred in the best courts, but that his good Nature, Charity, and Delight in doing good, and in communicating all he knew, exceed that of breeding.'

Towards the academic of the theological schools the doctor's attitude was the same as towards the academic of the historical and antiquarian. He was not like the man of whom Butler in *Hudibras* wrote:

> Profoundly skill'd in Analytick;
> He could distinguish, and divide
> A hair 'twixt south and south-west side;
> On either which he would dispute,
> Confute, change hands, and still confute.

Rather did he agree with the sentiments in George Herbert's poem *Divinitie*:

> Could not that wisdom, which first broach'd the wine,
>   Have thicken'd it with definitions?
> And jagg'd his seamless coat, had that been fine,
>   With curious questions and divisions?
>
> But all the doctrine which he taught and gave
>   Was cleare as heav'n from whence it came.
> At least those beams of truth, which only save,
>   Surpass in brightness any flame.
>
> *Love God and love your neighbour. Watch and pray.*
>   *Do as ye would be done unto.*
> O dark instructions; even as dark as day!
>   Who can these Gordian knots undo?
>
> But he doth bid us take his blood for wine?
>   Bid what he please; yet I am sure,
> To take and taste what he doth there designe,
>   Is all that saves, and not obscure.

It must be conceded, however, that this unconventional creature who appeared in his lecture-room in so jaunty a dress did more to destroy than to create confidence. His digressions might be entertaining, but Church history was hardly the place for them. In the first book, for example, the mention of Joseph of Arimathea reminded him of the flowering thorn at Glastonbury, which in turn reminded him of an oak near Lyndhurst in the New Forest that was said to put forth leaves at unseasonable times. When he did return to his proper subject he made his very contrition for the lapse the occasion for yet another tale: 'But I lose precious time, and remember a pleasant story,' he says, 'how two physicians, the one a Galenist, the other a Paracelsian, being at supper, fell into a hot dispute about the manner of digestion; and whilst they began to engage with earnestness in the controversy, a third man casually coming in, carried away the meat from them both. Thus while opposite parties discuss the cause of this hawthorn's budding on Christmas Day, some soldiers have lately cut the tree down, and Christmas Day itself is forbidden to be observed;[1] and so, I think, the question is determined.'

That is an instance of Fuller's dexterity in bringing himself back to the highway after an excursion into field, copse, or byway of recollection. In the next book—or chapter—he relates how the pagan temples were converted into Christian shrines when the people of Britain turned from the old religion to the new. The arrangement did not strike him as a very happy one. 'Surely,' he says, 'they had better have built new nests for the holy dove, and not have lodged it where screech-owls and unclean birds had formerly been harboured.' And as though that were not enough, he produces another image to make the custom seem still more incongruous: 'If the high priest amongst the Jews was forbidden to marry a widow, or divorced woman, but that he should take a virgin of his own people to wife, how unseemly was it, that God himself should have the reversion of profaneness assigned to his service, and worship wedded to the relict, yea (what was worse), whorish shrines, formerly abused with idolatry.'

Similar examples could be found in every book. If ever we are inclined to think that it is only the moderns who lack

---

[1] A reference to the Puritan ban on festivals.

a proper sense of the dignity of history, a glance through three or four pages of Fuller will put us right. Writing of religion in A.D. 501, which is hardly a date to suggest levity to the ordinary mind, he says: 'Needs then must religion now in Britain be in doleful condition; for he who expects a flourishing church in a fading commonwealth, let him try whether one side of his face can smile when the other is pinched.' It is to be doubted whether any writer ever combined such exuberance of fancy and raciness of style with such a burden of erudition. And his way of writing about every one—king or peasant, bishop or disputatious rebel—as though he had known them intimately all his life is most engaging. Thus Mellitus, Archbishop of Canterbury a thousand years before his chronicler's time, appears as 'a grave and good man, but much afflicted with the gout.' No man was ever less intimidated by great occasions or more at ease with his subject. The so-called artlessness of Izaak Walton is art concealing art. A man who wrote by nature as gracefully as Walton did would have written far more. A natural faculty will not be denied. Fuller, not Walton, was the natural writer of the age. He wrote because he couldn't help it. The words danced and sang in his brain and streamed across his pages, and all the bishops and critics in the world could never stop them.

The first intimation we have of such a work as the *Church History* being in progress appears in *The Holy State*, where he says that if better days came, 'God spinning out the thick thread of my life so long,' he would write an '*Ecclesiastical History* from Christ's time to our days, if I shall from remoter parts be so planted as to enjoy the benefit of walking and standing libraries.' That was in 1642—written probably in 1641—and the work was published in the first three months of 1656. We can imagine how he must have felt when he received his first copy from the press and sat back in his chair at Waltham Abbey to admire it. How unlikely it had seemed in the dark months of 1648 and 1649 that such a work would ever be completed! Was it not evidence that it is far easier to kill a man than to kill an idea? Such a thought may have crossed his mind, and if it did he would remember how

Cheynell tossed Chillingworth's book into the grave with its author, thinking he could make an end of it that way.[1]

Probably the work had been more than he had bargained for when he undertook it. Only the young conceive so mightily. Even the printing had been more than his own bookseller—or publisher—had been able to undertake. Parts had been let out to others, and, not unnaturally, the result was far from satisfactory. One small error pointed out by Heylyn is explained in a pleasant sentence: 'The posting press, which, with the time and tide, will stay for no man, mistaking my copy complete, and not attending my coming to London that morning from Waltham, clapped it up imperfect.'

On settling at Waltham Abbey, he probably expected to write quickly and have the work ready within three or four years at most. It was, in fact, entered at Stationers' Hall in September 1652, so the delay in production must have been greater than either publisher or author envisaged. One reason for this, as we shall see presently, was the increasing demands on the author as preacher and public figure. His calling came first. 'The historian,' he reminded himself, 'must not devour the divine in me.' But a still more important reason for the delay was that under the original plan the work had been intended to end with the death of James I. It was, of course, a bold design to include in so large a work events as recent as that, and Fuller confides that some of his friends had tried to persuade him to stop at the death of Elizabeth. A writer who had been playing for safety would have done so. But Fuller had his own views, and like a sensible man was ready to stand or fall by them. In explaining his reason for continuing, he tells the story of the young Greek who, when urged by his mother to marry, protested that it was too soon, and when the question was raised again some years later objected that it was too late. In the same way, says Fuller, 'some say, Truth is not ripe enough to be written in the age we live in; which proveth rotten too much for the next generation faithfully to report, when the impression of memorable matters are almost worn out. . . .

[1] See p. 120.

Sure I am, the most informative histories to posterity, and such as are most highly prized by the judicious, are such as were written by the eye-witnesses thereof—as Thucydides, the reporter of the Peloponnesian war.'

There, as in so many of his decisions, it is clear that the determining factor was common sense. But he was fully aware of the danger of recording contemporary events. Writing of the Lambeth Articles of 1595 he says: 'And now I perceive I must tread tenderly, because I go out, as before, on men's graves, but am ready to touch the quick of some yet alive. I know how dangerous it is to follow truth too near the heels; yet better it is that the teeth of an historian be struck out of his head for writing the Truth, than that they remain still and rot in his jaws, by feeding too much on the sweetmeats of flattery.' [1]

He deals also with an allied question. When the historian is writing of events he has witnessed, and in which, perhaps, he has taken part, ought he to remain only the detached recorder, studiously suppressing his own judgment? Fuller's ruling on this question is that because the historian like every other well-informed person must have his own opinions, he cannot remain completely detached—he himself, for example, wrote as 'a cordial Protestant'—but he is in honour bound never to intrude his own views 'to the prejudice of truth.' Where, however, the historian has sufficient knowledge of a subject to be able to pronounce an unbiased judgment upon it, then he ought to do so, in order to give others less privileged the benefit of his experience. Impartiality, he holds, as well as partiality, must not be allowed to prejudice the expression of truth. The first aim of the historian, in Fuller's view, is to record facts; the second, from a judicious appraisal of those facts, to state as much of the truth as the facts warrant.

Common sense was Fuller's salvation. His delight in the curious might so easily have led him from tradition to legend. and from legend to superstition. Indeed, it occasionally does so. But less often than we might expect. He enjoys telling his old wives' tales; but he is not often taken in by them; while for miracles, or anything else outside the

[1] *Church History*, book IX, section viii, § 28.

observable order of nature, he has the heartiest scorn.   After relating one superstitious story he exclaims: 'Fie for shame! he needs an hard place on his face that reports it, and a soft place in his head that believes it.'

The parts of this much discussed work that provoked the greatest number of comments were the dedications.   They abound in it.   The first is to 'the illustrious Esmé Stuart,' fourth Duke of Richmond and a kinsman of the martyred king.   The duke was a child of five!   Who but Fuller would have thought of giving pride of place in all this illustrious assembly of nobles and men of gentle birth to an infant? Who again would have been bold enough to set the name of Stuart in so prominent a place?   Together, these two surprising features were even more typical than they would have been separately.   Along with the whimsical humour of dedicating a ponderous folio to an unlettered infant, and the courageous defiance of dedicating it to one who bore the king's name, went the subtlety of naming a Stuart too young to be judged a traitor.   Heylyn viewed this dedication to a child somewhat differently, and sarcastically complimented Fuller on his good husbandry in now raising a nursery of young patrons to succeed the old ones he had cultivated so assiduously.[1]

Some of these dedications are turned with rare skill, and we can imagine the doctor, on his frequent rides between Waltham and St. Paul's Churchyard, chuckling to himself as yet another happy turn of expression occurred to him for yet another verbal bouquet.   Perhaps the neatest is that to Sir Richard Shugborough, a knight of the shire for Warwickshire: 'Master Haward returned this answer to Queen Mary (demanding the causes of his coming to Court), that it was partly to see Her Highness, and partly that Her Highness should see him—an answer, which though more witty than court-like, yea more blunt than witty, she took in good part. You will not be offended at this my dedication, partly that I

---

[1] Esmé Stuart had already received a dedication in *A Pisgah Sight of Palestine*.   The illustrations in that work are so incorrect that even Fuller apologized for them.   There could, however, be no offence in offering such a one for the amusement of a babe in arms, so he presents the plate to Esmé, 'until such time as he can read'!

may know you, partly that I may be known unto you.
Besides, being informed that you love to have your hospitable table handsomely attended with ancient servitors,
I presumed that this section, containing much of memorable
antiquity, would not be unwelcome unto you.' [1]

Fuller's dedications, though restrained and dignified in
comparison with most of his day, were lampooned by Robert
South, who, as *Terrae filius* for 1657, made sport of them in
his oration, describing them as begging epistles. Each of
the noble persons named, he implied, had been expected to
contribute ten gold pieces to the cost of production or the
author's profits, and all except one, he said, had done so.
The one who had excused himself had paid twenty gold
pieces to be left out! It is possible that in making this
thrust South had the third Duke of Richmond in mind,
who, if he had lived might have had the first dedication. He
died in 1655. The charge, however, is not to be taken
seriously, though it is obvious that so great a work could not
have been produced without financial assistance. What
stung Fuller in South's attack was a description of himself
running about London in his gown, with his great folio tucked
under one arm and his little wife tucked under the other,
attending banquets and luncheons, where his jests were
introduced between the courses, and his book as soon and as
often as opportunity arose. Fuller is further described in
this scurrilous attack as a somewhat greedy eater, and
likened to a butcher in appearance and manner, particularly
when wielding the knife.

One thing the attack does make clear is that Fuller and his
folio were much in the public eye. Any one who wishes to
ridicule the idiosyncrasies of a living author must choose
one who is before all else a 'character.' Fuller might even
have felt honoured if his wife and patrons had not been drawn
in. He did not, of course, reply; but he did say that he
thought South had gone beyond the limits permitted to such
jesters, and it is amusing to note that when South himself was
treated in a similar way by another *Terrae filius*, Lancelot
Addison, he jumped from his seat and exclaimed: '*O*

[1] *Church History*, dedication of section iii, book v.

monstrum horrendum, informe, ingens, cui lumen ademptum.'
Fuller himself says of his patrons that 'many, if not most . . .
invited themselves purposely to encourage my endeavours.'
If this is true, they may almost have become an embarrassment, and certainly he seems to have had difficulty in finding
anything to dedicate to some of them.   In one place he
smilingly remarks that it is fortunate for him that Henry VII's
law against keeping too many retainers does not apply to
patrons.   Nevertheless, these dedicatory epistles have their
biographical value, especially to students of Essex, the
county from which so many of the patrons were drawn.   It
shows also that Fuller was held in high esteem by many of the
most cultivated gentlefolk of his day.   And, still more noteworthy, as most if not all are Royalist, to flaunt them before
the public while the Republicans were in power showed considerable courage, and certainly not the time-serving spirit
with which some of his detractors charged him.

As history, the most valuable part of the work is in the
account of the Convocation of 1640, which, as we have seen,
he attended as proctor from the Bristol diocese: 'In these dis-
distracted times a parliament [1] was called with the wishes of
all, and hopes of most that were honest, yet not without the
fears of some who were wise, what would be the success
thereof.[2]   With this parliament began a convocation; all the
mediate transactions (for aught I can find out) are embezzled;
and therein it was ordered, that none present should take any
private notes in the house, whereby the particular passages
thereof are left at great uncertainty.   However, so far as I
can remember, I will faithfully relate, being comforted with
this consideration, that generally he is accounted an unpartial
arbitrator who displeaseth both sides.'   Whatever learned
judgment may pronounce on the merits of the earlier parts
of this enormous work—and clearly a detailed critical
examination is beyond the scope of this book—the accounts
of events in his own lifetime must remain important, if only
as giving the point of view of one of the wisest, sanest, and
most fair-minded men of his generation.   His detachment,

---

[1] The Short Parliament.
[2] See Clarendon's *Rebellion*, i. 232.

shown in his willingness to give full credit to those from whom
he differed, is remarkable. We may see this by referring to
his account of Laud, which was, as he confessed, 'though less
than his friends expected, more than I am thanked for.'

In writing of the 1640 convocation his phenomenal memory
would give him a great advantage over other reporters,
especially as the taking of notes in the House had been forbidden. He was also able to see both sides objectively,
because he could not agree with either. He had little sympathy with the Laudians, who dominated the conference,
while the Puritans, with whom he had more in common, were,
as he saw, already coming under the influence of Scotch
theology, an intoxicant as potent in that generation as
Scotch whisky is in ours. The extremists, he believed, were
destroying both Church and State between them.

Other and longer accounts of this convocation were to
appear later. Peter Heylyn, Fuller's bitterest opponent,
wrote an account from the point of view of a Laudian, and a
more detailed and important account than either was written
by Dr. Nalson. But Fuller's was the first to appear, and was
written entirely without the support of documents, which the
others made use of to bolster up their arguments. Heylyn,
in particular, had an axe to grind. When, on the 5th May,
Charles dissolved the Short Parliament, the members of
convocation were deeply embroiled in such problems as the
extent of regal authority in the Church, the growth of popery,
and the usual wrangle about ceremonies. With the dissolution of Parliament they were expected to disband; but the
divines were not to be cheated out of their quarrel. Heylyn
gleefully produced a precedent in Elizabeth's reign for convocation acting on its own authority after the adjournment
of Parliament. With Laud so powerful, it was in the king's
interest that convocation should continue, so a royal commission, signed by the Lord Privy Seal, the Lord Keeper,
and the Lord Chief Justice, along with other judges, was
brought in to silence the objectors. The distinction, however, was made that in their continued sitting they should
regard themselves as a synod, not a convocation.

It is difficult in a secular age to realize how important such disputes were to the seventeenth century. Why, Milton actually suggests that theological disquisitions are used to relieve the tedium of Paradise! Much of this preoccupation with the theory of religion had come with James, who esteemed his title, Defender of the Faith, above all the other honours of regal prerogative, and enjoyed nothing better than an ecclesiastical conference at which he could display his knowledge of theology. 'He doth wondrously covet learned discourse,' wrote Howard to Harrington. There was probably another reason for the canny Scot's interest in religion. He knew that the bishops were Royalists almost to a man, and James's churchmanship was political at least to the extent that his son's was artistic.

One of the liveliest parts of the *Church History* is that describing James presiding over the Hampton Court conference of divines in 1604. His Majesty is presented to us sitting in a withdrawing room of his palace, with Prince Henry on a stool at his side. All the lords of the Privy Council are in attendance, while the bishops and deans, led by the aged Archbishop of Canterbury, John Whitgift—whom Queen Elizabeth used to call her little black husband—defend the Church from the attack of a small contingent of Puritans, ably led by Dr. Reynolds. James was at the top of his form on this historic occasion. He was aware, as he joyfully confessed, that he was now sitting 'amongst grave, learned, and reverend men; not as before, elsewhere, a king without state, without honour, without order, where beardless boys would brave us to the face.' [1] Never before had he felt so exalted. And to give him his due, he was an admirable chairman. Those who were there to oppose conformity soon discovered that they had met their match, while Richard Bancroft, then Bishop of London, allowed his joy in so learned a prince to get the better of his judgment. Falling on his knees before this champion of the Kirk he exclaimed:

'I protest my heart melteth with joy, that Almighty God, of his singular mercy, hath given us such a king, as, since Christ's time, the like hath not been.'

Fuller, as a practical-minded man, was never drawn into

[1] *Church History*, book x, section i, § 20.

these niggling arguments. Perhaps he had not the kind of brain that follows them easily; almost certainly he disliked them, though this he showed in negative rather than positive ways. In the *Church History*, as in the *History of Cambridge*, if Fuller disliked a man he left him out of his work. And in the *Church History* this policy of omission involved the greater part of a race. He could rarely be induced to write about a Scot. They were too argumentative for him. In one place, after following James in one of his progresses as far as the Border, he declines to go beyond for fear of the moss-troopers. In another place he says that no one would pity him if he pricked his finger while meddling with a thistle. As a son of Merry England he distrusted the rigours of logic because, above everything else, he believed in the value of personality, and he knew that personal values cannot be defined in terms of logic. The *Church History* is full of his own personality, quickened and excited by his joy in others, for to Fuller the best things come through relationship. Not the least valuable part of the work is in its gallery of thumbnail sketches.

Because Fuller believed in the full development of personality he was puzzled and irritated by all the new and apparently unnecessary restrictions that the Scots brought with them. We say that he was puzzled, because it was not a question of deciding between two opposing principles. When there were two opposing principles you might almost always be sure that Fuller could accept neither. Yet though a son of Merry England he was also, by birth and upbringing, a son of the Reformation. He was, if you like, a Gospel minister. But, as with Dr. Johnson's friend Edwards, cheerfulness was always breaking in, and the jovial monk in him was constantly regaining possession. Nowhere do we see this more clearly than in the *Church History*. After a few pages of honest labouring with the doctrine men he breaks out again and again with something of this kind: 'The mention of Reading minds me of a pleasant and true story; which, to refresh my wearied self and reader, after long pains, I here intend to relate.'

Perhaps the question that exercised his mind most of all

in this matter of stricter discipline was the right observance
of Sunday.   An order issued by the Lord Mayor of London
in March 1643—while Fuller was minister of the Savoy—
will give us the background of the problem.   It forbade 'any
person or persons, in time of divine service, or at any time on
the Lord's Day, to be tippling in any tavern, inn, tobacco-
shop, alehouse, or other victualling-house whatsoever;
[or] any fruiterers or herb women to stand with fruit,
herbs, or other victuals or wares, in any streets, lanes, or
alleys . . . or any other ways to put those or any other things
to sale, on that day at any time of the day, or in the evening
thereof; or any milk-women to cry milk . . . or to do any
unlawful exercises or pastimes.'   Alongside such restrictions
there was the increased liberty allowed by the *Book of Sports*.
Fuller had been confronted by the Sunday problem while in
Dorset.   He was, on the whole, in favour of stricter observance.   In the third book of the *Church History* he says:
'Many complain that man's badness took occasion to be
worse, under the protection of these sports permitted unto
them.'

The first to enter the field as a champion of Sabbatarianism
was not a Scot, but a Suffolk country parson named Nicholas
Bownde, rector of Norton, seven miles east of Bury St.
Edmunds, who in 1595 published a book entitled *The Doctrine of the Sabbath*.   Fuller examined this work with great
care, and set down its main propositions under eleven heads.[1]
Except for some amusing exceptions in favour of 'lords,
knights, and gentlemen of quality,' Bownde was a strict
sabbatarian, and went much further than Fuller thought
desirable: 'It is almost incredible how taking this doctrine
was, partly because of its own purity and partly for the
eminent piety of such persons as maintained it, so that the
Lord's Day, especially in corporations, began to be precisely
kept, people becoming a law to themselves, forbearing such
sports as yet by statute permitted; yea, many rejoicing at
their own restraint therein.'   The last is a shrewd dig, and in
keeping with what he had said about will-worship in *The
Cause and Cure of a Wounded Conscience*.   'Learned men,'

[1] *Church History*, book IX, section viii, §§ 20, 21.

he goes on to say, 'were much divided in their judgments about these sabbatarian doctrines. Some embraced them as ancient truths, consonant to Scripture, long disused and neglected, now seasonably revived for the increase of piety. Others conceived them grounded on a wrong bottom; but because they tended to the manifest advance of religion it was a pity to oppose them, seeing none have just reason to complain, being deceived into their own good. But a third sort flatly fell out with these positions, as galling men's necks with a Jewish yoke, against the liberty of Christians: that Christ as Lord of the Sabbath had removed the rigour thereof, and allowed men lawful recreations: that this doctrine put an unequal lustre on the Sunday on set purpose to eclipse all other holy days, to the derogation of the authority of the Church: that this strict observance was set up out of faction to be a character of difference, to brand all for libertines who did not entertain it.'

That is a fair sample of Fuller at his best in dealing with such questions. Many of the old disputes have lost interest for us now, but this one between the three—or should it be thirty-three?—different opinions about Lord's Day observance is always with us, and, because so much of our social history is bound up in it, is interesting even to those who do not view the problem as Christians.

It is a pity that Pepys cannot join in the argument at this point. His views on the relationship between religion and pleasure were clear enough, and he was a reader of Fuller's *Church History*, as we know from the diary entry for 7th December 1660: 'I fell a-reading Fuller's History of Abbeys, and my wife in Great Cyrus, till twelve at night, and so to bed.' Pepys's criticism would not be Bishop Nicolson's. He would enjoy the asides as much as the main narrative, if not more. Perhaps the portraits would delight him most. Fuller can pass one at least of Clarendon's tests of a good historian, that of ability to present 'a lively representation of persons.' Take, for example, that of Richard III in book IV: 'Duke Richard was low in stature, crook-backed, with one shoulder higher than the other, having a prominent gobber-tooth, a war-like countenance which well enough

became a soldier.   Yet a modern author, in a book by him
lately set forth, eveneth his shoulder, smootheth his back,
planeth his teeth, maketh him in all points a comely, and
beautiful person.   Nor stoppeth he here, but proceeding from
his naturals to his morals, maketh him as virtuous as handsome (which in some sense may be allowed to be true), concealing most, denying some, defending others of his foulest
facts, wherewith in all ages since he standeth charged on
record.   For mine own part, I confess it no heresy to maintain a paradox in history; nor am I such an enemy to wit as
not to allow it leave harmlessly to disport itself for its own
content and the delight of others. . . .   But when men shall
do it cordially, in sober sadness, to pervert people's judgments, and thereby go against all received records, I say
singularity is the least fault can be laid to such men's charge.
Besides, there are some birds (sea-pies by name) who cannot
rise except it be by flying against the wind, as some hope to
achieve their advancement, by being contrary and para-
doxical in judgment to all before them.' [1]

Pepys could hardly fail to make use of the worldly wisdom
contained in that passage while conversing with his friends at
the Admiralty.   And who with any interest in the great
figures of the Church could forget the description of Richard
Hooker?

'Mr. Hooker's voice was low, stature little, gesture none
at all, standing stone-still in the pulpit, as if the posture of his
body were the emblem of his mind, unmovable in his opinions.
Where his eye was left fixed at the beginning, it was found
fixed at the end of his sermon: in a word, the doctrine he
delivered had nothing but itself to garnish it. . . .   His style
was long and pithy, driving on a whole flock of several clauses
before he came to the close of a sentence; so that when the
copiousness of his style met not with proportionable capacity
in his auditors, it was unjustly censured for perplexed,
tedious, and obscure.' [2]

At its worst, this intimate, personal way of looking at the
great seems to strip them of all their dignities and honours,

---

[1] *Church History*, book IV, section iv, § 8.
[1] Ibid., book IX, section vii, § 53.

and, if there is nothing behind these, to render them ridiculous. There is no such thing in Fuller as a man standing on his dignity. If he attempts it he finds such dignity a trap-door, and he is fortunate indeed if he does not fall through it when the doctor joins him. At its best the method can be singularly moving. We almost tremble when he reaches the death and burial of Charles I. We need not. The simplicity, nobility, and gentleness of his mind nowhere find more moving expression: with it he closes the last book and lays aside his pen:

'His hour drawing nigh, he passed through the Park to Whitehall: as he always was observed to walk very fast, so now he abated not any whit of his wonted pace. In his passage, a sorry fellow (seemingly some mean citizen) went abreast along with him, and in an affront often stared his Majesty in the face, which caused him to turn it another way. The bishop of London, though not easily angered, was much offended hereat, as done out of despiteful design, to discompose him before his death, and moved the captain of the guard he might be taken away, which was done accordingly.

'Entering on the floor of death, he asked of Colonel Tomlinson, who attended there, whether he might have the liberty to dispose of his own body, as to the place and manner of the burial thereof? The colonel answered that he could give his Majesty no account at all therein. . . .

'On the Wednesday sennight after, his corpse, embalmed and coffined in lead, was delivered to the care of two of his servants to be buried at Windsor; the one, Anthony Mildmay who formerly had been his sewer, as I take it; the other, John Joyner, bred first in his Majesty's kitchen, afterwards a parliament captain, since by them deputed (when the Scots surrendered his person) cook to his Majesty. This night they brought the corpse to Windsor, and digged a grave for it in St. George's chapel, on the south side of the Communion-table.

'But next day the Duke of Richmond,[1] the Marquess of Hertford, and Earls of Southampton and Lindsey (others, though sent to, declining the service, so far was their fear

[1] From whom Fuller had the account.

above their gratitude to their dead master) came to Windsor
and brought with them two votes passed that morning in
Parliament; wherein the ordering of the king's burial, for the
form and manner thereof, was wholly committed to the Duke
of Richmond, provided that the expense thereof exceeded not
five hundred pounds.   Coming into the castle, they showed
their commission to the governor, Colonel Whichcot, desiring
to inter the corpse according to the Common Prayer-Book of
the Church of England; the rather because the Parliament's
total remitting the manner of the burial to the Duke's discretion implied a permission thereof.   This the governor
refused, alleging it was improbable that the Parliament would
permit the use of what so solemnly they had abolished, and
therein destroy their own Act.

'The lords returned, that there was a difference betwixt
destroying their own act, and dispensing with it, or sus-
pending the exercise thereof.   That no power so bindeth up
its own hands as to disable itself in some cases to recede from
the rigour of its own acts, if they should see just occasion.
All would not prevail, the governor persisting in the negative,
and the lords betook them to their sad employment.

'They resolved not to inter the corpse in the grave which
was provided for it, but in a vault, if the chapel afforded any.
Then fall they a-searching, and in vain seek for one in King
Henry the Eighth's chapel (where the tomb intended for him
by Cardinal Wolsey lately stood), because all there was solid
earth; besides, this place, at the present used for a magazine,
was unsuiting with a solemn sepulture.   Then with their
feet they tried the quire, to see if a sound would confess any
hollowness therein, and at last (directed by one of the aged
poor knights) did light on a vault in the middle thereof.

'It was altogether dark, as made in the midst of the quire,
and an ordinary man could not stand therein without
stooping, as not past five foot high.   In the midst thereof lay
a large leaden coffin, with the feet towards the east, and a far
less on the left side thereof.   On the other side was room,
neither to spare nor to want, for any other coffin of a moderate proportion.

'That one of the order was buried there, plainly appeared

by perfect pieces of purple velvet (their proper habit) remaining therein; though some pieces of the same velvet were fox-tawney, and some coal-black (all dye of purple being put out therein), though all originally of the same cloth, varying the colour, as it met with more or less moisture as it lay in the ground. . . .

'The vault thus prepared, a scarf of lead was provided some two foot long and five inches broad, therein to make an inscription. The letters the duke did delineate, and then a workman was called to cut them out with a chisel. . . .

KING CHARLES, 1648

The plumber soldered it to the coffin about the breast of the corpse within the same.

'All things thus in readiness, the corpse was brought to the vault, being borne by the soldiers of the garrison; over it a black velvet hearse-cloth, the four labels whereof the four lords did support; the bishop of London stood weeping by, to tender that his service which might not be accepted. Then was it deposited in silence and sorrow in the vacant place in the vault (the hearse-cloth being cast in after it) about three of the clock in the afternoon, and the lords that night (though late) returned to London.'

After reading these words we cannot wonder that Coleridge was so carried away by Fuller's sincerity and command of his subject that at the end of his copy of the *Church History* he wrote:

'Next to Shakespeare, I am not certain whether Thomas Fuller, beyond all other writers, does not excite in me the sense and emotion of the marvellous: the degree in which any given faculty or combination of faculties is possessed and manifested, so far surpassing what one would have thought possible in a single mind, as to give one's admiration the flavour and quality of wonder! . . . *God bless thee*, dear old man! May I meet with thee! which is tantamount to—may I go to Heaven.'

CHAPTER XIII

CONTROVERSIAL PENS

. . . the controversial pen,
The holy strife of disputatious men.

CRABBE.

FULLER stands out among his contemporaries as an early manifestation of the easy-going Englishman of the modern world: tolerant, independent, and good-humoured. The type had already developed among the yeomen, quietly working the land, whose sons were to determine the character of the entire nation; but as yet it had found little expression in literature. Somehow, Fuller seems to have had a sense of it in his bones which saved him from much of the nonsense that so many of his fellows got into their heads about this time. When the Scots, an intellectual race, gained control of Church and State, they forced the poor, unhappy English to think. Few could realize what calamities would ensue, because few could know that when the English start thinking they reach such odd conclusions. As Fuller himself said of William Brightman's *Comment on the Revelation*, 'Sure I am that Time and Mr. Brightman will expound the hardest places in the Revelations; but what credit is to be given to the latter alone, I will not engage.'

In theology the resourcefulness—not to say the inventiveness—of these logicians passed all belief. Here, for example, is Dr. John Lightfoot (1602–75), Master of Catherine Hall, Cambridge, on the Creation: 'That the world was made at Equinox all grant, but differ at which, whether about the eleventh of March or twelfth of September; to me in September without all doubt. All things were created in their ripeness and maturity: apples ripe and ready to eat, as is too sadly plain in Adam and Eve's eating the forbidden fruit.' The learned doctor can even suggest the precise time of the Fall: 'About the sixth hour, or high noon most probably, as that was the time of eating.'[1] Can we wonder that Milton, in *Means to Remove Hirelings out of the Church*, says: 'Those theological disputations then held in the university by Professors and Graduates were such as tend least of all to the edification or capacity of the people, but rather perplex and leaven pure doctrine with scholastical trash than enable any minister to the better preaching of the gospel'?[2]

Fuller's first experience of love among the clergy came to him, as we saw in an earlier chapter, after the publication of his *Sermon of Reformation* in 1643, when John Saltmarsh, then holding a living in the East Riding of Yorkshire, accused him of flirting with Rome. His reply on that occasion was made in the bantering style that he used in controversy all his life. Gay clothes, he once remarked, are no armour for combat; yet he himself always rode into the field of battle gloriously caparisoned in cap and bells. Provided his adversary displayed his identity like an honest man, he could be assured of a gentlemanly engagement; but for the man who withheld his name, or who attacked him behind his back, he had nothing but contempt. 'I remember,' said he on one occasion, 'a speech of Sir Walter Raleigh: "If any," saith he, "speaketh against me to my face, my tongue shall give him an answer; but my back-side is good enough to return to him, who abuseth me behind my back."'

There was more in this than personal honour. Throughout the seventeenth century religious and intellectual thought, having slipped from their ancient moorings, were at the mercy of every tide of passion or wind of fancy. It had, therefore, become essential in Fuller's day that every man's credentials should be examined before granting him a hearing. All kinds of extraordinary persons had set up as prophets, claiming to have been favoured with new light on the Almighty's will for men. Fuller had little faith in these claims to peculiar favours of the Holy Spirit made by self-appointed prophets. If forced to it, he was ready to deal with them; but as a man whose entire cast of mind was

---

[1] Dr. Lightfoot was rector of Great Munden, Hertfordshire. After recording the execution of Charles I in his parish register he added '*murdered.*'

[2] *Prose Works*, iii. 37.

H

practical, he saw the futility of arguing with those who
claimed intuitive knowledge, and in any case he desired
above all things peace.   As he had written in his controversy
with Saltmarsh: 'Conceive me not to be of a brawling and
controversial disposition, who so desire and will pray for an
agreement from my soul, so long as my speech shall serve me.
Yea, if I should chance to be stricken dumb, I would with
Zacharias "make signs for table books," and write [that]
the name of that which I desire above all earthly things is
PEACE.   God send it.'

But this was no time to ask for peace, and after publishing
his *Church History* even Fuller could hardly expect to enjoy
it.   The attack, however, came from one he had studiously
tried to avoid offending, to wit, Peter Heylyn, one

> . . . that had the greatest Practice
> To prune and bleach the Beards of all Fantasticks.

Heylyn was eight years younger than Fuller, and by birth
and education an Oxford man.   Moreover, he was a good
historian.   He was himself working on a history of the
Church since the Reformation, and had enjoyed the use of
Sir Robert Cotton's library for that purpose.   He was able,
honest, and courageous, and such attacks as that of Carlyle,
who called him 'lying Peter,' are grossly unfair.   It is true
that he was quarrelsome.   He burned with a fierce Laudian
flame that had been lashed to a furious heat by the winds of
many controversies, and in consequence he had the utmost
scorn for the steady lambent glow of such churchmanship as
Fuller's.   Irritating as these precise men are, we ought in
fairness to admit that after they have worked hard to equip
themselves with detailed knowledge of their subjects they
have cause for annoyance at the easy success won by such
men as Fuller.   That Fuller was willing to acknowledge all
Heylyn's gifts, and to disclaim any animosity towards him
even in the face of attack, only increased the other's ire.
There was no compromise for Heylyn.   He lived in the
spirit of those words in Luke's Gospel: 'Between us and you
there is a great gulf fixed: so that they which would pass
from hence to you cannot; neither can they pass to us, that

would come from thence.' Unlike Fuller, he revelled in disputation, and spent his life, as became so learned a clerical
spider, spinning webs of erudition for the destruction of less
scholastic flies.

Heylyn's attack on Fuller did not appear until 1659, but
as it was provoked by the *Church History* it is most convenient to consider it here while that work is in our minds.
It was in a book entitled *Examen Historicum: or a Discovery
and Examination of the Mistakes, Falsities, and Defects in
some Modern Histories, &c.* The first part of the work was
devoted to what its author described as 'necessary animad-
versions' on Fuller's *History*, the second to Sanderson's
alleged errors in his writings on Stuart history. Fuller
replied in a work entitled *The Appeal of Injured Innocence*,
which in the reprint of 1840 was bound up in one volume with
the *Examen Historicum*. To Church historians it is an
important work because it is a public discussion of the tenets
of the English Church by two learned and acute men of
divergent views. In particular their reading of contemporary events was at variance. Both were honest; but what
was major to one was minor to the other. To Fuller the
Church was inclined to neglect her proper function—as he
saw it—of helping men to live good lives, by concentrating on
dogmas and reforms of Church order. 'At the last day of
judgment,' he said, 'when God shall arraign men and say:
"Thou art a drunkard, thou art an adulterer, thou art an
oppressor"; it will be but a poor plea for them to say: "Yea,
Lord; but I have been a public Reformer of Church and
State!"' And what had all this frantic reform achieved?
As Fuller saw it—rightly or wrongly—the answer was war.
Since starting work on his *Church History* in the pastoral
seclusion of his Dorset living he had studied the growing
divisions in the Church, and had viewed them with increasing
sorrow. Few of the points at issue were vital to Fuller's
conception of Christianity. To Heylyn they were, and in
the *Examen Historicum* Fuller's churchmanship is criticized
primarily because it shows such a lamentable lack of precision in defining the canons of the Church. Whether we are
interested in this or not, the dispute is of prime importance

in Fuller's life because it puts him in the dock, as it were, and forces him to face his critics, admirably represented by Heylyn, and defend himself. *The Appeal of Injured Innocence* is Fuller's apologia.

One of the doctor's most engaging qualities is that of taking the reader into his confidence, and in the *Appeal* he frankly admits that this quarrel was not of his seeking—that he had in fact been at some pains to avoid it, knowing Heylyn to be 'of a tart and smart style, endeavouring to down with all which stood betwixt him and his opinion.' Then he adds wittily that as no bird or beast of prey, unless 'sharp-set indeed,' would feed on its own kind, he had come to believe himself safe from Heylyn, seeing that both were Royalists. Shortly after the publication of the *Church History*, however, he had heard a rumour that Heylyn had gone into training for battle. One day Fuller happened to see the Animadvertor—as he called his adversary—in the street, and followed him to his lodgings at a stationer's—or bookseller's—house over against St. Dunstan's church. Sending up his name with a servant of the house, he asked for an interview, but received a curt reply that Heylyn was busy and could not see him. Even when the attack was launched he was half inclined to let it pass. He says he felt like a cow that had to suckle her own calves and at the same time yield milk again to the milkmaid:

Bis venit ad mulctrum, binos alit ubere foetus.

> She suckles two, yet does not fail
> Twice a day to come to the pail.

In other words, he had to feed his congregation with sermons, and at the same time produce material for his publisher, whereas Heylyn, in the fertile pasture of his retirement, only gave milk to relieve his own discomfort.

Finally he decided that it might be good for him to fight. He had, he confessed, found so much delight in the writing of history that he was afraid he had been guilty of neglecting his pastoral work for it. This attack would tend to discourage him in future: 'Mothers, minding to wean their

children, use to put soot, wormwood, or mustard on the
nipples of their breasts. God foresaw I might suck to a
surfeit in writing histories, which hath been a thief in the
lamp of my life, wasting much oil thereof.'

Nevertheless, though brought to book and apparently
prepared to declare everything, he was, in fact, by no means
guiltless of evasion. Heylyn alleged that Fuller was one
who accounted 'the Litany, the surplice, and other ceremonies, as superfluous and superstitious.' Fuller replied:
'This note might well have been spared. I appeal to such as
knew my conformity in the College chapel, country parishes,
and Cathedral of Sarum, to be my compurgators in this
unjust accusation.'[1] His outward conformity was not the
point. Heylyn might have produced in support of his summary of Fuller's attitude in general, passages in both *The
Holy State* ('The True Church Antiquary') and in *Joseph's
Parti-coloured coat*, where he says: 'But we would not have
religion so bedaubed with lace that one cannot see the cloth,
and ceremonies which should adorn, obscure the substance of
the sacraments and God's worship. . . . But let us love
religion not for her clothes, but for her face; and then shall we
affect it if she should chance (as God forbid) to be either
naked through poverty, or ragged through persecution. In
a word, if God hath appointed it, let us love the plainness of
his ordinance though therein there be neither warm water,
nor strong water, nor sweet water, but plain water of Jordan.'
Again: 'It is a true but sad consideration how in all ages men
with more vehemency of spirit have stickled about small
and unimportant points than about such matters as most
concern their salvation. So that I may say (these sorrowful
times having tuned our tongues to military phrases) some
men have lavished more powder and shot in the defence of
some slight outworks, which might well have been quitted
without any loss to Religion, than in maintaining the main
platform of piety, and making good that Castle of God's
service and their own salvation. Pride will be found upon
serious inquiry the principal cause hereof.'[2]

Fuller himself knew well enough that there were many

---

[1] *Appeal*, part ii., p. 494.   [2] *Collected Sermons*, i. 498–9.

aspects of Church history about which Heylyn was far better informed than he was, and probably the scholars of the day, who must at this stage have regarded Fuller's scholarship as superficial, expected Heylyn to win an easy and decisive victory. Those who witnessed the dispute would not be surprised to see Fuller evading, retreating, and cunningly returning to the attack behind the smoke-screen of a jest. What did surprise them was that usually Fuller's arguments were so forceful, and supported by so much learning, as well as by such readiness to cite authorities. In no other work do we see so clearly the gentle nobility of his character and the astonishing range of his studies. No matter how bitterly or unfairly he was attacked—and Heylyn fought a hard battle— he maintained his serenity and full command of his playful wit. It cannot be denied that Heylyn did find a few weak places. No man could write with equal knowledge and precision on every aspect of so large a subject. There are many mistakes in all Fuller's works, as indeed there are in Heylyn's, and as there must be in all such voluminous authors. We may say of Fuller what Sir John Buchan said of Sir Walter Scott: 'He has not the faultlessness of the minor masters, but his careless greatness has that "God's plenty" which Dryden found in Chaucer.' Belief in the infallibility of print is a superstition as foolish as any other concept of human infallibility. It is the attitude of an author to his mistakes when these are pointed out to him that shows grace or the lack of it, and Fuller proved himself a sensible and modest man by accepting the corrections gratefully, while very properly censuring the churlish way they were made. And when Heylyn missed the mark, how delightfully Fuller retorted! Here are two examples, found by opening at random in search of illustration:

'Well may the doctor run apace, drawing an empty cart after him. . . .'

'Nor did I ever say they were. Had I said so, the doctor's carping hand had had a handle to hold on, whereas now his teeth and nails must bite and scratch a fastening for themselves.'

Heylyn, however, was a skilful swordsman, and for all his

adversary's clever footwork he did, as we have said, pierce the armour occasionally, provoking such replies as this:

'I can patiently comport with the Animadvertor's jeers; which I behold as so many frogs, that it is pretty and pleasing to see them hop and skip about, having not much harm in them. But I cannot abide his railings; which are like to toads, swelling with venom within them. Any one may rail who is bred but in Billingsgate-College: and I am sorry to hear such language from the Animadvertor, a Doctor of Divinity; seeing railing is as much beneath a Doctor as against Divinity.'

It must not be thought that Heylyn himself was without humour. When free from provocation he could, we are told, be a lively companion; spinning, in fact, for the amusement of his friends yarns that would have done credit to Fuller. He could even slip an anecdote into a work of learning. His best-known book, *Cosmography*, was the occasion of one of the best of these. It relates that while riding through the forest of Whichwood, with a 'country customer' who had been sent with horses to fetch him from Oxford to his brother's house, Heylyn lost his way. The countryman began to suspect this, and asked if it would not be better to leave the forest and keep to the open fields. Heylyn, alas, had to confess that he did not know where he was, that he had never been in the place before, and that he did not, in fact, know which way to turn.

'That is strange,' remarked the countryman; 'I have heard my old master, your father, say that you made a book of all the world; and cannot you find your way out of the wood?'

This Fuller caps with a similar tale of his own. While walking in the park of Copt Hall, in his parish of Waltham Abbey, thinking out his sermon, the third son of the Earl of Dorset, 'a child in coats,' ran up to him and asked if he might come with the doctor. Fuller, afraid that he might not be able to keep an eye on his young friend while concentrating on his sermon, warned the child that if he came he might get lost.

'Then you must lose yourself first,' replied the child, 'for I will go with *you*.'

This homely incident he uses to point a moral. 'This rule

I always observe,' he smilingly confesses, 'when meddling
with matters of law: because I myself am a child therein, I
will ever go with a man in that faculty, such as is most
eminent in his profession, *a cujus latere non discedam*; so that
if he lose me, he shall first lose himself.'   In other words,
Heylyn would waste his time if he tried to catch Fuller out in
points of law.

History, however, was not a subject to be treated in so
light-hearted a way, and, says Heylyn, Fuller's work ought
to be called, not *The Church History of Britain*, but *Fuller's
Miscellanies*.   'But, above all things,' says Heylyn, 'recom-
mend me to his merry tales, and scraps of trencher-jests,
frequently interlaced in all parts of the History; which, if
abstracted from the rest, and put into a book by themselves,
might very well be served up for a second course to the
Banquet of Jests, a supplement to the old book, entitled
Wits, Fits, and Fancies; or an additional century to the
old *Hundred Merry Tales*, so long since extant.'

Fuller may have smiled at the suggested title for his work,
but when Heylyn proceeded to lay down the rules which in
his opinion the historian must observe, criticizing in particular the doctor's delightful use of odd scraps of verse to
relieve the tedium of the narrative, the reply came sharply:
'Let the Animadvertor keep those steel bodices for his own
wearing, and not force them on me.   What! not a plait or a
ruffle, more or less, but all must be done in number, weight,
and measure, according to historical criticism!   This is not
putting the book, but the author himself into the press.'
And in defence of his old wives' tales he says: 'It is as impossible to find antiquity without fables as an old face without wrinkles.'

It is clear throughout the discussion that above all things
Fuller desired a friendly conclusion to a dispute that he had
not sought, and that, for all his skill in conducting it, he did
not relish.   But while the one desired peace above everything
else, controversy was the breath of life to the other, and it is
hardly fair to reproach Heylyn for not accepting the proffered
handshake.   After all, the handshake was always Fuller's
trump card.   He was a master at reconciling opposites, and

that through a gift which Heylyn recognized and despised, the gift of being able to compromise. Heylyn was, in fact, far more heroic than Fuller—a stubborn fool, if you like, but heroic. He had stood to his Laudian guns throughout the quarrel between King and Parliament, and had taken his punishment like a man. He had not lived on good terms with a Regicide and afterwards bowed and scraped his way into a comfortable living, as Fuller, he would probably think, had done. Since the fall of Oxford early in the struggle Heylyn had been unbeneficed—a homeless scholar, depending on the charity of the Royalist gentry for food and shelter until at last he was able to settle modestly at Lacie's Court, near Abingdon, and take up his writing again with the help of the Bodleian library. He knew that his friendship with Laud, whose life he wrote, and the uncompromising way in which he had always expressed himself, gave him no hope whatever of finding any kind of profitable occupation while the Commonwealth continued. He had become irritable, too, during those exasperating years, and had made so many enemies that now it seemed as though the only way for him to relieve his vexatious spirit was by attacking one poor scholar after another. Nevertheless he could, when he wished, be a most attractive writer. In the eighteenth century he was, in fact, to enjoy a considerable vogue, as we may note from Prior's couplet, giving it as the mark of a student that he

> From breakfast reads till twelve o'clock
> Burnet and Heylyn, Hobbes and Locke.

Fuller, in his usual frank way, faces this charge of time-serving. He says: 'But it will be objected against me, that it is suspicious (at the least) that I have bribed the times with some base compliance with them, because they have reflected so favourably upon me. Otherwise how cometh it that my fleece, like Gideon's, is dry, when the rest of my brethren of the same party are wet with their own tears? I being permitted preaching, and peaceable enjoying of a parsonage.' It is, however, noteworthy that his reply to this assumed charge, though reasonable, and in the spirit of what has already been said, was rather longer than might have been thought necessary.

* H

The general effect of the *Appeal* was well expressed by one of the most learned of Fuller's nineteenth-century editors, James Nichols, who says: 'Published in the year prior to the Restoration, it displays to better advantage, perhaps, than any or all of his former productions, the multifarious acquirements and wonderful intellectual resources of Fuller. Highly as I am reputed to venerate his antagonist, Peter Heylyn, that staunch and sturdy Royalist, I feel no hesitation in pronouncing Fuller the victor in this contest; not only from the general justness of his cause, but also for that which exalts him as a man and a Christian—his playful wit, ingenuous candour, almost unfailing good humour, and remarkable moderation.'

In concluding his defence Fuller was as good as his word. He wrote a letter to Heylyn seeking a reconciliation. 'Why should Peter fall out with Thomas,' he says, 'both being disciples to the same Lord and Master? I assure you, Sir (whatever you conceive to the contrary), I am cordial to the cause of the English church, and my hoary hairs will go down to the grave in sorrow for her sufferings.' He then asked Heylyn to appoint a place where they could meet, 'that we, who have tilted pens, may shake hands together.'

Such blandishments, however, were cruel weapons to use against Heylyn — they were, indeed, those pitiless coals of fire which Christians have sometimes been inclined to glory in. Heylyn took his defeat badly, and with good reason. Fuller had refused to use the appointed weapons. When offered the sword, he had thrown it down as it were, taken the precaution of setting up a screen between himself and his challenger, and then, leaning on the screen, had simply smiled down on the man who wanted to fight him. Heylyn was not used to being treated thus. Indeed, it would appear that he expected his victims to admire even his skill in striking them, and

> In arguing, too, to own his wondrous skill,
> For e'en though vanquished, he could argue still.

Stubborn and quarrelsome though he was, there is much to be said for Heylyn. The world would be desperately dull if

all men were gentle and peaceable.   Soon after receiving
Fuller's reply, the old Laudian warrior returned to the attack;
but where in the *Examen Historicum* there had been only two
to dispose of, Fuller and Sanderson, in this second attack
there were five.   With splendid assurance he seems to have
thought himself capable of engaging them all at once.   So
in 1659 the *Certamen Epistolare, or the Letter-Combat*, was
published, bearing a dedication 'To my dear brethren the
poor remainders of the old regular and comfortable clergy of
the Church of England.'   The five to be demolished were
Richard Baxter, who had had the audacity to write disparagingly of the ejected ministers, Henry Hickman of
Magdalen College, Oxford, whom Heylyn described as 'a
whelp of the same litter,' Dr. Barnard, James Harrington,
and Fuller.

It had evidently been reported that Heylyn had asked
pardon of the two historians he had attacked in the *Examen
Historicum*.   This was the unkindest thrust of all.   How
could Peter Heylyn be expected to ask pardon of any man?
Far from begging Fuller's pardon he had written to him:
'I understand you have an answer in the press to my *Animad-
versions*, which I am very glad to hear of, because I hope the
truth will come out between us; if you can show me any
mistakes I shall be one of the first that shall give you thanks
for it, and do my endeavour to correct them.   If you can
charge me with any viciousness in life or conversation, do in
God's name, and spare not; I will not be thankful to you for
that neither, because I shall the better know what I am to
reform &c.'

He explains that he is anxious to dispose of his present
antagonists because he had recently drawn upon himself two
others, one of whom was Hamon L'Estrange, of Pakenham,
Suffolk, author of *The Reign of King Charles*, and brother of
Sir Roger, the pioneer English journalist.   By L'Estrange,
Heylyn complained, he had 'been handled in so rude and
scurrilous a manner as renders him incapable of any honest
correction, there being no pen foul enough to encounter him
which would not be made fouler by engaging in so foul
a combat.'   From Fuller, however, Heylyn said he had

received 'a well-studied answer, composed with ingenuity and judgment, not standing wilfully in an error of which he finds himself convinced, though traversing many points in debate between us, which with more honour to the truth might have been declined. And in the end thereof I find a letter directed or superscribed unto me, tending especially to the begetting of such a friendly correspondence betwixt us as may conduce to the establishment of a following peace.' All of this Heylyn thought very civil. 'But first I am to enter into consideration of some particulars relating to the late *Appeal*, to my adversary, to myself, and finally to some few differences which remain between us.'

He complains—not without reason—that Fuller had purposely ignored some of his points, while in dealing with others he had made use of all the subterfuges that wit and cunning could devise. Of course he had! Then to show himself a good fellow, and unjustly accused of malevolence in his attack on Fuller, he says: 'I shall be somewhat better-natured than the Lady Moore, of whom my author knows a tale, that coming once from shrift, she pleasantly saith unto her husband:

'Be merry, Sir Thomas, for I have been well shriven to-day, and mean to lay aside all my old shrewishness.'

'Yes, madam,' saith he, 'and to begin again afresh!'

Fuller's way of making light of small points that to Heylyn were grave offences provoked one of the Animadvertor's neatest retorts: 'I remember I have somewhere read of a famous wrastler who, being many times overthrown, did suddenly start up, and by an eloquent oration, persuaded the people that he rather fell by a slip of his own foot, than by the strength of his adversary. Such a wrastler I have met with in the present Appealant.'

The letter at the end, desiring a meeting to make peace, Heylyn thought against all the rules of such combat. He could not in honour 'embrace any of those civil and ingenious overtures which are made in the Appealant's letter,' until the truth had been established in all the points at issue between them. But, not to appear churlish, he offered to live on terms of mutual esteem with his genial opponent once they had settled their differences over points of fact and principle.

It is the old story. To Fuller the personal mattered more than the doctrinal. To Heylyn, doctrine, the facts of history, and absolute loyalty to king and Church were of paramount importance. It would be dishonourable to come to terms with a man who treated these questions as mere matters of opinion, taste, or temperament.

Fuller was perfectly happy to allow the doughty Peter to have the last word. He made a special journey to the other's lodging and Heylyn could no more resist the personal charm of the worthy doctor than a frozen lake can resist the rays of the sun. The pair of them laid their quarrel aside, and for the rest of their lives remained firm and devoted friends. At the Restoration Heylyn came out of his obscure retreat. His eyesight was failing, but he rejoiced that like Simeon he had lived to see what he regarded as the salvation of his people in the king's return. His prebend was restored to him, and he became a figure of veneration. He was one of the few who could come before his sovereign with a clean record of uncompromising loyalty. But the old high spirit was still there. He expected the reward that was his due. It was not to be. Inferior men were given bishoprics. The bough that will not bend must break. Poor old Heylyn fretted about the injustices he saw multiplied at the Restoration, until, shortly before his death, he had a curious dream. In it his late Majesty, Charles I, stood at his bedside and said, 'Peter, I will have you buried under your seat at church, for you are rarely seen but there or at your study.' So, when he died in the early summer of 1662, Heylyn was laid to rest in that very place—true to the last to his sovereign's wishes.

CHAPTER XIV

IN CAP AND BELLS

... Joking decides great things
Stronger and better, oft, than earnest can
                    MILTON.

HEYLYN'S contempt for Fuller's 'merry tales and scraps of trencher-jests' was not exceptional. Many of the learned divines of his day must have shared it. At least two who came later, Bishops Nicolson and Warburton, said plainly enough what they thought of this weakness for unseasonable pleasantries. To Bishop Warburton he was 'Fuller the Jester,' who wrote 'in a style of buffoon pleasantry altogether unsuitable to so grave and important a subject' as Church history, while Bishop Nicolson, as we said earlier,[1] remarked on reading the same work that it looked as if the man had 'designed to ridicule the annals of our Church into fable and romance.' When not directly under his influence, most men with any regard for the dignity of letters would agree that there are more than a few occasions when Fuller does go too far with his joking. But he does so because people to him, whether high or low, learned or simple, are such tremendous fun. His volubility does not arise from vanity, but from cheerfulness.

In his lighter moods Fuller has much in common with G. K. Chesterton—so much indeed that there are times when the latter might be thought to be a reincarnation of the former. In their works, both are moralists even while they are humorists. They rebuke with a joke, and find in the deserts of theology more occasions of mirth than the dull would find in a carnival. In their lives, both were men of charity, tolerance, and Johnsonian common sense. They might have worn each other's shoes, as it were, and in the same manner of speaking they did wear each other's ties. When Chesterton, with a supreme effort of will, succeeds in introducing the date

---

[1] See p. 182.

of his birth into his autobiography he does so with a phrase that Fuller might well have used. He says: 'I am firmly of opinion that I was born on the 29th of May 1874. . . .' Who else would have been 'firmly of opinion' on such a matter as that? Similarly, Chesterton might have referred, as Fuller did, to Chronology as a surly animal, apt to bite the fingers of those who handle it with greater familiarity than necessary. Both were in fact bitten more than once. And, incidentally, neither Fuller nor Chesterton was sufficiently egotistical to write either well or accurately about himself, yet both were practically incapable of writing an impersonal sentence.

Both Fuller and Chesterton had walked in Eden; but neither had eaten of that tree of knowledge from which men learn that it is wicked and foolish to write words simply for the excitement of playing with things so dangerous and sprightly. Fuller's style, when exuberant, might be defined as rococo, though the word itself was unknown to him. He is all bits and pieces, many of them fantastic and bizarre, yet never laboured or far-fetched. And this fragmentary make-up, which allows so much spontaneity and surprise in his work—if also irrelevance—has advantages. He is not like Humpty Dumpty. He can always be put together again.

Again like Chesterton, Fuller saw things pictorially. Both believed, as Fuller put it, 'that though reasons are the pillars of the fabric, similitudes are the windows which give the best lights.' The use of imagery was indeed the only elegance Fuller cultivated either as preacher or writer. He had no use for the usual oratorical flourishes. He spoke always in a simple, straightforward manner; but every sentence sparkled with wit, and this, supported by his handsome person and benign good humour, accounted for his popularity in the pulpit. His wit, however, was never sharp. It was playful —a thing of glancing lights and quirkish sallies. Who but Fuller—or Chesterton—would have attributed the plain style of the schoolmen to concern 'lest any of the vermin of equivocation should hide themselves under the nap of their words'? And no one else would have talked of peeping through 'the casement' of an index, or in writing a history

of Cambridge have told us how Matthew Parker—Archbishop of Canterbury, if you please—'squibs-in' a parenthesis.

Being a clergyman, Fuller did occasionally feel constrained
to limit the range of wit. 'Jest not with the two-edged
sword of God's word,' he said once. But he sometimes
forgot his own good counsel even in this. Enlarging on St.
Paul's command that we should not let the sun go down on
our wrath, he could not withhold the comment that if this
were taken literally, in Greenland men would have more
scope for revenge than St. Paul intended. He knew his own
weaknesses. He knew that he could no more hold back a
sally or a story than a toper can keep off the bottle. 'For-
give me, reader,' he says in one place, 'though I would not
write these things, they are so absurd, I cannot *but* write
them, they *are* so absurd.' In the warning against profanity
in jesting just quoted he says: 'Will nothing please thee to
wash thy hands in but the font? or to drink healths in but the
church chalice?' Such advice might help others to be more
restrained. It could have little effect on himself, for, as
he remarked after quoting a line from Horace, 'That fork
must have strong tines wherewith one would thrust out
Nature.'

But while Fuller was by nature a man of mirth, he may not
always have been conscious of his own humour. He cannot
have intended the prayer that God would 'pinch' him into
the remembrance of his promises to be quite so absurd as it
sounds to us. Similarly his deficiency in dramatic sense, and
in capacity for veneration, made some of his descriptions
more ludicrous than he can ever have intended them to be.
His description of Gunpowder Plot, for example, reads like
the account of a practical joke played by half a dozen school-
boys on their house-master. This inability to be suitably
impressed by greatness and importance, which was one of
Fuller's most marked characteristics, could, on occasion, be
an engaging quality—particularly because it means that we
can always be at ease with him. He is a comfortable sort of
fellow. But it could show itself as a serious flaw in his
make-up. Nowhere is this more marked than in his description of Salisbury Cathedral in the Wiltshire section of the

Worthies, which, in view of its personal associations, was the one building that might have been expected to draw out his pride. The truth is, of course, that he had none. He does begin by saying that the cathedral 'is paramount in this kind,' but then, before making any attempt to describe its beauty, he runs off into another of his merry tales: 'Once walking in this church (whereof then I was prebendary) I met a countryman wondering at the structure thereof.

'"I once," said he to me, "admired that there could be a church that should have so many pillars as there be hours in the year; and now I admire more, that there should be so many hours in the year as I see pillars in this church."'

In the next paragraph he gives himself away completely. 'I have been credibly informed,' he says, 'that some foreign artists, beholding this building, brake forth into tears, which some imputed to their admiration (though I see not how wondering can cause weeping); others to their envy, grieving that they had not the like in their own land.'

Such casual references as these belong to a different world from that of Milton, with his:

> But let my due feet never fail
> To walk the studious cloister's pale,
> And love the high embowèd roof,
> With antique pillars massy proof,
> And storied windows richly dight,
> Casting a dim religious light.

To Fuller, the odd little man in the cathedral was more interesting than the cathedral itself. Indeed he was amazed that mere architecture could stir men deeply. It seems a shocking attitude of mind in one who had undertaken to describe the wonders as well as the worthies of England; but after all he was only revealing again how very English he was. During the Second World War, when our national treasures were endangered by bombing, Englishmen were often heard remarking that the finest building in the land was not worth saving at the risk, however small, of endangering a single life. It is not an heroic view. Little would have been achieved if some men had not valued achievement above security, but it is one that Fuller would have shared to the extent of being astonished that any one could dissent from it.

Perhaps the most important result of this particular characteristic was that it made him a man of the people at a time when practically all literature, particularly secular literature, depended upon court favour, and was therefore courtly in tone.   Fuller was one of the first to take learning to the people and give it a human rather than a polite touch-stone of value.   He was not only typically and provincially English, but assured in his Englishness, and culturally the Englishman has seldom been assured.   He has had so little confidence in his native genius that all too often he has taken his art from this race, his literature from that, and his music from a third.   Occasionally, however, the native genius breaks through to produce a Chaucer, a Shakespeare, a Constable, or a Hardy.   Fuller was of this company.   While Milton was enriching the language with Latin, others with Italian, Spanish, and French modes of thought and expression, Fuller was content to use the Saxon words he had picked up in fields and cottages.   The richness of his idiomatic vocabulary has surprised several philologists.   Archbishop Trench said that few writers were more important than Fuller in this, while Coleridge, after reading a comment by John Nichols to the effect that much might be said in vindication of Fuller's language against the criticism of such sober-sides as Bishop Nicolson, burst out: 'Fuller's language! Grant me patience, Heaven!   A tithe of his beauties would be sold cheap for a whole library of our classical writers, from Addison to Johnson and Junius inclusive.   And Bishop Nicolson! — a painstaking old charwoman of the Anti-quarian and Rubbish Concern!   The venerable rust and dust of the whole firm are not worth an ounce of Fuller's earth.' [1]

The use of expressive old words, by which he gives a voice to the peasant no less than to the scholar, is part and parcel of Fuller's humour.   A village may be a 'dorp' in him; a narrow, projecting part of a field a 'spong.'   He uses the word 'hoit' for leap or caper—the word from which we may get

---

[1] *Notes Theological, Political, and Miscellaneous,* p. 101.

'hoity-toity.' You will find 'rank-riders' in Fuller. These were idle, dissolute fellows who lived by cheating innkeepers. They stayed the night and rode off next morning without paying the reckoning. In *The Merry Wives of Windsor* we meet them as cozeners. When Bardolph is asked where the host of the 'Garter's' horses are, he replies: 'Run away with the cozeners; for so soon as I came beyond Eton, they threw me off, from behind one of them, in a slough of mire; and set spurs and away, like three German devils, three Doctor Faustuses.' Sir Hugh, you may remember, says: 'Have a care of your entertainments: there is a friend of mine come to town, tells me there is three cozen-germans that has cozened all the hosts of Reading, of Maidenhead, of Colebrook, of horses and money.' While at Waltham Abbey, a town full of inns in those days, Fuller would hear many tales of rank-riders and cozeners.

Milton, the dominant literary figure of the age, could not give us its social background as convincingly as Shakespeare did that of the one before it. In the country, however, the older England was still there, and it is Shakespeare's rather than Milton's England that we find in Fuller, particularly in the *Worthies*. The society that Fuller knew, and that to him meant England, was not intellectual. The village squire was a farmer, even as the parson was, and both were far more at home in a labourer's cottage than in the kind of drawing-room that came into use towards the end of the seventeenth century, and increasingly in the eighteenth. Moreover memory counted for more in the seventeenth-century village than the modern town dweller can appreciate. Throughout the nineteenth century, and the first half of the twentieth, the past has been a shrinking portion of the average man's intellectual background; and this, as some of us think, to his great impoverishment. Folk memory, usually with a humorous twist in it, was a real asset to the people of Fuller's day. So was family memory. These we find everywhere in his work, and presented in a way that shows how much they meant to the common people. This aspect of his work comes out particularly well in his anecdotes. Perhaps one of the happiest instances is this: 'I could both sigh and smile at the witty simplicity of a poor old woman who had lived in the days of Queen Mary and Queen Elizabeth, and said her prayers daily both in Latin and English; and "Let God," said she, "take to himself which he likes best."'

He always enjoyed telling such tales, and was never happier than when the apparently simple countryman got the better of an argument.   He has a tale somewhere about a rich man who said he walked each day in order to get a stomach for his meat, to whom the poor man replied: 'And I to get meat for my stomach.'   He was also amused that for as long as he had known them shopkeepers had always complained that trade was dead.   'Wit,' said Coleridge, 'was the stuff and substance of Fuller's intellect.   It was the element, the earthen base, the material he worked in.'   Perhaps it was; but if so it was not the smart sort of wit that the twentieth century finds so amusing.   His was the wit of which Pope wrote:

> True wit is Nature to advantage dress'd,
> What oft was thought, but ne'er so well express'd.

There was none of the Oscar Wilde type of wit in Fuller.   He is full of light-hearted banter and shrewd comment rather than epigrammatic brilliance.   Such a remark as 'Some men's heads are like the world before God said unto it, Fiat Lux,' or 'All the whetting in the world can never set a razor's edge on that which hath no steel in it,' may not sparkle; but made by a natural humorist they go home, especially as they break out spontaneously with a score of similar odd sallies. Fuller is not a delicate plant that produces a few exquisite blooms after careful tending, but an enormous tree with every bough laden with blossom in spring and with fruit, ripe and succulent, in autumn.

Coleridge was probably right in saying that the wit Fuller worked in was the stuff and substance of his intellect.   No matter what his subject may be, it is there.   You find it especially in his biographies.

Writing of Andrew Perne, a Norfolk man who became vice-chancellor of Cambridge and Dean of Ely, he says that in the days of Queen Mary he was 'the screen to keep off the fire of persecution from the faces and whole bodies of many a poor Protestant; so that by his means no gremial of the university was martyred therein.

'I know he was much taxed for altering his religion four times in twelve years (from the last of King Henry the Eighth to the first of Queen Elizabeth); a Papist, a Protestant, a Papist, a Protestant; but still Andrew Perne. However, be it known, that though he was a bending willow, he was no smarting willow, guilty of compliance not cruelty, yea, preserving many who otherwise had been persecuted.

'He was of a very facetious nature, excellent at blunt-sharp jests, and perchance sometimes too tart in true ones. One instance of many; this dean chanced to call a clergyman *fool* (who indeed was little better); who returned, "that he would complain thereof to the lord bishop of Ely." "Do," saith the dean, "when you please; and my lord bishop will *confirm* you."

'Yet was Doctor Perne himself at last heart-broken with a jest (as I have been most credibly informed from excellent hands), on this occasion. He was at court with his pupil Archbishop Whitgift in a rainy afternoon, when the queen was (I dare not say wilfully, but) really resolved to ride abroad, contrary to the mind of her ladies, who were on horseback (coaches as yet being not common) to attend her. Now one Clod the queen's jester was employed by the courtiers to laugh the queen out of so inconvenient a journey. "Heaven," saith he, "Madam, dissuades you, it is cold and wet; and earth dissuades you, it is moist and dirty. Heaven dissuades you, the heavenly-minded man Archbishop Whitgift; and earth dissuades you, your fool Clod, such a lump of clay as myself. And if neither will prevail with you, here is one that is neither heaven nor earth, but hangs betwixt both, Doctor Perne, and he also dissuades you." Hereat the queen and the courtiers laughed heartily; whilst the Doctor looked sadly, and, going over with his grace to Lambeth, soon saw the last of his life.'

It is in his portraits that we get the best of Fuller, no matter which side of his make-up we are interested in. If we want his views on divinity, we find them most clearly expressed in his lives of divines, and so on. To him the truth about anything was personal, and conveyed to others through personality. Like Bacon he distrusted the abstractions of 'meddling intellect'; and like Wordsworth he believed that

> Wisdom oft
> Is nearer when we stoop than when we soar.

For Fuller as jester, then, we must glance through his portraits of jesters in various works. The best—and it is not without significance that it is one of the best of all his portraits—is that of Dick Tarlton in the *Worthies*. Tarlton has been identified by some as Shakespeare's Yorick. However that may be, he was Tarlton to Fuller, and needed no other title. We are told how a servant of the Earl of Leicester, while travelling towards his master's land in Denbigh, found Dick tending his father's swine, and was so taken by his ready wit that he carried him off to court, where he became the most famous of the queen's jesters.

It is while writing of Tarlton that Fuller answers those who speak disparagingly of the jester's calling. He tells us that some men argue that it is better to be a fool of God's making —born into the world without wit, or a fool of man's making —jeered at by his neighbours, than a fool of one's own making. According to these, Tarlton would have done better to have remained his father's swineherd. Others, however, he says, argue that 'jesters often heal what flatterers hurt,' and that in any case lawful delight is a worthy object. Whatever the argument, Fuller submits, all agree that 'Our Tarlton was master of his faculty. When Queen Elizabeth was serious (I dare not say sullen) and out of good humour, he could undumpish her at his pleasure. Her highest favourites would, in some cases, go to Tarlton before they would go to the queen, and he was their usher to prepare their advantageous access unto her. In a word, he told the queen more of her faults than most of her chaplains, and cured her melancholy better than all her physicians.

'Much of his merriment lay in his very looks and actions, according to the epitaph written upon him:

> *Hic situs est cujus poterat vox, actio, vultus,*
> *Ex Heraclito reddere Democritum.*

Indeed the self-same words, spoken by another, would hardly move a merry man to smile; which, uttered by him, would force a sad soul to laughter.

'This is reported to his praise, that his jests never were profane, scurrilous, nor satirical; neither trespassing on piety, modesty, or charity.'

There are many ways of describing a jester's function. Shakespeare may use one, and he, it may be remembered, said: 'Jesters do oft prove prophets.' It is for each to present them according to his humour. But only Fuller would have allowed the queen's jester to '*undumpish* her at his pleasure.'

It is a characteristic of Fuller's peculiar brand of wit that enables him to hit off a situation in a phrase. Pages have been written in every age discussing whether the scholars of the day are as good as their forerunners. How much energy would be saved each time if someone could interrupt the argument as Fuller did to observe: 'Grant them but dwarfs, yet stand they on giants' shoulders, and may see farther.[1] And how he loved to tease the pompous! He was a big man himself, but he seems to have had an affection for little people. 'Oft-times,' he says of tall people, 'such who are built four stories high, are observed to have little in their cock-loft.'[2] Again of a small man, he says: 'His soul had but a short diocese to visit, and therefore might the better attend the effectual informing thereof.'

In most wit—perhaps in all—there is an element of incongruity. As a rule, it requires a twist of mind that sees things in odd relationships or unusual proportions. Much of the Englishman's humour rises from understatement. He

---

[1] The dwarf on the giant's shoulder is proverbial. See John of Salisbury's *Metalogicus*, Herbert's *Jacula Prudentum*, Burton's *Anatomy*, Coleridge's *The Friend*, etc.

[2] Cf. *Holy and Profane States*, 'Andronicus,' section vi, § 19, 1:

'Often the cock loft is empty in those whom Nature hath built many stories high.'

Francis Bacon:

'My Lord St. Albans said that Nature did never put her precious jewels into a garret four stories high, and therefore that exceeding tall men had ever very empty heads.'

Apothegms, No. 17.

produces the incongruity by reducing rather than by magnifying. There is much of this in Fuller. Some of it came merely from his being an Englishman; but we cannot help suspecting that his emphasis on the value of small, undramatic, and unsensational matters was purposely cultivated. It may even have been a conscious protest against the prevailing influence of the Scots, who see heaven and earth, life and death, and all the rest of creation and experience in much more dramatic terms than mere Englishmen can conceive. At all events, it is worth noting that instead of dwelling on the magnitude of man's sin and the terrible darkness of his soul, Fuller kept harping on the commonplace faults that any man might stumble into. For the good of his soul he kept a record of his own shortcomings, and what an odd kind of record it is! Nobody but Fuller would have thought of this one:

'Lord, I discover an arrant laziness in my soul. For when I am to read a chapter in the Bible, before I begin it, I look where it endeth. And if it endeth not on the same side, I cannot keep my hands from turning over the leaf, to measure the length thereof on the other side.'

Fuller is often described as quaint. He is 'Quaint old Fuller.' And such is his delight in eccentricities that the epithet is not without point. Nevertheless, it is unfair to him. He has been the victim of a change in the meaning of that unfortunate word. In the seventeenth century it meant 'wise' and 'ingenious,' and therefore fitted him admirably. But when in the late eighteenth century its meaning degenerated to 'daintily odd' it was still left to hang like a faded garland about his neck. Charles Lamb—another who had much in common with him—writing in 1811 in Leigh Hunt's *Reflector*, realized what had happened and said: 'Without any intention of setting Fuller on a level with Donne or Cowley I think the injustice which has been done him in the denial that he possesses any other qualities than those of a quaint and conceited writer, is of the same kind as that with which those two great poets have been treated.'

Before we suggest that Fuller was sufficiently odd to be

singled out from among his contemporaries and described as quaint, we ought to glance at more of the titles of seventeenth-century books than the mere handful that have survived. If we do this we discover that the fantastic and grotesque in Fuller, which some have thought exceptional—in degree if not in kind—was common at the time he was writing, and that what seemed extravagant in him was restrained in comparison with much of the work of his day. Here are a few of the more eccentric seventeenth-century titles: *The Snuffers of Divine Love*; *Hooks and Eyes for Believers' Breeches*; *High-heeled Shoes for Dwarfs in Holiness*; *Crumbs of Comfort for the Chickens of the Covenant*; *A Pair of Bellows to Blow off the Dust cast upon John Fry*.

A Quaker who had been imprisoned for his faith, published a work entitled: *A Sight of Sorrow for the Sinners of Zion, breathed out of a hole in the wall of an earthen vessel, known among men by the name of Samuel Fisher*.

And here is another nest of them: *The Spiritual Mustard-pot to make the Soul sneeze with Devotion*; *Salvation's Vantage Ground, or the Louping Sand for Heavy Believers*; *A Most Delectable Sweet Perfumed Nosegay for God's Saints to Smell at*.

Many of these works had titles almost as long-winded as their contents. Here are two:

A Reaping Hook well tempered for the Stubborn Ears fo the Coming Crop; or Biscuits baked in the Oven of Charity, carefully conserved for the Chickens of the Church, the Sparrows of the Spirit, and the Sweet Swallows of Salvation.

Seven Sobs of a Sorrowful Soul, or the Seven Penitential Psalms of the Princely Prophet David, whereunto are also annexed William Hunnis's Handfull of Honeysuckles and divers Godly and pithy Ditties now newly augmented.

It was not in Fuller's nature to go against the fashions and conventions of his times, except where valued principles were involved. If this facetious squandering of words was the game men played, he was ready to play it with them. But with a difference. He has none of the fulsome piety found in most of these popular works of the day. Indeed, in considering them he sometimes seems puzzled to know what they are about, particularly when their authors indulge in the

somewhat luscious phraseology affected by the more extravagant among the Puritans. He may have had an inkling
that this was, in fact, what we in the twentieth century would
call inhibited sensuality. It did seem strange to him that
these critics of obscenity and lascivious living should know so
much about it. The Roman Catholics he had always understood to be wicked, so their excesses presented no problems
to him. With them he merely accepted what his uncle
Davenant and his father had told him. Consequently, as he
said of Matthew Paris, he seldom 'kisseth the pope's toe
without biting it.' But even as a son of the Reformation
there was no malice in him, so we find him joking even about
the Jesuits, of whom he says that such is their charity 'that
they never owe any man any ill-will—making present payment thereof.' There was nothing morbid about Fuller.
Anger, he held, had its place, but 'Heat of passion makes our
souls to crack, and the Devil creeps in at the crannies.'

Some of Fuller's topical allusions are now lost to us, but it is
an exciting game to try to discover the more obscure among
them. In writing of the army of the three kings (2 Kings,
iii, 9) who went against Mesha in *A Pisgah Sight of Palestine*
(iv. p. 26) he refers to 'that Paroyall of Armies.' The word
'paroyall' must have puzzled many readers who did not
happen to know that in cribbage it is the custom to refer to
three cards of equal value, such as three kings or three
queens, as a pair royal. Cribbage in Fuller's day was a
new game, and this use of a contemporary term in writing of
Palestine would delight some of his readers, and—to his
amusement—would shock others. It seems clear from
Fuller's manner of writing that he though more of his present
than of his future readers. We might describe his style as that
of a conversationalist rather than that of a writer. He wrote
with a sense of the reader's presence. Joubert once observed
that 'a book should have no more than the requisite tincture
of wit; but a superabundance is quite allowable in conversation.' Fuller certainly has a superabundance. As David
Lloyd said, he knew better where to spend his jests than
where to spare them, yet, curiously enough, he seems to have
known that it was possible to have too much joking. 'Harm-

less mirth,' he says, 'is the best cordial against the consumption of the spirits; wherefore jesting is not unlawful if it trespasseth not in quantity, quality, or season.'

But who thinks of a man's faults while under the spell of his wit? Whatever the critics may say about Fuller's jesting, the experience of most of his readers is that so well expressed by E. K. Broadus in his introduction to a volume of selections: 'When we turn the opening pages of any book of Fuller's, we are amused *at* him; as we read on we are amused *with* him; but by the time we have turned the last page, he will have us by the heart-strings.'

CHAPTER XV

MIXT CONTEMPLATIONS

Where no disputes, nor forc'd defence
Of a man's person for his sense,
Take up the time.

SUCKLING.

'MODERATION,' observed Fuller in one of his reflections, quoting Bishop Hall, 'is the silken string running through the pearl-chain of all the virtues,' and while it is true that with him the pearls of his wit may hide the silken string of his wisdom, on closer inspection we do find that this thread of moderation runs through his work and holds it in a single circuit. Early and late, his constant theme was the value of the golden mean. As divine and historian he kept to the middle way, and this by conviction not fear. His great sorrow was that during his lifetime moderation, and the tolerance that must always accompany it, was so nearly lost. In a preface he wrote to a collection of parliamentary speeches published in 1654 with the title *Ephemeris Parliamentaria*, he says: 'What by general error is falsely told of the Jews, that they are always crook-backed, warped, and bowed to the right or to the left; so hard it will be to find a straight, upright, and unbiased historian.' As for the theological arguments of his day, the anonymous biographer tells us: 'He was wont to call those controversies concerning episcopacy, and the new-invented arguments against the Church of England, with the answers and refutation thereof, ἡμερόβια, things of a day's life, and of no permanency; the Church being built upon a rock, as no storms could shake or move it, so needed it not any defences of art or learning; being of the same mind with Sir Henry Wotton, *Disputandi pruritus, scabies ecclesiae.*'

These disputes of his neighbours, however, never soured him. 'Indeed,' says the same anonymous biographer, 'the grace that was supereminent in the good doctor was charity.'

230

To illustrate this we have the story he uses to counsel men to accept with good grace the government of their country, even if it is not of their own choosing. It relates that when Lady Katherine Brandon, Duchess of Suffolk, along with other ladies present at a banquet with her, was invited to choose the gentleman she loved best, but *not* her husband, she surprised the company by choosing Stephen Gardiner, though every one knew she hated the man. Taking him by the hand she said:

'If I may not sit down with him whom I love best, I have chosen him I love worst.'

After telling this story Fuller confesses that 'Not to dissemble in the sight of God and man,' he preferred the old order, but if 'denied my first desire to live under that Church-government I best affected, I will contentedly conform to the Presbyterian Government, and endeavour to deport myself quietly and comformably under the same.'

The fanaticism found in the Church of Fuller's day was due to a variety of causes. One of them was that the clergy were fighting a losing battle and knew it. Ever since the Reformation there had been a trend towards the secularization of society, which involved the loss of much of the political power of the clergy. Fuller saw this, and accepted it with his usual good humour, or should we say with his ingrained English optimism and faculty for evading what would be disconcerting if faced? The canon law, he said, must now say to the common law: 'By your leave, sir,' before proceeding to a new venture. Most of the clergy were not so easily reconciled to their altered status, and it is hardly surprising that many of the bishops, as they looked backward wistfully towards pre-Reformation days, lost their Protestant fervour, while others pushed it to extremes. In 1641 we find Lord Falkland declaring that he knew bishops who were papists at heart, and were only held in the Church of England by their fifteen hundred a year. Whether this was true or false, it is certain that few of the bishops of Charles I, whether reactionary or progressive, were as easy in their minds about the future as Fuller appears to have been.

After the king's death, most of the laity were lost in a wilderness of disillusionment and frustration. Few found the Commonwealth all they had hoped it would be. For better or worse, Church and State were still tied to each other. Under Tudor and Stuart sovereigns, priestly power and regal power had been so interdependent that little was left of the one when the other was destroyed, and when the Church associated with the king was seen to be in ruins, the power that had displaced the Crown was expected to provide a new one.

Fuller was curiously detached from these problems that exercised the public mind of his generation. He acquitted himself well in such controversies as he could not avoid, but he had no love for them. He was designed by nature not 'for contentions, but for study and quietness.' This, as we have seen, was made evident to every one in his dispute with Heylyn, where he showed so plainly that he did not speak the same language as most of the professionally-minded church-men of his day, and could work up no enthusiasm for their battles. Like Izaak Walton, Sir Thomas Browne, Sir William Dugdale, and others who lived their own lives in their own ways, in spite of all distractions, he saw contemporary events against a larger background than that of the present. And it is worthy of note that it is these quieter men, not the contentious clerics, whom posterity has most delighted to honour. It was these men who proved that they had overcome in their own souls the world, the flesh, and the devil, and kept the lamp of faith burning with a flame steady enough to give light and assurance. 'Study to be quiet' was Izaak Walton's motto.

Fuller, obviously, could never renounce the world as completely as Walton did. Only part of his mind could be withdrawn. He was in the world to the extent of being one of its most fashionable preachers, one of its most popular authors, one of its most acceptable social figures. Could a man be all these things and still possess his soul in peace as more retiring men did? It seems improbable, yet it is certain that this friendly, amusing creature, who, when in company, told his tales and aired his learning with such relish, was in fact a being apart, whose richest hours were spent in the solitude of his own study. The anonymous biographer says: 'As to his books, which we usually call the issue of the brain, he was more than fond, totally abandoning and forsaking all things to follow them.'

It was from the private side of his life that he derived the strength that enabled him to maintain his stability and integrity throughout the civil wars. It was to him what night, with its sleep, is to day, with its restless activity; with the added force that this dreaming man in him belonged to his conscious as well as to his subconscious self. There was a Jacques and even a Hamlet in him. Ever since he lay on the banks of the Nene as a boy and of the Cam as a stripling he had found some of his purest pleasures—and how much of our strength comes to us from happiness!—in the thoughts that formed in his head unbidden and unexpected. Perhaps it was unfortunate that he had never had the leisure to cultivate the soil of his contemplative mind as he might have done, laying it out like a garden and tending its growth. The few years at Broadwindsor were probably the only years in his life when he had enjoyed freedom from anxiety and from the pressure of society. Leisure in a positive sense he never did know. He took no exercise except under compulsion until the Civil War forced him to wander from place to place, and then his natural curiosity made him explore each town and village he passed through for memorials and curiosities. Afterwards his only exercise was in his rides from Waltham or Cranford to London. If compelled to walk, the anonymous biographer tells us, it was a question which went fastest, his head or his feet. Lack of exercise probably accounted for his great bulk. Yet he was always healthy, probably because he was always a temperate, even an abstemious man. He ate only two meals a day and could never be persuaded to touch any but the plainest food. He drank little, did not smoke, and indeed his only vice was this excessive addiction to work.

In *The Holy State* we are told of the Lady Paula that she 'lived in an age which was, as I may say, in the knuckle and bending betwixt the primitive times and superstition, popery being then a-hatching.' Similarly Fuller lived in the knuckle and bending betwixt superstition and science, and but for the vigour of his personal life he might have been broken by it. He knew the value of his own exuberant personality both for himself and for others. It was his greatest asset. But there were times when he—like Chesterton and Johnson—worked it to excess. The greater our interest in Church history, for example, the less satisfactory must Fuller's great folio be to us. We are always far more conscious of him than we are of what he is discussing. But there are three of his books in which this personal note, through which he expressed his most characteristic wisdom, can be enjoyed without reservation. These are the two volumes of *Good Thoughts*, published in 1645 and 1647 respectively, and *Mixt Contemplations*, published in 1660. In these, with no obligations to history, divinity, or any other subject with standards of its own, he can gambol as he pleases while the reader sits back to enjoy the fun. And at the end of it, as the smile disappears from his lips, that same reader is conscious of the glow that comes only from contact with a man of rich humanity, clear of head and sound of heart. So these occasional writings mean a great deal to those who value Fuller for his own sake.

Incidentally, these minor works are useful reminders that all the normal pleasures of life do not necessarily come to an end with the outbreak of war. There are, of course, other such reminders. Sir Thomas Browne's *Religio Medici* came out in the very year of the Great Rebellion, 1642. And after reading one of Fuller's collections of *Good Thoughts* we may feel exactly as Sir Kenelm Digby felt after reading the *Religio Medici*. Writing to Lord Dorset, who had recommended the book to him soon after its publication, Sir Kenelm said: 'This good-natured creature [the book] I could easily persuade to be my bedfellow, and to wake with me as long as I had any edge to entertain myself with the delights I sucked from so noble a conversation. And truly, my lord, I closed not my eyes till I had enriched myself with, or at least exactly surveyed, all the treasures that are lapped up in the folds of these few sheets.'

CRANFORD CHURCH, MIDDLESEX

In times of national stress it is often—though not always—the lookers-on who see most of the game and assess most judiciously its points. Perhaps even where participants have the advantage it will be found that they are men who have the power to withdraw at least part of the time in order that they may survey the scene from a distance—men with mental and spiritual cottages-in-the-country, as it were, in the form of interests other than those of their everyday pursuits. We may think of Winston Churchill with his painting, Viscount Grey with his birds, and many others. It is indeed a national characteristic that we restore ourselves as professionals by what we do as amateurs. All successful nations believe that important things are worth doing well. But we English are remarkable in that we think so many things worth doing badly. We are a race of amateurs, and in this twentieth-century world, when the professionalism of a planned society tends to cut out the amateur, it may be worth our while to reflect on how much we run the risk of losing. Fuller, at all events, was pre-eminently an amateur. He dabbled in many arts, and if in consequence his work was less technically skilled than it might have been, his character was the more mature. This ripeness is reflected in his miscellaneous writings, in which we hear the man talking as he must have talked among his friends—such friends as Izaak Walton, whose *Compleat Angler* came out in 1653, or Henry Lawes, whose father had been vicar-general of Salisbury Cathedral. Henry had been court musician to Charles I, and wrote the coronation anthem for Charles II.

To Henry Lawes's collection, *Ayres and Dialogues for one, two, and three Voyces*, published in the same year as Walton's *Compleat Angler*, he contributed a Latin poem, and in glancing through this volume it is pleasant to note that in spite of all that had happened since the carefree Cambridge days of the twenties and thirties, many who contributed to such college collections as *Rex Redux* are represented. The cultured world of Fuller's day was small, and it was inclined to do what cultured circles always do—to form itself into a clique and shut out the rest. There is nothing new about the 'closed-shop' attitude either in art or in industry, and

I

however wrong the spirit behind it may be, it has its rewards of good fellowship, and congenial sharing of interests and pleasures. Clubs have their place as well as societies. Fuller, again like Dr. Johnson, was a clubbable man.

Perhaps the most interesting to the historian of several passages in praise of music in Fuller is the one in the *Worthies* where, in writing of Hooker, he says: 'Right glad I am that when music was lately shut out of our churches (on what default of hers I dare not to enquire), it hath since been harboured and welcomed in the halls, parlours, and chambers of the primest persons of this nation. Sure I am it could not enter into my head to surmise that music would have been so much discouraged by such who turned our kingdom into a commonwealth, seeing they prided themselves in the arms thereof, an impaled harp being the moiety of the same.' He thanked God that he had lived to see music restored since the nation came 'into right tune.' And while thinking of music it is interesting to find this man who had spent most of his life in pastoral, riverside country—Northamptonshire, Cambridge, Waltham Abbey, a man who had nothing of the mountaineer in his temperament, who had little interest in grandeur of any kind, or of the pride and stubbornness that it seems to engender, linking the sweetness of music with the kind of country that had held him practically all his life. In the last dialogue of the *Cause and Cure of a Wounded Conscience*, he says: 'Music is sweetest near or over rivers, where the echo thereof is best rebounded by the water. Praise for pensiveness, thanks for tears, and blessing God over the floods of affliction, makes the most melodious music in the ear of heaven.'

This pensive and reflective side of Fuller's mind, by which he could detach himself from the bustle and cruelty of the age he lived through, and by which he maintained moderation, produced some of his soundest observations. There are times when his relation to the contemporary scene is similar to that of a man whose house stands in a market square, and who, with the familiar objects of his own room about him—his books, his chairs, his lamp, his table—looks through his window on the jostling crowd outside, where men elbow and push their way, intent upon business that has no interest for him. The quiet assurance of his reflective writing must have been a comfort to the more nervous among his readers. As often as not he dispels their fears with an amusing story, like the one about the ape and the child, apparently Cromwell,[1] which Swift seems to have made use of for the *Voyage to Brobdingnag*: 'A careless maid, which attended a gentleman's child, fell asleep whilst the rest of the family were at church; an ape, taking the child out of the cradle, carried it to the roof of the house, and there (according to his rude manner) fell a dancing and dandling thereof, down head, up heels, as it happened.

'The father of the child, returning with his family from the church, commented with his own eyes on his child's sad condition. Bemoan he might, help it he could not. Dangerous to shoot the ape where the bullet might hit the babe; all fall to their prayers as their last and best refuge, that the innocent child (whose precipice they suspected) might be preserved.

'But when the ape was well wearied with his own activity, he fairly went down, and formally laid the child where he found it, in the cradle.

'Fanatics have pleased their fancies these late years with turning and tossing and tumbling of religion, upward and downward, and backward and forward; they have cast and contrived it into a hundred antic postures of their own imagining. However, it is now to be hoped, that after they have tired themselves out with doing of nothing, but only trying and tampering this and that way to no purpose, they may at last return and leave religion in the same condition wherein they found it.'

Fuller read what was in men's minds because he knew what was in their hearts. He understood human motives. Some of the men he caught and sketched for us in these miscellaneous writings are specially interesting because they show that the wars of the seventeenth century threw up exactly

---

[1] *Mixt Contemplations in Better Times*, pt. ii, xlvi: 'Some alive will be deposed for the truth of this strange incident, though I forbear the naming of place or persons.'

the same types as those of the twentieth.   There were the
new rich:

'England hath been tossed with a hurricane of a civil war.
Some men are said to have gotten great wealth thereby.
But it is an ill heap when men grow rich *per saltum*, taking
their rise from the miseries of a land. . . .   Can their pelf
prosper, not got by valour or industry, but deceit? . . .   Nor
will it prove happy, it being to be feared, that such who have
been enriched with other men's ruins will be ruined by their
own riches.'

There was the new pride:

'There is a disease of infants . . . called the rickets;
wherein the head waxeth too great, whilst the legs and lower
parts wain too little. . . .   Have not many nowadays the
same sickness in their souls? their heads swelling to a vast
proportion and they wonderfully enabled with knowledge to
discourse?'

There was the new lawlessness:

'Some sixty years since, in the university of Cambridge, it
was solemnly debated betwixt the heads, to debar young
scholars of that liberty allowed them in Christmas, as incon-
sistent with the discipline of students.   But some grave
governors maintained the good use thereof, because thereby
in twelve days they may more discover the dispositions of
scholars than in twelve months before.   That is a vigilant
virtue indeed, which would be early up at prayers and study,
when all authority to punish lay asleep.

'Vice, these late years, hath kept open house in England.
Welcome all comers without any examination.   No penance
for the adulterer, stocks for the drunkard, whip for the petty
larcener, brand for the felon, gallows for the murderer.

'God all this time tries us as he did Hezekiah, that he
might know all that is in our hearts.   Such as now are chaste,
sober, just, true, show themselves acted with a higher principle of piety than the bare avoiding of punishment.'

He saw through every kind of pretence, and must himself
have been as free from humbug as it is given to mere mortals
to be.   Nevertheless he had his peculiar little prejudices.
The prejudice against women that we suspected earlier seems

to have been well rooted. It produces several amusing passages. In one of his 'Meditations' he considers whether it is advisable for husbands to say their private prayers in the presence of their wives. He decides that it is not: 'It is not meet she should know all the secret bosom sins of him in whose bosom she lieth. Perchance being now offended for not hearing her husband's prayers, she would be more offended if she heard them.' Satan, he is quite sure, works through women.

It may seem odd when we first notice it that so many of Fuller's most amusing passages are with reference to prayer. This was certainly not due to any lack of sincerity in him. It rose rather from the natural and simple nature of his relationship with God, and if some of his comments seem naïve, others take us to the very heart of this good man's religion. Of these the most moving, when we think of it along with all the wild and incoherent petitioning of some of his contemporaries, is one in defence of set prayers:

'A good prayer is not like a stratagem in war, to be used but once. No, the oftener the better. . . . Despair not then thou simple soul, who hast no exchange of raiment, whose prayers cannot appear every day at heaven's court in new clothes. Thou mayest be as good a subject, though not so great a gallant, coming always in the same suit. Yea, perchance the very same which was thy father's and grand-father's before thee (a well-composed prayer is a good heir-loom in a family, and may hereditarily be descended to many generations), but know thy comfort, thy prayer is well known to heaven, to which it is a constant customer. Only add new, or new degrees of old affections thereunto, and it will be acceptable to God thus repaired, as if new erected.' [1]

This serenity and detachment of Fuller inevitably brought him increasing prominence as the high-falutin notions— the grandiose schemes for a new heaven and a new earth— of the upstarts were one by one discredited. This man, they saw, had the real substance of life in him. So as soon as Cromwell's ban on Royalist preachers was altered to exclude not all, but only political offenders, Fuller was again

---

[1] *Good Thoughts in Worse Times:* 'Meditations on all kinds of Prayers,' xii.

found in the London pulpits, preaching the same old doctrine to congregations as large and enthusiastic as ever, and nothing is more certain than that what took Fuller back into the forefront of public life was the people's recognition of the grace and integrity of his private life. Bailey said he must have been one of the first of the old Cavalier parsons to return to the city. He had, of course, an advantage in holding a living so near to London. Most of the Royalist clergy were still serving as chaplains in country houses. Many who had once been eminent were now practically forgotten, and even if known were no longer welcomed because they had got into the habit of airing their grievances on every possible occasion. It was often said of the Royalist parsons that they preached Charles martyred more often than Christ crucified.

If we glance at a remark made by Evelyn some time in 1650 we understand how London gentlemen of the better sort must have felt to see Fuller back again. Evelyn says that he had wandered into various churches and found the pulpits 'full of novices and novelties.' No doubt to such as Evelyn the new men seemed raw and inexperienced: their self-confidence the result of ignorance rather than knowledge. Perhaps the old men, on the other hand, seemed to be talking from a lost world, with voices that sounded like far-away echoes. Both have sounded thus to those who have lived through the revolution of the twentieth century, so we can imagine how they must have sounded to those who had lived through that of the seventeenth. With this in mind it is good to find that Fuller was still speaking with a living voice. As a shrewd observer he would note the changes, and as an historian he would be able to take the measure of them. The courtiers had gone. If the old nobility were still to be found, they were now impoverished. In their place were the new merchants, the men who were to re-establish the country's greatness. Fuller would have met several of them at Waltham Abbey, for not a few had built houses on the borders of the old royal forest. He had dedicated one of his books to Lady Roe, the wife of Sir Thomas Roe, one of the first of the new age. By comparing these new merchants with such men as Sir Francis Drake and Sir Walter Raleigh, the men who built up England in the previous century by more adventurous methods, about whom he had heard from those who had known them personally, he would see the trend of life, and no doubt be able to interpret it—encouraging what he saw good in it, and criticizing the whole constructively—to his influential congregations.

The first evidence we have of Fuller's reappearance in a London pulpit is in a vestry minute of St. Clement's, Clement's Lane, near King William Street, which he served as lecturer:

'The 5th of September 1651. Item, Whereas it was then declared that Mr. Thomas Fuller, minister, did resolve, according to his promise, to preach his weekly lecture in the parish church of St. Clement's: the persons then present did give their free consent that he should preach, and that the churchwardens should provide candles and other necessaries for the said lecture upon the account of the parish. And that the friends and auditors of the said Mr. Fuller may be accomodated with convenient pew-room, it was then ordered that the present churchwardens should cause to be made two decent and necessary pews of the two seats in the chancel where the youths of the parish do now sit.'

Archdeacon Churton, who copied this minute into an edition of Bishop Pearson's works, adds that it refers to Thomas Fuller, 'the jester,' and suggests that it was his droll, quaint way of preaching that made him popular. It was more than that.

Wherever we meet Fuller we always find him surrounded by personal friends, and in the records of St. Clement's we read names that are already familiar to us from earlier associations. There was Dr. Hamey, for example, a very good friend in the old Chelsea days, when Fuller was spending so much of his time in the Danvers household. Hamey has a place in the *Worthies*. As friendship meant so much to Fuller, it is not surprising to find a characteristic warning against the perils and discomforts of solitude in one of his published sermons first preached at St. Clement's. He says: 'Christ sent always His disciples by twos. . . . And this perchance was one reason why Christ, in the choice of His apostles and disciples, pitched on an even number—twelve of the one and seventy of the other—that if He should have occasion to subdivide them they should fall out into even couples, and no odd one lack a companion.'

How these London congregations must have enjoyed having their old friend back again! And how good some of his sallies are! There was one against the modern ranters who so rebelled against the old ordinances that they rejected even the old morality: 'Opposite are they,' said Fuller, 'to the man out of whom the unclean spirit being gone, "returned to an house swept and garnished," whereas these, leaving an house swept and garnished, return to the unclean spirit.' Warning them against being too complacent under the new order, he says: 'Pomp may be more in kingdoms, Pride may be as much in commonwealths.'

In preparing these Commonwealth sermons for publication he made a number of cuts, understanding by this time, better than earlier, the difference between the written and the spoken word. Lest any one should be disappointed by the pruning he says: 'Let them know that the hand, when the fist is closed together, is the same with the same hand when the fingers were stretched forth and palm thereof expanded.' The man was incurable!

CHAPTER XVI

THE GREAT TOM FULLER

'5th Jan. 1661. Home all the morning. Several people came to me about business, among others the great Tom Fuller, who came to desire a kindness for a friend of his who hath a mind to go to Jamaica with these two ships that are going, which I promised to do.'

PEPYS.

WE think of the Church of England of the eighteenth and nineteenth centuries, rather than that of the seventeenth, as a fashionable institution. But its social importance was considerable even in Fuller's time. Its divines, with the astuteness of their kind, were already making up socially for what they had lost politically. And the laity were nowhere prouder than in the place where they ought to have been most humble. You may remember how Pepys puffed himself out when he came into possession of a pew. When he first stepped into it he had precisely the same emotion as when he first stepped forth as a Cavalier, of which occasion he says: 'This day I first began to go forth in my coate and sword, as the manner now among gentlemen is.' That day he heard Dr. Fuller preach, and being so pleased with himself and the world, he recorded the fact approvingly. So Parson Fuller to Pepys was 'the great Tom Fuller.'

It is true that there were a few irreverent persons who refused to submit to the influence of these great city preachers. Even Stephen Marshall, to whose preaching John Cleveland referred in the lines:

> Or roar like Marshall, that Geneva bull,
> Hell and Damnation a pulpit full,[1]

could not impress Dorothy Osborne, who wrote refreshingly to Sir William Temple: 'Would you believe that I had the grace to go to hear a sermon upon a week day? In earnest, 'tis true; and Mr. Marshall was the man that preached, but never anybody was so defeated. He is so famed that I expected rare things of him, and seriously I listened to him

---

[1] *Poems*, p. 147. 'The Rebel Scot.'

as if he had been St. Paul; and what do you think he told us?
Why, that if there were no kings, no queens, no lords, no ladies,
nor gentlemen, nor gentlewomen, in the world, 'twould be
no loss at all to God Almighty. . . . I had the most ado to look
soberly enough for the place I was in that ever I had in my life.'

Dorothy Osborne would have found Fuller more to her
taste; but even he on one occasion disappointed Pepys, whose
diary entry for the 12th May 1661 runs: 'At the Savoy heard
Dr. Fuller preach upon David's words, "I will wait with
patience all the days of my appointed time until my change
comes"; but methought it was a poor dry sermon. And I
am afraid my former high esteem of his preaching was more
out of opinion than judgment.' This, however, we need
hardly take seriously. Fuller's popularity as a preacher is
not in doubt, and his was not a cheap success. He had never
flattered his congregations, or told them only what they
wanted to hear. Yet in spite of this they had called for him
again at the first opportunity.

But while their desire for him is not to be doubted, we
cannot help wondering how he himself felt about returning to
London—whether he really wished to be in the public eye
again. He had experienced a remarkable success at the
Savoy before the war, and had seen something of the hollowness of these city reputations—luminous bubbles that
floated on the air of popular favour but burst with the first
prick of adversity. He had become increasingly aware of the
difference between himself and both the Royalists on the
right and the Parliamentarians on the left. As the years had
passed he had felt himself being drawn closer and closer to
scholars, writers, and craftsmen who worked at their callings
in their own way and at their own time. These, he may have
felt, were the men who left permanent memorials. And if
only he could have the leisure he craved, it was most certainly within his power to make his *Worthies of England* even
better than his *Church History*, which, in spite of what the
more exacting scholars had said about it, had already given
him a considerable reputation. Again, the values of this
crude Cromwellian world were false to him. If he had been
a man of the prophetic type—burning with the fire of

reforming zeal—the divergence might have been a challenge. But he had never been passionate, or inspired, or capable of sufficient righteous indignation to make him effective as a reformer. With these things in mind, it does seem doubtful whether he can ever have desired a place in the London of the fifties in the way he had undoubtedly desired one in that of the thirties. The Tom Fuller of St. Clement's was an older and a wiser man than the Tom Fuller of St. Mary Savoy. But the greatness he may not have sought was inescapable. And when invited, he would certainly feel it his duty, if not his pleasure, to accept. Had he not said, 'the historian must not devour the divine in me'? Moreover, he still loved the people. His weariness, as he admitted, was for the men of his own profession who went about 'sowing of schism, setting of errors, and spreading faction, whilst our Savour "went about doing good."'

As far as we know, in conducting services he conformed to the Commonwealth rules where these were strictly enforced, though we may be sure that he would take advantage of any liberties allowed. These may have been greater than is commonly thought. It is quite possible that he used the Prayer Book service at Waltham Abbey. Where the local ecclesiastical boards raised no objection, it frequently did remain in use. In London there seems to have been far more tolerance than in most parts of the country. It is true that in the eastern counties, where Puritanism was so strong, the use of the liturgy was almost unknown; but in the corner of Essex near London there was a pocket of loyalty to the Prayer Book. In 1649 we find the people of Woodford, a few miles across the forest from Fuller's Waltham Abbey, making a collection for the chaplains and servants of the king, forty of whom, it was stated, were in great distress. As Waltham Forest was an ancient royal hunting ground it had many Royalists and their dependants. This part of the county, therefore, tended to have a different political outlook from that of the weaving towns of North Essex, with their centre in Colchester.

Cromwell himself, we must remember, was always a supporter of religious toleration and had no bitterness against the Church as such. 'I had rather that Mahommedism were permitted amongst us than that one of God's children should be persecuted,' he said. He disliked Laudians because they were Royalists, not because they were churchmen. At heart he was an English country gentleman, and Lathbury is quoted by Bailey as saying in the *History of English Episcopacy* (p. 295) that 'in London the presence and influence of the Protector were sufficient to protect the clergy; but in the country the letter of the declaration against the Common Prayer was strictly observed.'

Fuller's personal attitude is best seen in the amusing story of his interview with the 'triers,' the men who came to examine him in conformity. When one of them raised a delicate point, hoping to catch him, he said:

'Sir, you may observe that I am a pretty corpulent man, and I am to go through a passage that is very strait: I beg you would be so good as to give me a shove and help me through.'

A man with that approach was not likely to get into much trouble of his own making, but, in the winter of 1655, something happened that compelled Cromwell to tighten restrictions on the Royalist clergy. This was the rising in the west under John Penruddock, in which Fuller's brother-in-law, Hugh Grove, was involved.[1] Here, as so often elsewhere when reports came in of stirrings of discontent, it was found that the Cavalier parsons were behind the rebels. But even after this, Cromwell was still inclined to allow as much liberty to the clergy as was consistent with government security— even to those who were known to have Royalist sympathies. The edict that followed was framed primarily to check schoolmasters, private tutors, and chaplains, because these were raising another generation of Royalists. It was laid down that in future no 'delinquents' were to keep such persons, or allow their children to be taught by them. The hardship resulting from this decree can be imagined when we reflect that most of the Royalist clergy were employed in one or more of these capacities, and had no other means of support. There are references in Evelyn which show how bitterly this edict was felt by the most loyal adherents of the

[1] See pp. 77–8.

old Church. On Fuller himself it would have little effect. The anonymous biographer says: 'The good doctor forbore not to preach as he did before; the convincing power either of his doctrine or his worth defending and keeping him out of the hands of that unreasonable man, Cromwell.'

Three years later, early in 1658, another living fell into the doctor's lap, thrown into that capacious receptacle by Lord Berkeley, the nobleman to whom he had referred in one of the dedications to the *Church History* as 'the paramount Maecenas of my studies.' It was the living of Cranford in Middlesex, where his church, recently restored, stands to-day in a public park, formerly the grounds of Cranford House, a seat of the Berkeleys, though his parish is rapidly being converted into a built-up area as part of the borough of Heston and Isleworth. In the following August the old Lord Berkeley died, and was succeeded by his son, a scholar and devout churchman, one of the founders of the Royal Society and a benefactor to Sion College, which Fuller used so freely. He had a seat, Durdans, near Epsom, mentioned by Pepys, who said that he had been very merry there when a little boy. But he spent much of his time at Cranford.

On moving to his new home, Fuller resigned his Waltham living, and there is a curious tradition in the abbey town that he was the better pleased to do so because of strained relations between himself and his patron, the Earl of Carlisle. Misunderstandings are so rare in Fuller's life that we may be forgiven if we are eager to know the cause of this one. Thereby hangs a tale. It is said that Fuller once recited some witty verses on a scold to the earl, who was so amused that he asked for a copy of them. For once Fuller's wit, sharpened by his ingrained hostility towards women—real or jocular— got the better of him. 'What need of that, my lord?' he replied, 'you have the original.' The remark, it appears— doubtless because it was appropriate—was never forgiven.

Cranford had several features in common with Waltham. It was approximately the same distance from London; it was the gift of a wealthy patron who was a friend of many years' standing;[1] it was near a great open space. At Waltham

---

[1] Fuller had first preached at Durdans years previously.

the open space had been a forest, at Cranford it was a common, and both were notorious haunts of highwaymen and other disreputable characters. The churches, however, were different. St. Dunstan's, Cranford, must have seemed small to him after the great abbey church at Waltham. It was, in fact, the smallest church he had ever had, and the living, though adequate financially, must surely have been accepted in the hope of affording greater leisure for writing. At the same time Cranford had the kind of tradition he had rejoiced in at St. Bene't's and at St. Mary Savoy. There had been a church on the site, with a resident priest, when Domesday Book was compiled in 1086. Afterwards this ancient building was the chapel of the Knights Templars, and remained such until the order was suppressed in 1310. Since then, though inconveniently placed, because at a distance from most of the houses, it had served as the parish church of what long remained a small and rural village.

In these circumstances his life at Cranford must have been similar in many ways—though more leisurely—to what it had been at Waltham until, as the Commonwealth passed into the shadows, the rising hopes of the Royalists again transformed the London scene to his advantage.

When Cromwell died in September 1658 it was clear to Fuller's friends that the gathering fire of the doctor's renown was ready to break into flame. His *Andronicus* had given him a vogue among the exiled Royalists in Holland; his return to the London pulpits had brought him before their friends at home. Nevertheless, his startling political intervention in the winter of 1659-60 was as unexpected as it was timely. This dramatic event came in the form of a pamphlet, published in January or February 1660, entitled *An Alarm to the Counties of England and Wales*, which, as to authorship, was described mysteriously as the work of 'A Lover of his Native Land.' A second printing followed quickly, but only with the third was the author's name disclosed. The avowed object of the work was to rouse the people of England to demand the immediate election of a free Parliament, and its special significance was that it appeared only a few days before General Monk's famous letter of the

11th February, declaring for the same need. Practical as ever, Fuller stated in his alarum that the increasing miseries of the land were due to two causes. The first was the decrease of trading; the second the increase of taxation, 'so that every hour the burden groweth weightier, and the back of our nation the weaker to support it.' This was not perhaps the kind of theme to be expected from a Cavalier parson. But he was sound enough in his main submissions. He enlarged on the unemployment in the old weaving towns and the insecurity of the trade routes at sea. And he got in many shrewd digs at those who were aggravating the national troubles. There were the new 'Grandees, greatened by the times,' who were impoverishing the country by depositing their money in foreign banks: 'The increase of taxes must inevitably cause the ruin of our nation: for though still there be wealthy men left (as they show it in their cowardice, and fear to engage for the general good), yet they grow thinner every day, whilst such as are left no root of their own, rather than they will wither will turn suckers on the stock of others. So that the greatest happiness rich men promise to themselves, is only to be last devoured, though the comfort of the lateness will not countervail the sadness of the certainty of their destruction.'

The new Parliament that Fuller called for must be full as well as free—'no cripple, but entire and complete in all the members thereof. Our land hath lately groaned under the most grievous monopoly as ever was, or can be, when a handful of men have grasped to themselves the representing of a whole (not to say three) nation, most of them being but Burgesses, who though equal in votes, are not equal in their representation with the Knights of the Shires. . . . That what pertaineth to all should be handled by all is a truth so clear and strong, that they must offer a rape to their own reason that deny it.'

The men now needed by the nation, he declared, were genuinely godly and well-affected men, not such as assumed these virtues only by 'the canting language of the times'; they were men of estates, since, he said, such 'will be tender in taxing others, as striking them through themselves, whilst such who bear nothing care not how much they burden others, as if paying were as easy as voting, and money as free as words.' They should also be men of spirit, but not such as stood to gain by the continuance of the army. Above all, they should be 'men of moderation, a quality not opposed to diligence, but to violence, not unacting men, but regulating their activity.'

This remarkable pamphlet was published along with several others, in the manner of the age, by John Williams, Fuller's usual publisher and by this time a well tried friend, under the title *A Happy Handful, or Green Hopes in the Blade.* It bore as its motto the doctor's favourite text: 'Seek peace and follow after it,' and the dedicatory epistle, though signed by the publisher, reads like Fuller's work. It was addressed to General Monk, the man expected by the writers to deliver the nation from its present rulers.

Fuller's association with Monk at this critical turning explains much. If Coleridge had known his history better he might have refrained from his ridiculous outburst against Fuller for writing somewhat extravagantly—perhaps foolishly —in praise of Monk. 'I remember,' says Coleridge, 'no other instance of flattery in this no less wise than witty, and (for one speck in a luminary does not forfeit the name) not less honest than liberal writer, though liberal and sensible to a degree unprecedented in his age, and unparalleled. . . . These paragraphs, however, form a glaring exception. The flattery is rancid. A more thoroughly worthless wretch than Monk, or of meaner talents could not History furnish where-with to exemplify the caprice of Fortune; or shall I not rather say the judgment of Providence in righteous scorn by chastisement of a thankless and corrupt nation, bringing in one reptile by the instrumentality of another, a lewd, lazy, mean tyrant by a brainless, avaricious, perjured traitor— and to this hateful ingrate alone Charles II showed himself not ingrate.' Coleridge, it will be seen, himself lacked the virtue of moderation that Fuller was so eloquent in extolling His frequently quoted praise of the doctor, found in several places, is certainly discriminating at times, and illumines the doctor's talent with a flash such as only genius could strike;

but at other times his adulation is stupid with a profundity that mere talent could never encompass. On the whole, Fuller's reputation has suffered more during the last century from the excessive praise of Coleridge than it has from any one else's detraction.

We get a much truer picture of what Monk meant to the London of February 1660 from Pepys, who on the 11th of that month wrote: 'I heard the news of a letter from Monk, who was now gone into the city again, and did resolve to stand for the sudden filling up of the House, and it was very strange how the countenance of men in the Hall was all changed with joy in half an hour's time. So I went up to the lobby, where I saw the Speaker reading of the letter; and after it was read, Sir C. Haselrigge came out very angry, and Billing standing at the door, took him by the arm, and cried: "Thou man, will thy beast carry thee no longer? Thou must fall!" We took coach for the City to Guildhall, where the Hall was full of people, expecting Monk and Lord Mayor to come thither, and all very joyfull. Met Monk coming out of the chamber where he had been with the Mayor and Aldermen, but such a shout I never heard in all my life, crying out, "God bless your Excellence."'

Pepys goes on to describe how there were bonfires along Cheapside, and along the Strand, so that in one place he could count thirty-one, and how, as he went home, all the bells of London were set a-ringing. There were rumps carried on sticks; there was burning and roasting, and drinking to the new House—'The butchers at the May Pole in the Strand,' he says, 'rang a peal with their knives when they were going to sacrifice their rump.'

Fuller himself, in *Mixt Contemplations in Better Times*, mentions this date as a national turning point. Under the inspiration of this rise of the national spirit, and in the faith that 'its old good manners, its old good-humour and its old good-nature' would be restored to it, he collected his reflections on the signs of promise, and again showed himself a shrewd political observer. His old arguments were still there. Moderation was needed as much as ever if the nation were 'safely to digest and concoct her own happiness, that she

may not run from one extreme to another, and excessive joy
prove more destructive to her than grief hath been hitherto.'
And while pleading for moderation he pleaded also for
toleration, particularly in the Church: 'As for other sects . . .
we grudge not that gifts be bestowed upon them.   Let them
have a toleration (and that, I assure you, is a great gift
indeed), and be permitted peacefully and privately to enjoy
their consciences both in opinions and practices.'

He had known eighteen years of political misery; but asked
only that it should be forgotten: 'Let us forget all our
plunderings, sequestrations, injuries offered unto us, or
suffered by us.   The best oil is said to have no taste, i.e.
no tang.   Though we carry a simple and single remembrance
of our losses unto the grave, it being impossible to do otherwise (except we raze the faculty of memory, root and branch,
out of our mind), yet let us not keep any record of them with
the least reflection of revenge.'

Mixt Contemplations in Better Times was dedicated to
Lady Monk, who would be well known to him by repute if not
personally.   She was the daughter of a farrier, who followed
his craft in that part of the Strand which lay in his old parish
of St. Mary Savoy.   Her first husband was another farrier,
named Radford.   She had met Monk while he was a prisoner
in the Tower by serving him there as a sempstress.   All kinds
of disparaging things have been said about Lady Monk.
Pepys and Aubrey were far from complimentary, and there
may have been reason in some of their imputations.   Arthur
Bryant says that Lady Monk, like Lady Suffolk of Audley
End, conducted a profitable business in public offices, 'using
her husband's unique position to demand a "rake-off" from
every aspirant to employment in the state.'[1]   Fuller, like
Pepys, makes it clear that Lady Monk was given to inter-
fering in public affairs, but unlike Pepys he approved.   Or
was it only that his experience with Lady Carlisle had cured
him of rudeness towards women?   'You are eminently
known to have had a finger, yea, an hand, yea, an arm
happily instrumental therein.   God reward you with
honour here, and glory hereafter,' he said of her part in the

---

[1] *Samuel Pepys: the Man in the Making*, p. 109.

Restoration. And evidently he saw no indelicacy in referring to her humble birth, for he reminded her that he 'had the happiness, some sixteen years since, to be minister of that parish wherein your Ladyship had your nativity.'

The social classes were not as far from each other then as they were later, but in any case humble birth was no reproach in Fuller's eyes, and—who knows?—old Clarges, the farrier, may have been as worthy a character, and as widely esteemed, as old Hobson the carrier.

But Lord Berkeley, not Monk, was Fuller's chief patron, and the worthy doctor was not the man to disregard the fact. Berkeley, moreover, was a national figure at this time, and came into still greater prominence in May, when he was one of the six commissioners of the House of Lords sent to The Hague to bring home the king. Fuller was in the earl's retinue, and the anonymous biographer, who is consistently well informed about these last years of the doctor's life, says that Lord Berkeley had arranged for Fuller to preach before His Majesty. This design to bring the witty and learned divine to the notice of a sovereign so well disposed towards the virtues that Fuller had exalted all his life—if not ill disposed towards some of the vices that he had no less consistently condemned—was unhappily frustrated by the necessity of bringing His Majesty to England with the greatest dispatch.

At least four of the six commissioners of the House of Lords, to say nothing of his many friends there from the Commons, were friends of Fuller. Besides Lord Berkeley, they were Viscount Hereford, Lord Brook, and his former parishioner, the Earl of Middlesex of Copt Hall. Edward Montagu, shortly afterwards to become Earl of Sandwich, who was there to assure the king of the loyalty of the Fleet, was a cousin of Fuller's old patron, Edward Montagu of Boughton, and as we glance through the list of those who waited upon Charles on this occasion, we recognize so many of Fuller's patrons among them that we realize at once how auspiciously placed the doctor was at the opening of the new reign.

Pepys, of course, was at The Hague, and on the 17th May 1660 noted that while on his way to pay his respects to the

Queen of Bohemia he met Dr. Fuller, and sent him to a tavern with Mr. Pickering.

When the never-to-be-forgotten day of Restoration, the 29th May, arrived, 'the good doctor,' says the anonymous biographer, 'was so piously fixt as nothing else might presume to intrude upon his raised gladded spirits.' Alas, it was so, and his enthusiasm ran to verse! He composed a poem of forty-two stanzas about this time, twenty-five of which he characteristically ran into the *Worthies* after describing the battle of Worcester. If ever a man took to heart the sacred injunction to 'gather up the fragments that remain, that nothing be lost,' that man was Fuller. There are times, indeed, when he seems to repeat the miracle of filling twelve baskets with the fragments from five barley loaves. But that is by the way. At the end of his poem on the Restoration he had the grace to promise that he would forbear in future: 'And here my Muse craves her own *Nunc Dimittis*, never to make verses more; and because she cannot write on a better, will not write on another occasion, but heartily pray in prose for the happiness of her lord and master.'

Charles would have enjoyed one of Fuller's sermons far more than he could possibly enjoy his poem. Whether it was the poem that delayed too late his expected advancement in the Church or not we cannot discover. Doubtless the speculation is frivolous; but it is a curious fact that in the unseemly scrimmage for ecclesiastical preferments that followed the Restoration Fuller got practically nothing. Perhaps he himself would have explained that by this time he was no longer nimble enough to gain anything in a scramble! He was, however, restored to his prebendal stall in Salisbury Cathedral, and in August 1660, by royal mandate, Cambridge at last conferred on him the degree of Doctor of Divinity, 'as a scholar of integrity and good learning who had been hindered in the due way of proceeding.' But the expected bishopric failed to materialize. Perhaps when he preached at the Savoy on the 12th May 1661—the sermon Pepys thought so little of—taking as his text 'I will wait with patience all the days of my appointed time until my change comes,' he was dropping a hint. For once the astute Samuel may have missed the point. There was, however, one last favour, which the anonymous biographer calls his 'last felicity.' Though he never preached before the king, he was appointed 'Chaplain in Extraordinary' just before his sudden death in 1661. If he had lived a few months longer he would almost certainly have received either Exeter or Worcester. The anonymous biographer says that Lord Berkeley, the queen mother, and the Duchess of Orleans, who visited England that year, urged the appointment and Willmott, in his *Life of Bishop Taylor*, says: 'Who among Jeremy Taylor's contemporaries could prefer an equal claim? Hall, the imaginative and devout, and Ussher, the sagacious and learned, in the same year were called to their crown, without beholding the faintest dawn of the renovation of that Church, which they defended by their talents, and beautified by their lives. Hammond and Fuller enjoyed a clearer prospect; they perished in the hour of victory; henceforward to be numbered with the chosen worthies of England.'

Either Exeter or Worcester would have been a fitting award, and would have provided scope for his great gifts; but looking backward across the history of the Church from this twentieth century, we may feel that the one position for which Fuller was perfectly fitted was not in the west, but at the heart of his beloved London. It is with Nowell and Donne that we see him. He would have made a great Dean of St. Paul's. But it was not to be.

Soon after the Restoration he visited the west country again, calling at Broadwindsor, where he heard John Pinney preach, and after receiving favourable reports of his ministry from old friends in the village, relinquished in Pinney's favour all claim to the living, which he might now have resumed. Exeter also he visited, after fifteen years' absence, and found fewer churches than when he lived there as chaplain to the princess. 'The demolishers,' he remarked, 'can give the clearest account how the plucking down of churches conduceth to the setting up of religion.'

On his return to London early in August he became ill, an unusual experience for him. It was thought that he had caught infection in Salisbury, where fever was rife at the time of his visit.   Dr. Nicholas, Dean of St. Paul's, who had been in Salisbury about the same time as Fuller, fell a victim to the same sickness.   However that may be, on the 12th August it was clear to his family that Fuller was gravely ill; but having promised to preach a marriage sermon that day for a kinsman who was to be married on the 13th, he refused to stay in bed. And here we must allow the anonymous biographer to take up the narrative:

'Being in the pulpit he found himself very ill, so that he was apprehensive of the danger; and therefore before his prayer, addressed himself thus to his congregation:

'"I find myself very ill, but I am resolved by the grace of God to preach this sermon to you here though it be my last."

'A sad presage, and more sadly verified!

'He proceeded in his prayer and sermon very perfectly, till in the middle (never using himself to notes, other than the beginning word of each head or division) he began to falter, but not so much out, but that he quickly recollected himself, and very pertinently concluded.   After he had a while sat down, he was not able to rise again, but was fain to be led down the pulpit stairs by two men into the reading place. He had promised also to christen a child (of a very good friend of his) then in the church, and the parent did earnestly importune him to do it, and the good doctor was as willing as he desiring; but the doctor's son showing him the extreme danger there was of his father, he desisted from his request.

'Much ado there was to persuade the doctor to go home in a sedan; he saying still he should be well by and by, and would go along with them; but at last, finding himself worse and worse, he yielded to go, but not to his old lodgings (which were convenient to him in the Savoy), but to his new one in Covent Garden.'

His friend and parishioner at Cranford, Dr. Scarborough, afterwards chief physician to Charles II, was called; but he was away from London, and Dr. Charlton, another eminent doctor, physician in ordinary to both Charles I and Charles II, came instead.   Dr. Charlton, says the anonymous biographer, 'addressed himself to the recovery of the good doctor. The disease was judged to be a malignant fever, such as then raged everywhere, and was better known by the name of the New disease, which like a plague had swept away a multitude throughout the kingdom.' Blood letting was resorted to, but the paroxysms continued, 'his fever being so fierce and pertinacious, and which resisted all remedies.' Neither the skill of his doctors nor the care of his family could save him. He died on the following Thursday, protesting to the end that he would be well by and by, talking as usual about his books, and constantly asking for pen and ink, because, he said, there was something he wanted to write, and presently he would be strong enough.

When, on the 17 August 1661, his body was carried to Cranford for burial, two hundred of his fellow clergy rode in the cortège, a tribute, says the anonymous biographer, 'scarce to be paralleled.'

CHAPTER XVII

BIOGRAPHER IN BRIEF

'Tis opportune to look back upon old
times and contemplate our forefathers.
SIR THOMAS BROWNE'S *Hydriotaphia.*

WHEN he died at the early age of fifty-three, Fuller had been engaged on *The History of the Worthies of England* for at least seventeen years. This and *The Church History of Britain* had long been in mind as the two great works of his life, and it is sad to reflect that while the *Church History*, which gained only qualified praise, was published in his prime, the *Worthies*, the crowning glory of his learning and industry, did not appear until after his death. It was ready for the printer at the beginning of 1660, if not earlier; but Heylyn's attack on the *Church History* made further revision advisable. Consequently, this enormous folio, a most ambitious undertaking for those days, had to be seen through the press by John Fuller, the doctor's eldest son, afterwards fellow of Sidney-Sussex.

The *Worthies* was designed as a sequel to the work of 'learned Master Camden and painful Master Speed.' They, said Fuller, had described the counties of England as so many rooms in the national house; he would describe the furniture, and do it, he hoped, in such a way as to gain five objects: first, 'some glory to God; secondly, to preserve the memories of the dead; thirdly, to present examples to the living; fourthly, to entertain the reader with delight; and lastly (which I am not ashamed publicly to profess), to procure some honest profit to myself.' In *English Biography before 1700* (p. 238) Mr. D. A. Stauffer reminds us that this is the first considered appearance in England of 'entertainment as well as profit' as a 'legitimate end for biography.' It is probably the first considered appearance of personal profit as a legitimate end for any kind of authorship. In order to achieve the entertainment—and doubtless with the profit equally in view—Fuller introduced many 'pleasant passages,' disarming such criticism as Heylyn's beforehand by the frankness of his admission that he had introduced, not as meat, but as condiment,' a generous number of anecdotes, so that if the reader did not leave the book '*religiosior* or *doctior* —with more piety or learning,' he would at least depart '*jucundior*—with more pleasure and lawful delight.' Legitimate or not, it was as well to state in that apparently ingenuous fashion that entertainment was one of his objects, though he knew full well that he could no more stop joking than the average parson can stop preaching.

The plan of the work was to describe each county under such regular headings as Boundaries, Buildings, Natural Commodities, Manufactures, Wonders, Battles, Proverbs, and so forth, followed by short biographies of all its most eminent natives, and these last, of course, form the most important section. The arrangement was orderly, and on the whole it was followed with care, though in value the various subsidiary sections are naturally unequal. Most of the proverbs, for example, are from Heywood, so, however interesting in themselves, Fuller cannot take much credit for them. But even while ostensibly writing of proverbs he slips in an amazing amount of curious and unexpected information, particularly in the London section. For example, after quoting 'He is only fit for Ruffian's Hall,' he says: 'A ruffian is the same with a swaggerer, so called because endeavouring to make that side to swag or weigh down, whereon he engageth. The same also with swash-buckler, for swashing, or making a noise on bucklers.' We then learn that West Smithfield, by this time a horse market, was formerly called Ruffian's Hall, because it was the favourite resort of those who met 'to try masteries with sword and buckler.'

In the same section, after writing of cockneys that they are Londoners born within sound of Bow Bell, commonly laughed at by country folk for their ignorance of nature, he greatly improves the lesson by adding: 'One merrily persuaded a she-citizen, that, seeing malt did not grow, the good housewives in the country did spin it.

'"I knew as much," said the Cockney, "for one may see the threads hang out at the ends."'

The cockney, happily, is still with us; but now that less useful and adaptable members have been eliminated from the English family, a valuable, if minor, attribute of Fuller's work is that in it they are preserved for us, drawn from life by the hand that delineated rascals as merrily as worthies. Thus, in the Cumberland section we have moss-troopers, so called because 'dwelling in the mosses, and riding in troops together.' These people dwell, he explains, in the waste land between two kingdoms and obey the laws of neither: 'Their sons are free of the trade by their fathers' copy. . . . They may give for their motto, *Vivitur ex rapto*, stealing from their honest neighbours what sometimes they regain. They are a nest of hornets; strike one, and stir all of them about your ears.'

Most counties had their lawless elements, and Fuller can seldom have failed to note them. In Essex he found the Waltham Blacks, in Devonshire the Gubbings, of whom he writes that though he cannot explain their name it is well known that parts of fish that are of little worth are called gubbings, 'and sure it is they are sensible that the word importeth shame and disgrace.' These west country outlaws lived on the edge of Dartmoor, and rumour had it 'that some two hundred years since, two strumpets being with child, fled hither to hide themselves, to whom certain lewd fellows resorted, and this was their first original. They are a peculiar of their own making, exempt from bishop, arch-deacon, and all authority either ecclesiastical or civil. They live in cots (rather holes than houses) like swine, having all in common, multiplied without marriage into many hundreds.'

As we should expect, half the fascination of the *Worthies* is in the digressions. By this time the doctor had accumu-lated such a store of out-of-the-way knowledge and tales of odd coincidences that his asides had become gloriously unpredictable, if at times no less gloriously irrelevant. We cannot nod while reading Fuller, though he sometimes assumes the bland inconsequence of a dream. Who, for example, while reading about dotterels in Lincolnshire, would expect to be told a tale about apes in India? Yet so it is in Fuller. And the tale is a good one. It relates that the natives catch apes by dressing and undressing a boy in sight of the ape, who, on seeing the clothes left behind, gets into them himself, and when sufficiently entangled is easily caught, the clothes hampering his movements in trying to escape.

The various sections of the *Worthies* are almost equally productive of these miscellaneous delights, and many of them are as useful to the historian and biographer as they are entertaining to the general reader. While writing of leather as one of the manufactures of Middlesex he recalls an anecdote about the great Cecil asking a cobbler to explain to him the process of tanning. He would probably hear this story at Waltham Abbey, because Theobalds, Cecil's home, was near by, and Enfield, the town beyond—in which incidentally, Fuller's widow was living at the time of her death—was a tanning centre. Most of the hides from the London slaughter-houses were tanned there. Another amusing story about Cecil in the *Worthies* relates that his rooms at Theobalds were hung with maps of England. When young men came to ask him to sign their passports, he would examine them in the geography of their own country, and if their knowledge did not satisfy him, bid them stay at home and discover their own land first.

In the same casual way, reflections of seventeenth-century post-war conditions find a place in the record, and these not infrequently resemble comparable conditions in the twentieth century. We learn, for example, that servants were completely out of hand, and would obey their masters only when they thought fit.

In every section of the work we have the same wise, witty, and well informed observer, recording his impressions for our profit and delight. His generalizations are as just as they are lively, and some of them are of considerable historical value. For example, there is the observation that estates in the home counties change hands more frequently than those in the north and west. It is found, either repeated or amplified, under several headings. In the Berkshire

section it runs: 'The lands in Berkshire are very skittish, and
often cast their owners; in Middlesex it is observed that the
gentry seem sojourners rather than inhabitants.' 'Is it not
strange,' he asks after giving a fifteenth-century list, 'that of
the thirty-three forenamed families, not three of them were
extant in the shire one hundred and sixty years after, viz,
anno domini 1593, as appeareth by the alphabetical collection
set forth by Mr. Norden in that year?[1]   I impute the
brevity (as I may term it) of such gentry in this county to the
vicinity of London to them, or rather of them to it; and hope
that worshipful families now fixed in Middlesex will hereafter
have longer continuance.'   When he comes to the north of
England he notes no less vividly the opposite.   Writing of
Northumberland, he is reminded of the fable of the sun and
the wind vying with each other to remove the traveller's
heavier garments.   'The wind made him wrap them closer
about him; whilst the heat of the sun soon made him to part
with them.'   Then he sums up the evidence he has collected
in the various counties by adding: 'This is moralized in our
English gentry.   Such who live southward near London
(which, for the lustre thereof, I may fitly call the sun of our
nation), in the warmth of wealth, and plenty of pleasures,
quickly strip and disrobe themselves of their estates and
inheritance; whilst the gentry living in this county, in the
confines of Scotland, in the wind of war (daily alarmed with
their blustering enemies), buckle their estates (as their
armour) the closer unto them; and since have no less thriftily
defended their patrimony in peace, than formerly they
valiantly maintained it in war.'   The climate he finds to be
the determining factor, for, he says, 'sure I am, that northern
gentry transplanted into the south by marriage, purchase, or
otherwise, do languish and fade away with few generations, whereas southern men on the like occasions removing
northward acquire a settlement in their estates with long
continuance.'

The scientific study of such questions was not to be
expected in the seventeenth century; but if Fuller could not
aspire to be scientific, he was invariably sensible.   Good

[1] In his *Speculum Britanniae*, p. 42.

sense was always prominent in his work, and not least when his own profit was involved. He was much more acute than most topographers in the way he contrived to be frank without being offensive—speaking the truth with humour where he could not speak it with charity. But perhaps the greater marvel from this point of view is in the way he bestows so many garlands without once becoming entangled in their ribbons. But having sat at Camden's feet he had learned the art of saying that none surpassed the county under review, without, however, claiming for that county sole pre-eminence. As he says in the Herefordshire section, Camden 'never expresseth which is first, too politic to adjudge so invidious a pre-eminence. And thus keeping the uppermost seat empty, such competitor counties are allowed leave to put in their several claims.'

Although many of the counties he reviews must have been completely unknown to him, he gives the impression of being familiar with all, even to the point of knowing most of their family jokes. Thus Cornishmen are taunted with having only two oaths, or at most three, and Coggeshall in Essex is 'Jeering Coxhall,' known already for its practical jokes— conscious and unconscious.

As he was writing in the seventeenth century and we are reading him in the twentieth, it is not surprising that some of the counties can hardly be recognized from his descriptions. It is curious, for instance, to hear that the best wheat in England grows in a vale south of Harrow. On the other hand, Colchester, we find, was already famous for oysters, and Manchester for cotton. But cotton was not the principal product of Lancashire. There were others of equal if not greater importance, and among them oats, which must have disappeared from that county, as hops disappeared from Essex, until the twentieth-century revival of agriculture. Alas, in appearance Manchester was to Fuller, as to Leland, a different city from that of the present: 'For when learned Leland on the cost of King Henry the Eighth, with his guide, travelled Lancashire, he called Manchester the fairest and quickest town in this county; and sure I am, it hath lost neither spruceness nor spirits since that time.' Spruceness

and spirits it still possesses; but no one could call it fair
to-day. It still, however, has the bonny lasses that Fuller
found there.

Several of his descriptions of county commodities in the
Worthies are among the most delightful of all Fuller's
writings. And what fun he has with some of them! Writing
of Leicestershire, for instance, he tells us that the county is
called Bean-belly Leicestershire, and that 'those in the
neighbouring counties use to say merrily:

'"Shake a Leicestershire yeoman by the collar, and you
shall hear the beans rattle in his belly."
But those yeomen smile at what is said to rattle in their
bellies whilst they know good silver ringeth in their pockets.'
Moreover, he reminds those who would ridicule the bean-
bellied yeomen of Leicester, 'their plenty argueth the goodness of their ground; for, whereas lean land will serve for
puling peas and faint fetches, it must be strong and fruitful
soil indeed where the masculine beans are produced.' The
flowers of Norwich, described incidentally as 'either a city in
an orchard, or an orchard in a city,' induce such reflections as
'Single flowers are observed much sweeter than the double
ones (poor may be more fragrant in God's nostrils than the
rich); and let florists assign the cause thereof, whether
because the sun doth not so much dry the intricacies of such
flowers which are duplicated.'

His moralizing, sometimes a little obtrusive for modern
taste, is at its mellowest in such passages, and while writing
of honey as one of the natural commodities of Hampshire he
falls into discourse as pleasant as that of Walton himself:
'Honey,' he says, 'is useful for many purposes, especially that
honey which is lowest in any vessel. For it is an old and
true rule, "the best oil is in the top; the best wine in the
middle; and the best honey in the bottom." It openeth
obstructions, cleareth the breast and lights from those
humours which fall from the head, looseneth the belly; with
many other sovereign qualities, too many to be reckoned up
in a winter's day.

'However, we may observe three degrees, or kinds rather,
of honey: *Virgin honey*, which is the purest, of a late swarm

which never bred bees.—2. *Chaste honey*, for so I may term all the rest which is not sophisticated with any addition.—3. *Harlot honey*, as which is adulterated with meal and other trash mingled therewith. Of the first and second sort I understand the counsel of Solomon, "My son, eat honey, for it is good."'

Honey was a subject well suited to one so smooth and sweet of tongue. Indeed, his kindness did occasionally go so far as to bring into suspicion either his judgment or his candour. Though the Pouletts, with their kinsman, the Marquess of Winchester, had done so much to deserve his admiration and gratitude, they must have wondered how others would receive his comment on Sir Robert Naunton's disclosure about the first marquess. In *Fragmenta Regalia* Sir Robert had said that this nobleman acquired, spent, and bequeathed more wealth than any subject since the Conquest. 'Indeed,' remarks Fuller, 'he lived at the time of the dissolution of abbeys, which was the harvest of estates; and it argued idleness if any courtier had his barns empty.'

Of his personal observations on the life of the land in his day perhaps the most interesting is the account of the plough he saw at Stockbridge in Hampshire when a young man. This machine, he tells us, 'might be drawn by dogs, and managed by one man, who would plough in one day well nigh an acre of the light ground in this county. . . . But the project was not taking, beheld rather as pretty than profitable; though in the judgment of wise men this groundwork might have been built upon, and invention much improved by the skilful in mathematics; for I have heard that some politicians are back friends (how justly I know not) to such projects, which (if accomplished) invite the land to a loss, the fewer poor being thereby set a-work; that being the best way of tillage, which employeth most about it, to keep them from stealing and starving; so that it would not be beneficial to the state, might a plough be drawn by butterflies, as which would draw the greater burden on the commonwealth, to devise other ways for the maintenance of the poor.'

But it is of persons that he writes most delightfully. His anecdotes are full of lightning sketches of Elizabethan and

Jacobean characters caught off their guard.   Fuller's subjects are never posed.   There is Lord Hunsdon, for example, who lived in the great house of that name associated with Mary Tudor, near the Hertfordshire-Essex border.   While travelling towards London with a retinue befitting his importance he chanced to meet his neighbour, Mr. Colt of Nether Hall, Roydon, with whom he had a quarrel.   Lord Hunsdon, says Fuller, was 'a valiant man, and lover of men of their hands; very choleric, but not malicious.'   On recognizing Mr. Colt he rode up to him and struck him a blow on the ear.   Colt naturally returned the blow.   Immediately Lord Hunsdon's retinue swarmed about him.   But they were called off.

'You rogues,' cried his lordship, 'may not I and my neighbour Colt exchange a blow but you must interpose?'

Lord Hunsdon was one of the queen's favourites.   He was her cousin, and when he suppressed a rising in the north in 1569 she wrote to him: 'I doubt much, my Harry, whether that the victory given me more joyed me, or that you were by God appointed the instrument of my glory.   And I assure you, for my country's good, the first might suffice; but for my heart's contentation, the second more pleaseth me.' [1]

Thrice this valiant Harry was in the way of being created Earl of Wiltshire, a high honour for Elizabeth to consider bestowing, for she was as niggardly with peerages as her successor was lavish.   But each time something intervened, until 'When he lay on his death-bed, the queen gave him a gracious visit, causing his patent for the said earldom to be drawn, his robes to be made, and both to be laid down upon his bed; but this lord (who could dissemble neither well nor sick) "Madam," said he, "seeing you counted me not worthy of this honour whilst I was living, I count myself unworthy of it now I am dying."'

Everywhere in the work we have Fuller's vivacity and unabashed familiarity with every rank and condition of men. Scores of his anecdotes are now familiar to every one without their source being known.   The Vicar of Bray is here.   'The vivacious vicar hereof living under King Henry the Eighth,

[1] *Worthies:* Hertfordshire.   Sir Henry Cary.

COPT HALL, ESSEX

CHARLES LE SECOND
ROY DE LA GRANDE
BRETAGNE

Que Pallas soit votre guide, Gardons votre Doigt.
Mars & Cupidonne qui conduise votre couraige
Que votre Sceptre montre sont le Pegase aus.
Ses Mercure comme laquais toujours a votre coste
Que la Fortune soit en votre, au heureux secours
Tu ne qui sur nos très bee éte jusques ici iustice.

King Edward the Sixth, Queen Mary, and Queen Elizabeth, was first a Papist, then a Protestant, then a Papist, then a Protestant again. He had seen some martyrs burnt (two miles off) at Windsor, and found this fire too hot for his tender temper. This vicar being taxed by one for being a turncoat and an inconstant changeling—"Not so," said he; "for I always kept my principle, which is this, to live and die the vicar of Bray."' Here also is the story of Spenser presenting his poems to the queen. It was the occasion on which Her Majesty commanded Cecil to give him £100. The sum was too large, objected Cecil; whereupon he was ordered to give what he thought reasonable and the poet, either by design or negligence, received nothing. After a suitable time had elapsed Spenser addressed to the queen these lines:

> I was promised on a time,
> To have reason for my rhyme;
> From that time unto this season,
> I received nor rhyme nor reason.

It is, indeed, the manner as much as the matter that makes the *Worthies* so rich. Fuller's open-mindedness and insatiable curiosity keep him free from dogmatism. He seldom sits in judgment, though he is not afraid to venture a shrewd comment on a theory when he thinks this might help a reader less well informed than himself. As a rule his inborn common sense and restless wit make these occasional remarks as valuable as they are delightful. And, incidentally, the personal element in Fuller tells us as much about his age as about himself. He was, as we have seen, a highly successful publicist, and such a man must always interpret to itself the mind of his own generation. The respect and popularity that Fuller enjoyed make it plain that a very substantial proportion of his contemporaries did accept his reading of their thoughts. So the mere selection of subjects, whether commodities, manufactures, or persons, and the relative value set upon each, may be taken as reflecting in the main the popular estimate of his age as well as himself. With this in mind it is interesting to see what he has to say about Shakespeare, Donne, and others whose fame has

K

increased with time. Ben Jonson, we find—not unexpectedly —appears as 'paramount in the dramatic part of poetry, and taught the stage an exact conformity to the laws of comedians.' His plays, says Fuller, 'will endure reading, and that with due commendation, so long as either ingenuity or learning are fashionable in our nation.' Of Shakespeare we read 'that though his genius generally was jocular, and inclining him to festivity, yet he could (when so disposed) be so solemn and serious, as appears by his tragedies; so that Heraclitus himself (I mean if secret and unseen) might afford to smile at his comedies, they were so merry; and Democritus scarce forbear to sigh at his tragedies, they were so mournful.

'He was an eminent instance of the truth of that rule, *poeta non fit sed nascitur* (one is not made but born a poet), indeed his learning was very little; so that, as Cornish diamonds are not polished by any lapidary, but are pointed and smoothed even as they are taken out of the earth, so Nature itself was all the art which was used upon him.

'Many were the wit combats betwixt him and Ben Jonson; which two I behold like a Spanish great galleon and an English man-of-war: Master Jonson (like the former) was built far higher in learning; solid, but slow, in his performances. Shakespeare, with the English man-of-war, lesser in bulk, but lighter in sailing, could turn with all tides, tack about, and take advantage of all winds, by the quickness of his wit and invention.'

But though Fuller, in order to provide entertainment for them and profit for himself held up the mirror to his friends and contemporaries, and reflected to us their estimates of national heroes, he did remember his obligations to later generations. No serious student of the *Worthies* can doubt that it was designated by its author to take its place in line with the medieval encyclopaedias. Sooner or later, then, we must lift our minds from the work itself and see it in relation to similar works. In particular we must compare Fuller's biographical sketches with those of his contemporaries. If we compare him with other scholars of his day we see that he is remarkable for the range rather than for the exactness of his studies. As a biographer he is more difficult to place. The full-length biography had not, of course, developed in his day; but the art was practised with considerable skill. The book mentioned a moment ago, *English Biography before 1700*, by Donald A. Stauffer,[1] is at present the only adequate treatment of the subject, and would have to be read by any one who wished to understand precisely what Fuller's place was in the history of biography. At first glance his stature is not increased by seeing him in relation to his contemporaries. Let us take three with whom he might quite legitimately be compared, Clarendon, Izaak Walton, and John Aubrey. While he has something in common with all, he lacks their distinguishing qualities. That is to say, he lacks Clarendon's expansive view of history and his power of relating each subject to its environment; he lacks Walton's sympathetic insight into personality as well as his grace of expression; and lively as he is, he has nothing as scintillating as Aubrey's best sketches. Nevertheless, he has his place, and it is far from being a lowly one. Incidentally, the word 'biographist' was his invention, and the word 'biography' made its first appearance in English literature in the anonymous *Life*.

The truth is that it is only when we examine the development of his own work, from the *Holy War* and *The Holy State* to the *Church History* and the *Worthies*, that we see the nature and value of his contribution to the art of biography. What he did for it in his own practice, he did for it by influence in the practice of others. In discussing *The Holy State* we saw that Fuller's literary gift, and in particular his part in the development of the essay, sprang neither from intellect nor conscious artistic sense, but spontaneously from the sanity of his mind and the richness of his personality. His gift to biography was similar, only here it is seen in half-realized form in *The Holy State*, and fully mature only in the *Worthies*. By turning from the one to the other we see how he moved from the moralizing studies of the former, where the person was a comment on a type, to a form in which the person fashions his own mould and is something in his own right. This was, of course, done by our masters of biography

[1] Harvard University Press, 1930.

consciously and with studied skill, whereas Fuller did it, and
was one of the first to do it, simply by the grace of God.
His success is, perhaps, no great credit to him.   He arrived
at the gates of heaven, as it were, in this as in so many other
things simply by following his nose; but it is evidence of the
rightness of his instincts and the soundness of his judgment
that he did arrive.   Even in his delight in trifles, which so
scandalized the grave divines of his own day, he was right.
Truth may be in trifles.   'Nor is it always in the most distinguished achievements that men's virtues or vices may be
best discerned,' said Plutarch; 'but very often an action of
small note, a short saying, or a jest, shall distinguish a
person's real character more than the greatest sieges, or the
most important battles.' [1]

Fuller's joy in the small things that make up so much of life
arose, it is worth noting, from the delight he found in this
world, which has always been a fault in him to the stricter
brethren.   In Fuller's day men whose lives were considered
worthy of a biographer's interest were not expected to show
interest in the pomps and vanities of earthly life.   Fuller's
subjects, however, are all too often men of the world, though
if they are also men of charitable inclinations so much the
better.   Thus he writes approvingly of Humphrey Chetham
(1580–1653), the Manchester philanthropist, a clothier and
private banker, for having 'signally improved himself in
piety and outward prosperity.'   But Chetham was not there
solely because he had bequeathed money to endow a public
library of 'godly English Bookes . . . proper for the edification of the common people,' which were to be chained in the
local parish churches.   He was a man who had done very
well for himself, and to Fuller there was no reproach in that.
Indeed he was rather more complacent about such things
than we, with our awakened social consciousness, can always
approve.   He finds nothing but satisfaction in quoting the
reply of Dr. Edington, Bishop of Winchester, when offered
Canterbury.   'Canterbury,' said the bishop, 'is the higher
rack, but Winchester is the better manger.'   On the other
hand he did hold it against another bishop of Winchester,

---

[1] *Life of Alexander*, Langhorne's translation

Henry Beaufort, that he held the sees of Lincoln and Winchester for fifty years, and was 'so far from being weaned from the world, he sucked the hardest (as if he would have a bit off the nipples thereof) the nearer he was to the grave.'

This interest in worldly prosperity, and the gaining of possessions, though still uncommon among scholars, was another reflection in Fuller of the popular as distinct from the academic mind of his age. The scramble for land was at its height, and consequently many of his curious stories deal with it. One of the best is found in the Devon section. It relates how a gentleman named Child, 'being of ancient extraction at Plimstock in this county, and great possessions. It happened that he, hunting in Dartmoor, lost both his company and way in a bitter snow. Having killed his horse, he crept into his hot bowels for warmth; and wrote this with his blood:

> He that finds and brings me to my tomb,
> The land of Plimstock shall be his doom.

That night he was frozen to death; and being first found by the monks of Tavistock, they with all possible speed hasted to inter him in their own abbey. His own parishioners of Plimstock, hearing thereof, stood at the ford of the river to take his body from them. But they must rise early, yea, not sleep at all, who over-reach monks in matter of profit. For they cast a slight bridge over the river, whereby they carried over the corpse, and interred it. In avowance whereof, the bridge (a more premediate structure, I believe, in the place of the former extempore passage) is called Guils Bridge to this day. And know, reader, all in the vicinage will be highly offended with such who either deny or doubt the credit of this common tradition. And sure it is, that the abbot of Tavistock got that rich manor into his possession.'

After reading such tales as these, can we wonder that Pepys, when he first met with the *Worthies* on the 10th February 1662, sat and read it till two o'clock before he noticed the time, so engrossed did he become?

CHAPTER XVIII

THE WORTHY DOCTOR

For his religion, it was fit
To match his learning or his wit.

Hudibras.

FULLER'S place, then, was not with the bold and heroic of that
rebellious age. He was a public figure and always ready to
volunteer for duty; but the richest side of his nature was
reflective. And if he had been no more than a distinguished
clergyman of the period, like Heylyn or Baxter, he would be
remembered only by those students of Church history, most
of them clerics, who remember the Heylyns and the Baxters.
As it is he is remembered also, and with affection, by the
many to whom the seventeenth century means men like
Izaak Walton, Pepys, Sir Thomas Browne, and Sir William
Dugdale. In a longer range he is with Leland and Camden.

From one point of view it may seem curious that antiquarian research should have flourished in the restless seventeenth century. From another it might be argued that this,
like every other exercise of the spirit, could not fail to thrive
the better for opposition. It certainly did so. Fuller's was
a great age for such as he. The Elizabethans: John Leland,
John Stow—'the merry old man,' as Henry Holland called
him—and modest, friendly Camden, who had lit the fire and
trimmed the lamp of antiquarian research in England so
genially, had been succeeded by Sir William Dugdale, who
with his *Antiquities of Warwickshire* was the first of the great
county historians, and whose major works came from the
press at the same time as Fuller's. While Dugdale was
working in Warwickshire, John Habingdon was collecting
material for a history of Worcestershire. And only a few
years later John Aubrey came to the fore with his works on
Wiltshire and Surrey. All these admirable men may have
felt that there was no place for them in the raw and uncouth
civilization into which they had been born. But they did

their work quietly in spite of distractions, and their laurels are still green.

But bright as these laurels are, they have not the freshness they had when first placed on those august but genial brows. Antiquaries and men of learning, whether of this or an earlier age, are respected to-day; but they are not the national figures they were in the smaller literary world of the seventeenth century, when the scholar was usually a man of good family, interested in buildings and pedigrees as well as in abstract and speculative studies. As an illustration, we can hardly imagine an eminent playwright of our own day referring to the writings of a regional historian and antiquary as 'the glory and light of the kingdom,' yet that is what Ben Jonson called William Camden. But the creative artist did not always enjoy the pre-eminence accorded him to-day. At the time when Fuller was writing, learning and wit were set above imagination. One reason for this, of course, was that writers used Latin, which, with its greater conciseness, was better suited to the less vivacious and fanciful subjects. The great libraries of the day had few books in English, and most of these were theological or historical. Approximately half the books published during Fuller's lifetime were religious.

The legal and courtly background of Tudor and Stuart England favoured historical studies, which accounted for most of the other half. In a work of 1568 entitled *The Institucion of a Gentleman*, the author says: 'Ther can be nothynge more meete for gentlemen then the readyng of histories. . . . By them we lerne to knowe howe princes and rulers of thys worlde have passed their lives.' That was what most of the young gentlemen of the day wanted to know. From Oxford or Cambridge they went either into the Church or into the inns of court, usually with the service of the king or one of his nobles in view. Church and State were closely associated then. George Herbert, as we know, was a courtier during much of his life, and even Baxter, the leader of the Nonconformists, had thoughts of trying his fortunes at Court. He stayed with Herbert's brother, Sir Henry Herbert, Master of the Revels, for a month, but reconsidered, we are told, after seeing a stage-play on a Sunday when he thought there ought to have been a sermon.

Fuller, as divine, was neither a Herbert nor a Baxter. He was, perhaps, midway between them. He was too much of a divine to be a courtier like Herbert, and too little of a saint; he was too courtly to be as serious as Baxter, and too worldly. He was of the same mind as Baxter's neighbour, Sir Ralph Clare, who expressed his distaste of 'precisions and extempore praying and making such ado for heaven.' The truth is, he lacked the spiritual gifts that would have placed him either with these or with Laud, Andrewes, and Jeremy Taylor. As a churchman he belonged to yet another company, that of the Christian humanists. There was Renaissance as well as Reformation influence in him. English as he was, and presently our last word must be of that, he had something of the spirit animating Erasmus and Montaigne. Like them he abhorred superstition and loved reason, rejecting those writers who filled their folios with tales of miracles, 'swelling the bowels of their books with empty wind in default of sufficient food to fill them.' He would not be drawn away from the simple truths that could be expressed in plain statements and were acceptable to common sense. The 'Lo, here!' and 'Lo, there!' prophets never attracted the worthy doctor. His guiding star was not

> A light that falls down from on high
> For spiritual trades to cozen by:
> An *ignis fatuus* that bewitches,
> And leads men into pools and ditches.
>
> *Hudibras.*

On the contrary, his appeal as a churchman was always to history and reason. Any kind of infallibility, whether of the pope or Calvin, he distrusted. And equally he distrusted 'the dead reckoning of logic.' For so eminent a churchman, Fuller has curiously little significance for the student of seventeenth-century ecclesiastical history. He was one of the great Cavalier parsons but not one of the great Caroline divines. He belonged, in fact, to the Church of Elizabeth, not the Church of either James or Charles, which is another way of saying that he belonged to Hooker's Church, not

Laud's, for it was Hooker who saw that the voices of reason and learning, and the witness of moral evidence, would be silenced if the infallible discipline of the Puritans was allowed to replace the infallible discipline of the pope.

He did side with the Puritans, however, when it was necessary to go into either one lobby or the other. But his sympathy lay with the Puritanism of the earlier, more thoughtful and less emotional kind, rooted in that English humanism which tried to cut away from religion its superstition, so that it might be transformed under God into a more spiritual faith.

Outside the Church, his mind was progressive, and indeed we may say that his churchmanship was conservative simply because he saw that Hooker's Church was more sympathetic than that of Laud or the Presbyterians towards such progress as he thought sound. He had supped with the humanists, as it were, and had no appetite for the fare served up by the Scots theologians. Perhaps he realized, either in his mind or in his heart, that there was a great movement for intellectual expansion afoot, and that it was one of the major misfortunes of the times that the Stuarts should have barred its progress by introducing the academic and reactionary conception of their own divine function and their people's duty. The locked gates opened by Henry VIII and Elizabeth, however, proved too heavy for James and Charles—with their reactionary conception of their divine right—to close, and the people passed through them. Fuller was too loyal a Cavalier to acknowledge this publicly; but he must have known it. Perhaps he realized also that the other great trend of the times, Protestant thought, which had been forced into a narrower bed by the Puritans, was carrying men away from that freedom of thought which his own and Hooker's conception of the Church allowed. Cavalier and Protestant as he was, his constant pleading for moderation suggests that he knew full well the dangers of both extravagant Royalism and unrestrained Protestantism.

But whether Fuller saw the full purport of these trends or not, we see it, and we see what he could never see: the sanity and wisdom of his own bearing. And may we not read into

* K

Fuller's relationship with his age something more? This conflict between the Roundheads and the Cavaliers was, in fact, the supreme expression in English history of the permanent conflict between two irreconcilable conceptions of the good life, which, for our western civilization, is first seen in the conflict between the legalistic Hebrews and the pleasure-loving Hellenes. These are the two splay-footed feet that our western civilization stands on. In Fuller's day the English, talked into it by the Scots, became aware as never before of these rival ideologies, and not yet having developed their national gift for compromise, they went sadly astray. In all the confusion that followed, Fuller, perhaps better than any other public man of his generation, kept his head and expressed what is now accepted as the typically English point of view. To put it figuratively, he was an early master of the difficult art of walking on two intellectual legs, with feet that point in opposite directions.

The odd thing about this art is that it is so difficult to master intellectually, so easy physically. Perhaps we should be more deft with our brains if we worried less about this 'dead reckoning of logic,' which Fuller, with his usual sagacity, distrusted. We ought to be frank here and admit that he did evade many problems that a more intellectually courageous man would have faced. Like one of his own worthies, Dr. Parsons, he 'knew well how to lay his thumb on what he would not have seen.' But he did so in order to make the persons more prominent than their vexatious and soul-destroying problems. Labels he hardly noticed. When, in his controversy with Heylyn, he asked what sense there was in Thomas quarrelling with Peter, he summed up his whole attitude to these differences that troubled others so much. His fellow creatures were not Protestants and Catholics, Parliamentarians, Cavaliers, and all the rest of it; they were not even Heylyns and Fullers; they were Thomases and Peters. And those names received at baptism were theirs by the grace of God, not by the terms of that Utopian heresy which evolves a human and limited conception of a social ideal, and then proceeds to select or train men to fit it, rejecting the irregular. Fuller exulted in human nature as

he found it, accepting it in all its rich variety and judging its
weaknesses charitably. 'For,' said he, 'those who endeavour
to make the way to heaven narrower than God hath made it,
by prohibiting what he permits, do in event make the way to
hell wider, occasioning the committing of such sins, which
God hath forbidden.' Like his own James Cranford, a
Warwickshire worthy, 'he had, as I may say, a broad-chested
soul, favourable to such who differed from him. His moderation increased with his age, charity with his moderation; and
he had a kindness for all such who had any goodness in them.'
So the splay-footed nature of reason—or the horns of its
dilemma, if you prefer the usual term—which sends one man
to the left, another to the right, never troubled him.

There was room in Fuller's capacious soul, then, for everybody, and every oddity of thought and action. And somehow the boundless charity of his personality holds the entire
and ill-assorted company together. Even the joylessness of
the extreme Puritan drew from him a censure too gentle to
give offence. He quietly pointed out that 'the Lord
alloweth us sauce with our meat, and recreation with our
vocation,' and left it at that. You may find Fuller at one
moment telling the tale of the origin of bottled beer in England, at another speculating on the derivation of 'bean-belly
Leicestershire,' at a third discussing patiently the curious
ways of Providence. The beggar gets in as good a word as
the bishop. On being asked how he could go about practically naked he replied that he supposed all his body must be
face. And would any one but Fuller, in writing about so
exalted a person as Archbishop Laud, have thought of an old
gipsy custom when he had to mention the danger of trying to
pronounce judgment so soon after death? 'Indeed,' he
said, 'I could instance in some kinds of coarse venison, not fit
for food when first killed; and therefore cunning cooks bury
it for some hours in the earth . . . so the memory of some
persons newly deceased are neither fit for a writer's or
reader's repast, until some competent time after their
interment.'

Indeed, his mind was so hospitable that he was like the
chamberlain of the inn, of whom he wrote that he wondered

how he, 'being but one, is to give attendance to many guests.'
The doctor's head was always a full inn.   It was, in fact, an
inn—particularly on the literary side—that yielded more
hospitality than profit, for, disguise it as we may, there is a
hard core of self-interest in the first rank of men of letters no
less than in the first rank of men of business.   Fuller was too
much at the beck and call of every sympathy to do with his
great gifts and brilliant intelligence what a better economist
would have done.   Thus, while he contributed to the development of the essay, the biography, history, and miscellaneous
literature in England, and left work of value in each form, he
achieved pre-eminence in none.   Here was abundance, but
not perfection.

But what he lost, as it were, in height, he gained in breadth.
After all, perfection is inhuman, and Fuller, before everything
else, was human.   He had no wish to be one of the superior
few.   His heart was with the many.   And he liked the many
to dine at his table.   We may see this in the hospitality he
offered in the *Worthies* to representatives of the new trading
classes as well as to the old nobility.   In his lists for the
various counties he gives honourable places to men in local
as well as in national government, pointing out that though
'generally of mean extraction, they raised themselves by
God's providence, and their own faithfulness.'   He was, we
may say, an early champion of the middle classes, and it is
from this sympathy with the middling people, who in course
of time were to determine the character of the new, com-
mercialized England, that Fuller gained what is perhaps his
outstanding characteristic as a writer from the merely professional point of view.   He was the first of our modern
popularizers of learning, and in this twentieth century, when
we have a host of writers trying to evolve styles that will
enable them to reach those millions of readers whose grand-
fathers were illiterate and whose fathers never opened a book,
he is particularly worthy of study.   In his attitude towards
his public he is far nearer in spirit to the writers of to-day,
who hide rather than display their academic distinctions,
than to those of the eighteenth century, who were obliged to
set up as pundits because otherwise they could not hope to

engage the attention of the small highly-educated minority who read.

All this varied interest and exercise of talent leads to the conclusion that it was in the core of his being that Fuller was an amateur. If he had applied himself to one form only as the born professional would have done, he might have been a master. It was not in his nature to do so. His sympathies were too wide. The consequence was that the professional historians and biographers of the eighteenth century had no use for him and his fame was obscured until the men of the Romantic movement, with their broader sympathies—men such as Coleridge and Lamb, who wished to humanize scholarship—restored him to favour. These men gave him a niche in the Temple of Fame they had built so zealously. To-day his claims to the niche still hold good, but there is no longer a temple. The twentieth-century iconoclasts have destroyed it. But does this matter to Fuller? With the disappearance of the temple all those priestly and erudite authors who were once honoured above all the rest of mankind have lost the only place where they could declaim their noble periods. They undoubtedly belong to the past and have no successors. Their line is extinct. Fuller, however, was never of their company. So although his canonization by Coleridge, Lamb, and the rest of them no longer means anything, he is still a living author, while many to whom he was inferior as divine, historian, biographer, are dead.

The reason is that though the general attitude of the Romantics towards Fuller was extravagant it was not so foolish as at first it appears. Coleridge's claim was this: 'Shakespeare! Milton! Fuller! Defoe! Hogarth! As to the remaining mighty host of our great men, other countries have produced something like them. But these are uniques. England may challenge the world to show a correspondent name to either of the five. I do not say that, with the exception of the first, names of equal glory may not be produced *in a different kind*. But these are genera, containing each only one individual.' At first it seems absurd to place Fuller in such company. But on reflection we find that there was something unique in Fuller as a writer, and,

paradoxically, the unique element was that through which
he expressed the mind of the common man. And that
common man, whether lord or labourer, was distinctively an
Englishman. The ordinary Englishman seldom does find
expression in literature. In Fuller he has it as he has it in
Chaucer, Shakespeare, and a few others of that large-
hearted kind.

It was the Englishman in Fuller that made him so contented with middle rank, and that explains the amateur in
him. The real Englishman has little desire to lord it over his
fellows, either as man of letters or man of estate. Fuller had
this normal English attitude instinctively; but at the same
time it seems clear enough that it was part of his considered
philosophy of life, for he lived by the golden mean, distrusting
extremes in everything. Again, he showed his English
character in his consistent habit of trying to reduce the airy
speculations of theology into everyday religion.

It was also the Englishman in him that distrusted intellect
and would never allow him to press a theory beyond its
practical utility. And having said that, we can narrow this
insularity in him still further and say that he belonged body
and soul to the east of England, for he was to Vaughan and
Traherne, the mystics of his day, what Crabbe was to Wordsworth, which is only another way of saying, what the flat,
breezy eastern counties are to the romantic mountains of the
west and north.

So as writer we find him yet again where we found him as
thinker and as churchman, in the give-and-take England of
the Tudors rather than in the doctrinaire England of the
Stuarts. As he belonged to Hooker's Church rather than to
Laud's, he belonged to Shakespeare's company rather than to
Milton's, and it was this Shakespearian universality of sympathy that enabled him to hold up the mirror to the England
of his time in the *Worthies*, and show us the developing social
trends in a way that a man of academic mind could not have
done. For all his love of the past, he was ready to accept the
present and look forward confidently towards the future.
What he said of Bacon was equally true of himself. He was
'a great honourer of ancient authors, yet a great deviser and

practiser of new ways of learning.' Even in his portrait of
the Church Antiquary, where his love of the old might be
expected to get the better of him, he says that his subject
'doth not so adore the Ancients as to despise the Modern.'

For such largeness of mind as this, there must surely have
been more in the worthy doctor than the wit that Coleridge
said was the stuff and substance of his intellect. There was;
and it was something in the heart and soul of the man.
It may have been wit that drew the Cambridge of the
1630s to him; it was something more that captivated his
many discerning admirers, such as Leslie Stephen. It was
humanity. He was a man who loved and enjoyed his kind.
He had his quips and cranks of expression, but there were no
tricks in his mind. He faced his fellow men squarely.
Common sense was his guide and measure. Indeed it is more
than likely that his fooling was as deliberate as his preaching.
He had a tale of 'A notable fellow, and a soldier of Alexander,' who, 'finding first admission to be the greatest
difficulty, put feathers into his nose and ears, and danced
about the court in an antic fashion, till the strangeness of the
show brought the king himself to be a spectator. Then this
mimic, throwing off his disguise,

'"Sir," said he to the king, "thus I first arrive at your
majesty's notice in the fashion of a fool, but can do you
service in the place of a wise man, if you please to employ
me."'

The same may be said of Fuller.

AN ALPHABET OF FULLERISMS

A

AFFECTIONS, like the conscience, are rather to be led than drawn; and, it is to be feared, they that marry where they do not love, will love where they do not marry.

ANGER is one of the sinews of the soul; he that wants it hath a maimed mind.

B

BISHOPS. Let canvas be rough and rugged, lawn ought to be soft and smooth. Meekness, mildness, and mercy being more proper for men of the episcopal function.

C

CAVILLERS. Such find a knot in a bulrush, because they themselves before had tied it therein; and may be compared to beggars, who breed vermin in their own bodies, and then blow them on the clothes of others.

CELIBACY. Though there be no fire seen outwardly, as in the English chimneys, it may be hotter within, as in the Dutch stoves.

CHEESE   Poor men do eat it for hunger, rich for digestion.

CHEMISTRY is an ingenious profession, as which by art will force somewhat of worth and eminence from the dullest substance, yea, the most obdurate and hardest-hearted body cannot but shed forth a tear of precious liquor, when urged thereunto with its intreaties.

CLOTH sure is of the same date with civility in this land. . . . Well may the poets feign Minerva the goddess of wit and the foundress of weaving, so great is the ingenuity thereof.

D

DEER, when living, raise the stomachs of gentlemen with their sport; and, when dead, allay them again with their flesh.

DIARIST.   Now he can hardly be an ill husband who casteth up his receipts and expenses every night; and such a soul is, or would be good, which enters into a daily scrutiny of its own actions.

DIARY.   An exact diary is a window into his heart who maketh it; and, therefore, pity it is that any should look therein, but either the friends of the party, or such ingenuous foes as will not (especially in things doubtful) make conjectural comments to his disgrace.

DRUNKARDS are distinguished from the king's sober subjects by clipping the coin of the tongue.

E

ELDER BROTHER.   One who made haste to come into the world to bring his parents the first news of male posterity, and is well rewarded for his tidings.

EYES.   The eyes being the grace of the body, as windows are of buildings.

F

FAME is the echo of actions, resounding them to the world, save that the echo repeats only the last part, but fame relates all, and often more than all.

FANCY.   It is an inward sense of the soul, for a while retaining and examining things brought in thither by the common sense.

FAVOURITE.   A favourite is a court-dial, whereon all look whilst the king shines on him; and none when it is night with him.

FLOWER.   A flower is the best-complexioned grass . . . and daily it weareth God's livery, for 'He clotheth the grass in the field.'

G

GARLIC. Indeed the scent thereof is somewhat valiant and offensive; but wise men will be contented to hold their noses, on condition they may thereby hold or recover their health.

GIBEON, whose inhabitants cozened Joshua with a pass of false-dated antiquity. Who would have thought that clouted shoes could have covered so much subtility?

GILGAL, where the manna ceased, the Israelites having till then been fellow-commoners with the angels.

GRAVITY is the ballast of the soul, which keeps the mind steady

GRUEL (though homely) is wholesome spoon-meal physic for the sick, and food for persons in health. . . . Now gruel imperfectly mixed is wash rather, which one will have little heart to eat, and get little heart thereby.

GUNPOWDER is the emblem of political revenge; for it biteth first, and barketh afterwards, the bullet being at the mark before the report is heard; so that it maketh a noise, not by way of warning, but triumph.

H

HOPE is the only tie which keeps the heart from breaking.

HORSES. These are men's wings, wherewith they make much speed. A generous creature a horse is, sensible in some sort of honour, made most handsome by that which deforms men most—pride.

I

INDEX. An index is the bag and baggage of a book, of more use than honour; even such who vehemently slight it, secretly using it, if not for need, for speed of what they desire to find.

J

JEWS. These Jews, though forbidden to buy land in England, grew rich by usury . . . so that in the barest pasture, in which a Christian would starve, a Jew would grow fat, he bites so close unto the ground.

K

KNIVES are the teeth of old men ... whereof the bluntest, with a sharp stomach, will serve to cut meat.

L

LANCASHIRE, a frontier country, as I may term it, of papists and Protestants, where the reformed religion had rather a truce than a peace.

LEAD is not churlish but good-natured metal, not curdling into knots and knobs, but all equally fusile; and therefore most useful for pipes and sheets; yea, the softness thereof will receive any artificial impressions.

LIGHT, God's eldest daughter, is a principal beauty in a building.

LOGIC. It is seldom seen that the clunch-fist of logic (good to knock down a man at a blow) can so open itself as to smooth and stroke one with the palm thereof.

M

MARRIAGE. Though bachelors be the strongest stakes, married men are the best binders, in the hedge of the commonwealth.

MARTYRS. If they had not been flesh and blood, they could not have been burnt; and if they had been no more than flesh and blood, they would not have been burnt.

MUSIC is nothing else but wild sounds civilized into time and tune.

N

NEEDLE. It is the woman's pencil; and embroidery is the masterpiece thereof.

NEGROES. The image of God cut in ebony.

NOBLEMAN. He is a gentleman in a text letter, because bred, and living in an higher and larger way.

NONCONFORMISTS.

1. Ancient . . . who desired only to shake down the leaves of episcopacy.

2. Middle . . . who struck at the branches thereof.

3. Modern . . . who did lay the axe to the roots of the tree.

O

OBSTINACY.   Some think it beneath a wise man to alter his opinion . . . it matters not though we go back from our word, so we go forward in the truth and a sound judgment.

P

PHILOLOGY properly is terse and polite learning, *melior literatura* . . .; being that florid skill, containing only the roses of learning, without the prickles thereof, in which narrow sense thorny philosophy is discharged, as no part of philology.

PIKES.   Fresh-water wolves; and therefore an old pond pike is a dish of more state than profit to the owners, seeing a pike's belly is a little fish-pond.

PINS fill up the chinks betwixt our clothes, lest wind and weather should shoot through them.   A pin is a blind needle.

PIPES are chimneys portable in pockets, the one end being the hearth thereof.

PROVERB.   A proverb is much matter decocted into few words.

PYRAMIDS.   The pyramids, doting with age, have forgotten the names of their founders.

Q

QUARRELS.   When worthy men fall out, only one of them may be faulty at the first, but, if such strifes continue long, commonly both become guilty.

R

REPUTATION.   A good name is an ointment poured out, smelt where it is not seen.

S

SALMON. A dainty and wholesome fish. . . . Being both bow and arrow, it will shoot itself out of the water an incredible height and length.

SALT is most essential to man's livelihood, without which neither sacrifice was acceptable to God, nor meat is savoury to man. It is placed on the board with bread, to show that they are equally necessary to man's sustenance.

SECRETS. Some men's souls are not strong enough, but that a weighty secret will work a hole through them.

SLEEP. Sleep and Death are two twins: sleep is the elder brother, for Adam slept in Paradise; but Death liveth longest, for the last enemy that shall be destroyed is Death.

T

TAPESTRY is a kind of gardening in cloth.

TOMBS are the clothes of the dead: a grave is but a plain suit, and a rich monument is one embroidered.

V

VOCATION. To prevent such foot-travelling, it is good to be mounted on a gainful vocation, to carry one out of the mire, on all occasions.

W

WOOLL, must needs be warm, as consisting all of double-letters.

Y

YEOMEN. The good yeoman is a gentleman in ore, whom the next age may see refined.

(THE DAVENANT FAMILY HAD BEEN SETTLED AT SIBLE

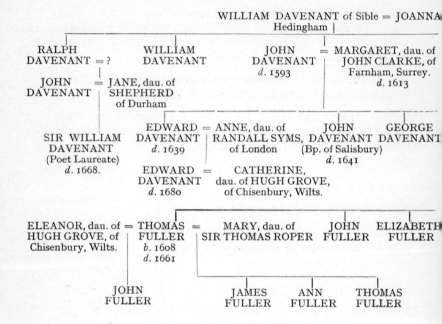

WILLIAM DAVENANT of Sible = JOANNA
Hedingham

RALPH
DAVENANT = ?

JOHN = JANE, dau. of
DAVENANT | SHEPHERD
of Durham

WILLIAM
DAVENANT

JOHN = MARGARET, dau. of
DAVENANT | JOHN CLARKE, of
d. 1593 | Farnham, Surrey.
d. 1613

SIR WILLIAM
DAVENANT
(Poet Laureate)
d. 1668.

EDWARD = ANNE, dau. of
DAVENANT | RANDALL SYMS,
d. 1639 | of London

EDWARD = CATHERINE,
DAVENANT | dau. of HUGH GROVE,
d. 1680 | of Chisenbury, Wilts.

JOHN   GEORGE
DAVENANT DAVENANT
(Bp. of Salisbury)
d. 1641

ELEANOR, dau. of = THOMAS = MARY, dau. of
HUGH GROVE, of | FULLER | SIR THOMAS ROPER
Chisenbury, Wilts. | b. 1608
d. 1661

JOHN   ELIZABETH
FULLER   FULLER

JOHN
FULLER

JAMES   ANN   THOMAS
FULLER   FULLER   FULLER

dau. of JOHN FREAR, of Clare, Suffolk.

JOANNA DAVENANT	A daughter	ANNE DAVENANT

WILLIAM DAVE-NANT	JAMES DAVE-NANT	RALPH DAVE-NANT	JUDITH DAVE-NANT	= THOMAS FULLER (2nd husband)	MARGARET DAVENANT	= ROBERT TOWNSON (Bp. of Salisbury), d. 1621.

MARGARET FULLER	MARIA FULLER	JUDITH FULLER	ANNE FULLER

BIBLIOGRAPHY

FULLER'S WORKS

1. 1631   *David's Heinous Sin.* (A poem.)
2. 1639   *The History of the Holy War.*
3. 1640   *Joseph's Parti-coloured Coat.*
4. 1642   *The Holy State and The Profane State.*
5. 1642   *A Fast Sermon Preached on Innocents' Day.*
6. 1643   *A Sermon on His Majesty's Inauguration.*
7. 1643   *A Sermon of Reformation.*
8. 1643   *Truth Maintained.*
9. 1644   *Jacob's Vow, a Sermon Preached before His Majesty.*
10. 1645   *Good Thoughts in Bad Times.*
11. 1646   *Fear of Losing the Old Light.*
12. 1646   *Andronicus, or the Unfortunate Politician.*
13. 1647   *The Cause and Cure of a Wounded Conscience.*
14. 1647   *Good Thoughts in Worse Times.*
15. 1647   *A Sermon of Assurance.*
16. 1648   *A Sermon of Contentment.*
17. 1649   *The Just Man's Funeral.*
18. 1650   *A Pisgah-Sight of Palestine.*
19. 1652   *A Comment concerning Christ's Temptations.*
20. 1653   *Perfection and Peace.*
21. 1653   *The Infant's Advocate.*
22. 1654   *A Comment on Ruth.*
23. 1654   *A Triple Reconciler.*
24. 1655   *Life out of Death.*
25. 1655-6   *The Church History of Britain with The History of the University of Cambridge and The History of Waltham Abbey.*
26. 1656   *A Collection of Sermons.*
27. 1657   *The Best Name on Earth.* (Sermons.)
28. 1657   *A Sermon Preached at the Funeral of Mr. George Haycock.*
29. 1659   *The Appeal of Injured Innocence.*
30. 1660   *An Alarm to the Counties of England and Wales.*
31. 1660   *Mixt Contemplations in Better Times.*

32. 1660   *A Panegyric to His Majesty.*   (A poem.)
33. 1662   *The History of the Worthies of England.*
34. 1781   *Observations of the Shires.*
35. 1891   *Collected Sermons*, edited by J. E. Bailey and W. E. A. Axon.

WORKS TO WHICH FULLER CONTRIBUTED

1. 1631   *Genethliacum.*
2. 1633   *Rex Redux.*
3. 1640–1   Colet, John: *Daily Devotions.*
4. 1651   *Abel Redevivus.*
5. 1651   Holdsworth, R.: *Valley of Vision.*
6. 1652   Sparke, E.: *Scintillula Altaris.*
7. 1653   Lawes, H.: *Ayres and Dialogues.*
8. 1654   *Ephemeris Parliamentaria.*
9. 1657   Smith, H.: *Sermons.*
10. 1658   Spencer, J.: *Things Old and New.*
11. 1659   *Pulpit Sparks.*
12. 1660   *The House of Mourning.*
13. 1662   Josephus Ben Gorion: *History of the Jews.*

BIOGRAPHIES

1. 1661   Anonymous: *The Life of that Reverend Divine and Learned Historian, Dr. Thomas Fuller.*
2. 1750   Oldys, William: Memoir of Fuller in *Biographia Britannica.*
3. 1844   Russell, Arthur Tozer: *Memorials of the Life and Works of Thomas Fuller, D.D.*
4. 1874   Bailey, John Eglington: *The Life of Thomas Fuller, D.D., with Notices of his Books, his Kinsmen, and his Friends.*
5. 1884   Fuller, Morris Joseph: *The Life, Times, and Writings of Thomas Fuller, D.D., the Church Historian*
6. 1935   Lyman, Dean B.: *The Great Tom Fuller.*

MISCELLANEOUS SOURCES

Aubrey, John   *Brief Lives*, edited by Anthony Powell (1949).

Ball, Thomas   *Life of Preston*, 1651, edited by E. W. Harcourt (1855).

Barker, Arthur   *Milton and the Puritan Dilemma* (1942).

Bate, George   *The Lives*, etc., of the Regicides (1661)

Broadus, E. K.   Intro. to *Thomas Fuller: Selections* (1928).

Broome, A.   *Selections from Fuller and South* (1815).

Bulstrode, Sir Richard   *Memoirs and Reflections* (1721)

Carter, Charles Sydney   *The English Church in the Seventeenth Century* (1909).

Cartwright, Julia   *Madame: the Life and Letters of Henrietta, Duchess of Orleans* (1894).

Chandler, Richard   *A History of Basing House* (1827).

Choate, J. B.   *Wells of English* (1892).

Christophers, S. W.   *Homes of Old English Writers* (n.d.).

Coleridge, S. T.   *Literary Remains*, vol. ii (1836); *Notes on English Divines* (1853); *Notes Theological, Poli tical, and Miscellaneous*, ed. by T. M. Raysor (1936).

Cotton, William   *Gleanings from the Municipal and Cathedral Records of Exeter* (1877).

Cross, F. L.   *Anglicanism: the Thought and Practice of the Church of England* (1935).

Crossley, J.   Article on Fuller's *Holy and Profane States* in the *Retrospective Review* (1821).

Currier, A. H.   In *Biographical and Literary Studies*. Boston, New York (1915).

Davenant, John, and Evans, Bergen   'Letters in Tanner Collection,' The Bodleian. *Review of English Studies*, Oct. 1931, pp. 452–3.

D'Ewes, Sir Simonds   Autobiography (1845).

Evelyn, John   Diary

George, E. A.   *Seventeenth Century Men of Latitude* (1909).

Gibson, Strickland   *A Bibliography of the Works of Thomas Fuller, D.D.* Oxford Bibliographical Society (1936).

Gray, J. H.	*The Queens' College, Cambridge* (1899).
Grierson, Sir Herbert	*Cross-Currents in English Literature of the Seventeenth Century* (1929).
Harleian MSS.	3739, 4944, 6065.
Heath, James	*An Elegy upon Dr. Thomas Fuller, that most Incomparable Writer.* Single sheet, Bodleian.
Henson, H. H.	*Studies in English Religion in the Seventeenth Century* (1903).
Hewlett, Maurice	*Last Essays* (1922).
Houghton, W. E.	*The Formation of Thomas Fuller's 'Holy and Profane States.'* Cambridge, Mass. (1938),
Jessop, Augustus	*Wise Words and Quaint Counsels of Thomas Fuller* (1892).
Jordan, W. K.	*The Development of Religious Toleration in England*, vol. iv (1932).
Kellett, E. E.	*Reconsiderations* (1928).
Lamb, Charles	Works (1818).
Lloyd, David	Memoirs (1668).
Macaulay, Rose	*They Were Defeated.*
Mackie, J. D.	*Cavalier and Puritan* (1936).
Macnamara, F. N.	*Memorials of the Danvers Family* (1895).
Manchester Public Library	The Fuller Collection (Bailey bequest).
Masson, David	*Life of Milton* (1859–80).
Masterman, J. H. B.	*The Age of Milton* (1897).
Mede, Joseph	*The Works of Joseph Mede* (with prefatory Life) (1672).
Minchin, H. C.	'Glimpses of Dr. Thomas Fuller,' article in the *Fortnightly Review* (July 1908).
Motier, M. M.	*Henrietta Ann (of England)* . . . (1929).
Mullinger, J. B.	*History of the University of Cambridge* (1873–84).
Notes and Queries	May, July 1918.
Nichols, J.	*The Progresses and Public Processions of Queen Elizabeth* (1788–1821).
Oman, Carola	*Henrietta Maria* (1936).
Pepys, Samuel	Diary.
Richardson, C. F.	*English Preachers and Preaching, 1640–1670* (1928).

Rogers, H.   'An Essay on the Life and Genius of Thomas
                    Fuller,' *Edinburgh Review*, Jan. 1842.
Rushworth, John   *Historical Collections* (1692).
Russell, T.   'A Broad Chested Soul,' *Gentleman's Maga-
                    zine* (1897).
Saintsbury, G.   *Cambridge History of English Literature*,
                    vol. vii.
Shirley, F. J.   *Richard Hooker and Contemporary Political
                    Ideas* (1949).
Spectator, The   4th April 1885 : 14th May 1892.
Stephen, Leslie   'Fuller, Thomas,' *Dictionary of National
                    Biography*; *Cornhill Magazine*, Jan. 1872.
Stauffer, Donald A. *English Biography before 1700* (1930).
Symonds, Richard   *Diary of the Marches kept by the Royal Army
                    during the Great Civil War*, Camden
                    Society (1859).
Thompson, E. N. S. *Literary Bypaths of the Renaissance* (1924).
Tullock, John   *Rational Theology in the Seventeenth Century*
                    (1874).
Waltham Abbey   Parish Registers and Churchwardens'
                    Accounts.
Walten, M. G.   *Fuller's Holy and Profane States*, with an
                    essay and voluminous notes. Columbia
                    University (1938).
Ward, Samuel   *Two Elizabethan Puritan Diaries, by Richard
                    Rogers and Samuel Ward*, edited by
                    M. M. Kappen. Chicago (1930).
Whitaker, W. B.   *Sunday in Tudor and Stuart Times* (1933).

INDEX